MARY

Founder of Christianity

MARY

Founder of Christianity

Chris Maunder

A Oneworld Book

First published by Oneworld Publications in 2022

Copyright © Chris Maunder 2022

The moral right of Chris Maunder to be identified as the Author
of this work has been asserted by him in accordance with the
Copyright, Designs, and Patents Act 1988

ISBN 978-0-86154-264-2
eISBN 978-0-86154-265-9

Typeset by Tetragon, London
Printed and bound in Great Britain by Clays Ltd, Elcograf S.p.A.

Oneworld Publications
10 Bloomsbury Street
London WC1B 3SR
England

Stay up to date with the latest books,
special offers, and exclusive content from
Oneworld with our newsletter

Sign up on our website
oneworld-publications.com

For Natalie, fellow pilgrim,
with love

Contents

Preface

There has been an increasing interest in the women in the New Testament over the last few decades as we become more aware of the marginalization of women in all religions and traditions around the world, and in their texts. No woman has attracted more attention and discussion than Mary, the mother of Jesus. In this book, I ask the following question: how important was Mary in the foundation of the Christian faith, and what did she contribute?

The thinking behind the book goes back to the 1980s and has been developed in articles that I have written in *The Month* (December 1996), *Mary: the Complete Resource* (edited by Sarah Jane Boss, 2007), *Origins of the Cult of the Virgin Mary* and *The Oxford Handbook of Mary* (both edited by myself, 2008 and 2019). In this book, I want to bring the conclusions together and offer them to a wider audience than those who read academic literature.

Despite being a member of the Catholic community, I will not be starting out from the point of view that Catholic or

Orthodox doctrines are absolute and not to be questioned. I will be going back to first principles, exploring what the New Testament has to say about Mary and following contemporary directions in biblical studies.

There is a centuries-old definition, attributed to Anselm from the end of the eleventh century, of theology as 'faith seeking understanding'. I am a person of Christian faith; for many years I have taken an active part in Marian devotion, partaking in pilgrimage and helping to maintain a medieval chapel dedicated to Mary in my hometown. At the same time, I have spent over three decades as an academic researcher into Mary and her shrines and apparitions. Even as I honour Mary in daily prayer and practice, I also want to understand the traditions about her intellectually as well as spiritually and emotionally. Honest reflection leads me to believe that there are many challenges in some of the ways that she has been regarded over the centuries, and that there is no disrespect in posing some searching questions about Mary as a person who lived in history and who is represented in the New Testament.

I completed this book during the coronavirus lockdown of 2020–1. Therefore, the person to whom I am most indebted for supporting me in writing it is my wife, Natalie. She has been a constant help throughout and has read the manu-script, offering advice. I would also like to thank York St John University, where I worked from 1992 to 2020, for creating an environment in which research is encouraged and facilitated, and the Centre for Marian Studies, founded in 1995, for pro-viding friends and colleagues with passion for the study of Mary that complements my own. Finally, I am most grateful to the publishers, Oneworld Publications, for placing their trust in me while responding promptly and helpfully to all my questions.

1

Introduction

WHO WAS MARY?

Mary the mother of Jesus of Nazareth is as important in the world today as she has ever been. Christianity continues to grow as a global religion. Among Roman Catholic and Eastern Orthodox communities, and others which are associated with them, Mary continues to be revered and venerated. It would be true to say that, while Jesus Christ as God Incarnate is at the centre of the Christian faith, Mary is indispensable to an understanding of Jesus in the many branches of the Catholic and Orthodox Churches. Belief in the Incarnation means that the context in which Jesus lived is important, as a Jew growing up in Galilee in the Roman Empire under Augustus and Tiberius, and as the son of Mary. Protestants also understand that Mary plays an important part in the Christian story as proclaimed in the New Testament, even if, generally, they do not share the devotion that she inspires in other denominations.

This book sets out to ask the question 'who was Mary?' based on an investigation of the New Testament texts, just as many others have done but in a new and radical way, taking into account modern trends in biblical studies. Major theological, political, and social developments have changed the way in which we approach the Bible. There are many interesting questions that can be asked about the virgin conception of Jesus and Mary's contribution to Jesus' ministry. There is also an interesting and long-standing mystery concerning Mary's involvement in the events of the crucifixion, burial, and resurrection of Jesus. The answers suggested in this book will cast a new light on Mary's role in the story of Christian salvation.

In world religions and philosophies, we are used to the idea of a founder. Jesus Christ, Muhammad, and Gautama Buddha stand at the origin of great world religions. Abraham is the forefather of the Jewish tradition, and Moses the one who received and established the *Torah*. Confucius could be said to have founded a philosophy rather than a religion; perhaps that is true of Buddha too. Zoroaster was the founder of a smaller but still influential religion named after him. Western philosophy looks back to Socrates, Plato, and Aristotle, who created the baseline for everything that came after them. More recent philosophers have also created traditions that acknowledge them as founders: Descartes, Kant, Hegel, and Marx, for example. Eastern philosophers as founders of systems of thought include Sankara and Ramanuja.

When you ask people to name a woman who founded a religion, they struggle to answer. You can suggest Ann Lee, who brought the Shakers into being, the Fox sisters, unwitting originators of Spiritualism, Madame Blavatsky for Theosophy, and Mary Baker Eddy for Christian Science. These are new names to many. Even to those who have heard of them, how much more marginal these movements appear beside global religions and philosophies! This, of course, reflects our patriarchal world in which initiatives in society, politics, and religion have been thought to reside within the province of males.

This book argues that the global religion with the most adherents, Christianity, has its origins in the mission and vocation of its most famous female, Mary the mother of Jesus, along with other women who accompanied her, including Mary Magdalene. Despite the often-held assumption that the Bible says little about Mary, there are plentiful signs in the New Testament that she preceded and inspired her son in the emergence of a new faith, planted in Jewish soil but eventually extending to all regions and peoples of the globe after its adoption by the Roman Empire.

It is easy, in a patriarchal religion focused upon a male saviour, to fall back on a general principle that 'behind every great man you find a good woman', or some such words. This presupposes that the male is primary in the events, and that the contribution of the female must therefore be subordinate or secondary. This is the assumption of the social world into which Jesus and Mary and their associates were born, and it has survived almost to our own times. In this thinking, Mary was the stereotypical good mother in a male-dominated world: loving and well-meaning, not always understanding what men must be about, prioritizing the safety of the family over urgent social and political projects, and therefore subject to the heartbreak of having her concerns and fears dismissed and then realized. This, of course, was always a stereotype, even in the first century. However, it does intrude into the New Testament and the way in which it has been interpreted in Christian tradition. But there is much more to it. Recent important changes in the way that we conceive of the relationship between the genders (changes which are still slowly coming to pass across the world with much resistance) mean that we can consider afresh the role of females in the formation of the Christian faith, and the pleasant surprise is that the gospels themselves contain clear indications that will help us do this.

In 2002, I was involved in a BBC programme on Mary. It investigated the social history of women in first-century Judea and Galilee. That seems a very sensible way to approach the subject, and one that New Testament historians would take today. However, I had one major reservation with the way that the programme presented Mary. There is the danger that, if you concentrate on the social history alone, you will end up reconstructing a Mary who is 'everywoman', a typical first-century Jewish woman from Galilee. I think that the programme sailed too close to this tendency. Whichever century or place a person lives in, while their life may share some general contextual outlines with others, this will not change the fact that people are *individuals*. A typical twenty-first-century person living in England would have a car, a smartphone, and a social media presence. That is not 100 per cent guaranteed, but even if it is an accurate generalization, it does not tell you much about any particular person as a unique individual. In all times and places, while many people fit the broad outlines of 'everyperson', they are all different, and some of them are especially remarkable, achieving things that most other people either cannot or would not do. Building a portrait of a typical first-century Jewish woman overlooks the possibility that Mary was a remarkable or unusual person, which is something that one strongly suspects in the case of the mother of Jesus. While women in her society were limited in terms of opportunities for political power or religious functions, historians have established that some women in the ancient Mediterranean did achieve considerable independence and positions of leadership.

The obvious starting point for a biblical investigation into the person of Mary is the conception and birth narratives of

Matthew and Luke. However, it is also necessary to take the whole life of Jesus into account when trying to understand his mother, given that the New Testament tells us that she outlived him. Her life encompassed his and Acts 1.14 confirms that the early Church remembered her as one of its first members. Therefore, this book includes chapters which summarize research into Jesus' life and ministry, the context for the life of Mary. This requires careful sifting as to what we can conclude historically rather than assuming that every single gospel passage relates events as they actually happened.

The book also explores the history of the family of Jesus, who are mentioned in the gospels. Mark's Gospel is especially important in this respect; Matthew follows Mark, and John has other information. The wider family are not much in evidence in Luke, but they appear in his second book, the Acts of the Apostles. Who were the brothers and sisters, and what was their relation to Mary? This is an area where it is particularly important not to start out with presuppositions based on doctrine, which could skew the research into Mary's role as a mother in this family; we need to go back to first principles.

The death of Jesus, the events that led up to it, and what happened immediately after it form the focus for several chapters. What role did Mary play in these events? She appears to be mentioned in John's Gospel alone as far as the death of Jesus is concerned, and then briefly in Acts after the Ascension of Jesus, but there might be more to discover than first meets the eye. Because this is a study of what we can know about Mary from the New Testament, we will not be entering into any discussion about her own death, which is nowhere described in any biblical text. Yet it is possible to sketch some outlines of her place in the earliest Church based in Jerusalem.

Before we begin the task of exploring what the New Testament has to say about Mary and how this might lead us to understand something about the Mary who actually lived as the mother of Jesus, we need to establish certain important principles that will help us to direct the research.

APPROACHING THE BIBLICAL TEXTS

A New Testament researcher who is intellectually honest will admit that biblical interpretation will always be subjective. We all have presuppositions. Biblical interpretation is usually done for a purpose, to achieve something and to change Christian thinking. One has an instinct or insight that an established way of reading the Bible relating to contemporary belief, devotion, or moral practice is no longer helpful, and then one pursues a new approach. Biblical study is like a mirrored glass through which it is difficult to see the reality of the first century. George Tyrrell (1861–1909) famously said that scholars trying to discover the 'historical Jesus', that is, the Jesus who really lived in first-century Israel, were simply discovering their own reflection at the bottom of a deep well. This note of caution applies to the historical Mary as well.

We will be undertaking a critical investigation of the New Testament, although not a destructive one. Mainstream biblical scholarship today accepts certain tenets of critical analysis. These will form the basis of the research in this book; they are summarized here and developed more fully in the chapters to come.

The New Testament and Gender

In a modern approach to scholarship, it is essential to adopt a critical perspective which explores the way in which gender and sexuality are discussed in the biblical text. The New Testament was written in a patriarchal world, which accredited women with neither equal opportunity nor equal voice; this is reflected in the texts, although it is possible to find positive images of women and their contribution to the Church. This is extremely relevant to any interpretation of the figure of Mary in the New Testament.

History and Story in the Gospels

Biblical scholarship generally accepts the existence of symbol and metaphor in the gospels. The narratives present evangelistic messages through story. This does not mean that the story may not also have happened in history, at least in some form; it is a key aspect of faith that God speaks through human events and relationships. Nevertheless, there are some narratives where the evidence suggests that the event described did not happen in history, and what we have is a metaphorical story with a theological message. Mary's story is subject to this possibility as much as any other biblical character, and maybe more so, because portrayals of her as virgin mother are symbolically significant.

The New Testament's Relationship with its Jewish Origins

Since the Second World War and the Holocaust, there has been a radical rethinking of the way in which the New Testament depicts the Jewish community. There are places in the New Testament which appear to be polemical against Jews in ways that have encouraged antisemitism in the history of the Church; the gospels and the Acts of the Apostles were written in a time when Christianity and Judaism were moving on divergent trajectories. Nevertheless, Christianity arose in a Jewish context; Jesus, his followers, and the first Christians were Jews.

Mary, as the mother of Jesus and a prominent member of his family, is of special importance in this respect: how far do the depictions of her obscure the fact that she was Jewish with aspirations for her family within Jewish cultural traditions?

Therefore, while the New Testament is to be respected as the inspirational collection of writings that it is, it can be conceded that there are aspects of it which represent the history of Jesus' life in particular ways, and that these may suggest things on the surface which we might want to question. Those sections which appear to portray women as the silent and uninfluential partners of the male disciples reflect a patriarchal world where texts generally did not represent the actual everyday lived practices and actions of women. Many passages which appear at first sight to be descriptions of what happened as events may be metaphorical rather than historical in order to present the theological ideas which the early Christians believed. Texts which appear to suggest that the Jews were collectively hostile to Jesus, or legalistic, or pedantic, or even murderous, originate during a stage of Christianity when relations to mainstream Judaism were breaking or had broken down. Fortunately, there are clues in the New Testament text itself to the ways in which some of these misconceptions can be challenged.

However, some contemporary books go much further than this. They claim that the gospels and Acts are tendentious fictions. For example, they suggest that Jesus was really a violent revolutionary so that, decades later, the New Testament texts pacified his image to avoid conflict with Rome, or that Jesus was made to look more religiously radical than he really was by the New Testament writers in order to attack Jewish custom and practice, or that Christianity was actually founded by St Paul in a way that was wholly alien to its origins.

There may be germs of truth in some aspects of these theories, but this is not the route that I will be taking. Questioning the very basis of the New Testament and its faith by taking a particular perspective on historical research is legitimate, but it is just as speculative as any other approach and the claims made cannot be proven. I do understand that sometimes these critiques are written or read by people who may have been hurt by the more unfortunate developments of the Christian faith, such as antisemitism, colonialism, misogyny, the abuse of power, or simple intransigence. However, the Bible is a deposit of faith for a very wide range of people, and to condemn it as an outright fraud attacks all those who have based belief, practice, and ethics on its scriptures. If Jesus really was a promoter of violent revolution, and Paul actually did create a mythical figure wholly unrelated to the historical Jesus, this would completely contradict the fundaments of the New Testament, and there would be little point in proceeding to undertake a biblical analysis unless one wished to undermine and oppose Christianity per se. This is not something I am interested in.

In analysing the gospels with respect to how they portray the figure of Mary, I am mindful of the fact that these texts have inspired people for two thousand years and that they have helped to shape the ethical, moral, and religious framework of cultures across the world. Therefore, critical investigation needs to be undertaken with a large helping of reverence and respect.

I am going to proceed according to these general assumptions:

- The New Testament is a collection of texts that present a genuine articulation of faith by first-century Christian communities;
- The writers of the gospels made selections from the sources and traditions that they inherited, edited their material for the purposes of presenting the early

Christian faith as they saw it, and created scenarios that illustrated points of faith;

- A researcher can seek to uncover the sources and traditions behind the texts based on as much evidence as is available, but always with an awareness that this work will be speculative;

- In the absence of clear evidence to the contrary, it is best to accept the plain reading of the text, while accepting that the genre of any given narrative may mean that it is metaphorical with a theological purpose rather than a description of actual historical events.

For the most part, the gospels are not eyewitness reports established during Jesus' ministry and then handed down. While they may include accurate memories of events, these are not easy to separate out and identify. The New Testament is the product of about seventy years of development in the early Church's spread across the Mediterranean, and so it represents diversity and evolution in its pages. What we know as the 'gospel message' was inspired by Jesus, his life, ministry, crucifixion, and the events of the first Easter, but it was not all created ready-made by him. The gospels represent the inspirational creativity and faith response of more than one generation of Christians.

The traditions about Jesus emerged from different circumstances across several decades; they reflect those changing and diverging contexts. Bodies of material such as Matthew's 'Sermon on the Mount' are collections of material, some of which may go back to Jesus himself, and some of which may have been constructed by Christians who believed themselves to be inspired by his Holy Spirit. There were oral traditions which fed into the New Testament and so it is important to recognize the existence of early Christian 'folk culture', mostly handed down by word of mouth.

There is a scholarly consensus as to the general outlines of the development of the New Testament which will provide a basis for the arguments in this book. In summary, some of the letters of Paul (and possibly that of James) are the earliest writings in the New Testament, dated in the 50s CE; the gospels came later, between about 70 and 100 CE and were written in this order: Mark, Matthew, Luke, and John, with each of the succeeding gospels having some access to a version of Mark (see Appendix 1 for the detail).[1] The story of Mary unfolded as the gospels developed (see Appendix 2 for a full list of the passages involving women called Mary in the New Testament).

---

[1] Matthew, Mark, and Luke are known as the 'synoptic gospels', as they have a lot of material in common.

2

Women in Early Christian Tradition

WOMEN'S CONTRIBUTIONS TO CHRISTIAN ORIGINS

It is often claimed that there is not a great deal written about Mary in the New Testament, and that would certainly be true if we did not have the first two chapters of Luke. But how far can this relative silence be explained by the fact that she was a woman in a patriarchal age?

Feminist analysis of the Bible might seem to some to be a niche subject, a political take which has more to do with the social changes of the twentieth century than the circumstances of the first century in which the gospels were written. But this is a wrong impression. While feminism is a modern social movement which has initiated new ways of reading the Bible, nevertheless its central question is one that is unavoidable and should have been asked many centuries earlier. It concerns the Christian witness of around one half of the members of the early Church: the women.

What was their contribution to a Church that was led by men, its founding documents supposedly written by men? Can we recover anything of their voices? Did they offer a perspective which we might have lost? The context of a person shapes their thinking and their experiences. Social demarcation between male and female in ancient Jewish culture in terms of roles, expectation, and opportunities means that the female perspective on the revolutionary events of the first Easter and its aftermath will have contrasted to a male one in some respects.

We are faced with the fact that the world in which the Church was born and has developed right up until now has been patriarchal, in that men have had priority over women in terms of controlling and shaping the world in which we live; Christian texts and beliefs reflect that world. There are two main responses: the first is to abandon the Christian faith, because it is so thoroughly and irredeemably male-dominated. Some feminists have done this, along with many other people who feel that Christianity is no longer relevant to the modern situation. The second is to find a way to reform it. Given that Christianity is based on the Bible, because its texts tell us about the centre and origin of the Christian faith, Jesus Christ the Word of God Incarnate, any reformation requires radically new interpretations of the Bible, especially the New Testament.

If male supremacy, or indeed the domination of any group of human beings over others, is regarded as a sin, something to be challenged and changed, then it is impossible for a Christian to accept that Jesus Christ promoted it. If Jesus Christ is God, then his teaching must be universal, for all times and places. The Son of God, the Word who speaks the truth of God to all generations through history, cannot be sexist and misogynist, bound to a patriarchal context. While the first-century context will reflect the way in which Jesus' teaching was first received and will colour the way in which it was originally presented, nevertheless it must be possible to find the liberation of all people at its heart. Fortunately, there is nothing in Jesus' own practice in the gospels to suggest that he was committed to the right of males to retain power in society, nor that he approved of any form of domination or marginalization.

Of course, the writers of the gospels and Acts, who belonged to a culture far removed from ours, have presented their material in such a way that women's voices are not as prominent as men's, even though we find strong females in the text. There is also the problem that instructions enforcing the silencing and subjugation of women can be found in some of the epistles traditionally ascribed to Paul (for example, 1 Cor. 14.34–35, 1 Tim. 2.12–14). Yet elsewhere, Paul states that 'there is no longer male and female; for you are all one in Christ Jesus' (Gal. 3.28),[2] which is likely to have been an early strand of tradition, as Galatians is one of the first of Paul's letters, one of those probably written by Paul himself. For these reasons, feminist analysis has suggested a distinction between the ethos of Jesus and his original community, and the practice of the Church at the time when the later epistles and gospels were written.

The claim in feminist biblical studies that Jesus' original community was egalitarian cannot be proved, and it can be challenged on the grounds that it is 'golden age' thinking rather than genuine history of the origins of Christianity. Nevertheless, it does have support in the general observation that religious movements are often highly radical at the outset, and then gradually accept the social world in which they are forced to operate. This has been referred to as the

---

[2] All biblical quotes in the book are from the New Revised Standard Version unless otherwise indicated.

'routinization of charisma', a concept suggested by the sociologist Max Weber. It can be applied to any religion or denomination. This general phenomenon does lend some weight to the idea that Jesus was more egalitarian on the question of gender than the New Testament texts might suggest.

Susan Hylen, in her book *Women in the New Testament World*, shows that research on women in the ancient Greco-Roman Mediterranean reveals a picture that is far from uniform. This diversity also applies to Jewish culture. Although women were often instructed to remain passive and silent in male writing on ideal behaviours (and this includes the Pauline epistles), this was far from the reality of everyday relations between the sexes. While denied the very highest positions in the imperial hierarchy (except when deriving power from their husbands, as with the empress), women participated fully in many other areas of life, and did assume positions of responsibility and leadership. The common view that women only had a say in the 'private sphere' is complicated by the fact that the virtues of the domestic situation were projected into the public and civic environment, so that virtues such as modesty, industry, and loyalty were at the same time domestic and social. For this reason, women had a role to play in a range of social activities, save perhaps for the highest level of politics and the legislature. Women, it is true, were subordinate to men as a general rule, but this subordination was only to men of equal or higher rank.

Because the New Testament was formed in the Greco-Roman world in which this complicated cultural situation existed, we can therefore expect to find this complexity reflected in the New Testament and the communities from which it emerged: the ideals of female subordination as expressed in male writing versus the everyday reality of women's participation and responsibility, even leadership. The area in which women were most obviously subjugated was in *written texts*, and the New Testament is a collection of texts. It may not represent fully the female voices and activities at the origins of Christianity.

It would not be right to suggest that women in ancient Jewish culture suffered more greatly from patriarchal suppression than in other nations of the time or in the Christian tradition which was to come; Jewish women did participate and had some influence in both religious and civic life. There is evidence that women had leadership roles in synagogues (which strengthens the case for women's leadership in Christianity).[3] Yet, it would appear that the higher the social class, the rarer the opportunities for women in the Jewish culture of that time to assume any position which had power or responsibility, such as in the monarchy, the main institutions of government, or the priesthood. These were the agents of power in ancient Mediterranean society, and therefore women for the most part had no say in the most important factors that determined their lives, unless they were able to influence men of power (as portrayed through stereotypes in the legend of Herodias manipulating her husband Herod Antipas to execute John the Baptist).

Hylen shows that widows in ancient Mediterranean cultures were sometimes women of means. They often lived with their sons and other male relatives, but this did not mean that they were powerless within the family; on the contrary, they had social and religious influence (for example, see Judith in the book of Judith,[4] and Anna in Luke 2.36–38). Some widows remarried, while many others regarded staying single as remaining faithful to their first husbands. There is a common assumption that Mary was a widow at the time of the ministry

---

[3] As demonstrated in the research by Bernadette J. Brooten, *Women Leaders in the Ancient Synagogue*. We will discuss this further in Chapter 15.
[4] In the Protestant canon, the book of Judith is placed among the apocrypha (see footnote 5).

of Jesus, which is a reasonable one given that women usually married men who were older and that Joseph plays no part in the narrative of Jesus' adulthood.

WOMEN AND THE BIBLE

The process of finding female voices in biblical history, where one has been used to hearing and reading male voices, is known as *reclaiming*. Stories are shaped by contexts and experiences. One could make a very good case for the argument that women in the early Church were involved in the storytelling and creation of the narratives, if not their written forms (and it has been suggested that women may have written some of the texts, although this is not the mainstream academic view).

In the New Testament, women's contributions to early Christianity were given less prominence than those of men, and women are portrayed in particular ways that reflect a patriarchal culture. In some ways, the Old Testament comes off better than the New! It is true that there are extremely misogynistic texts in the Hebrew Scriptures and Old Testament apocrypha[5] but there are also strong female characters. There are the foremothers of Israel: Sarah, Rebekah, Leah, Rachel, and Sarah's slave, Hagar. Ruth has a book in her name, and her relationship with her mother-in-law Naomi is an enduring story in the Bible. To these we can add women whose major contribution is not simply mothering: the judge Deborah; Judith, and Jael, the assassins of leaders of enemies of the Israelites; Esther, the Jewess who became a Persian queen

---

[5] Hebrew Scriptures: the collection of books that the Protestant denominations refer to as the Old Testament based on the Jewish canon or *Tanakh*. The Roman Catholic and Orthodox traditions include other books that are usually referred to as the Old Testament apocrypha.

and interceded to save the Jewish people, the third woman who is the subject of an entire book. In the Song of Songs, we read about love from the perspective of the female partner. Women's lives are reflected in the Hebrew Scriptures, even if often we encounter stereotypes rather than real women of the period (and this can be said of men too). Given that women were readers and hearers of scriptural texts as well as men, it is not surprising that the canon includes something of the female experience.

The New Testament contains strong indications that women were ministers or householders in the early Church: Chloe ('Chloe's people', 1 Cor. 1.11); Phoebe the deacon of Romans 16.1; Lydia, who is baptized with her household (Acts 16.15); the 'leading women' of Acts 17.4. 'Nympha and the church in her house' is mentioned in Colossians 4.15, and Acts 12.12 describes 'the house of Mary, the mother of John whose other name was Mark, where many had gathered and were praying'. These expressions suggest female Christian leadership at a time when worship was confined to private houses, as the head of the house led liturgy and worship.

Nevertheless, in the gospel passages that describe Jesus' ministry, the emphasis is on male disciples as the confidants of Jesus. He sometimes takes aside the leading three disciples, Peter and the sons of Zebedee, as in the Transfiguration narrative (Matt. 17.1–13; Mark 9.2–13; Luke 9.28–36). The calls to the first of Jesus' followers in all four gospels refer only to males, and the twelve disciples listed in three of them are all male. On other occasions, the twelve seem to be alone with him, as at the Last Supper in Matthew 26.20 and Mark 14.17 (the term 'apostles' at Luke 22.14 is less specific and John does not specify the total number present). There is no female disciple explicitly present at the Last Supper, which includes some of the most important passages of Jesus' teaching and the institution of the Eucharist.

Each gospel has an average of twenty-one separate pieces of narrative[6] which refer to male disciples by name or refer to 'the twelve', who are clearly male. There are another twenty-three on average which refer to 'the disciples' or 'the apostles', where probably males are implied (possibly one could argue that men *and* women might have been intended by these expressions). Contrasting with this: outside the group of named disciples, and also excluding the birth and infancy narratives and those concerning John the Baptist, each gospel has an average of nine sections where named or anonymous women encounter Jesus, and twelve with named or anonymous men.[7]

There are, of course, notable exceptions to the general rule that men are more prominent in the gospels: the birth and infancy narratives in Luke and the empty tomb stories in all four gospels are examples where women act as the main subjects of the text. We might expect women to be prominent in texts which involve birth and death. In the cultures of the ancient Mediterranean, women were the primary agents in funerary rites and were associated with death and the supernatural in drama and literature. There are also important encounters between individual women and Jesus: with the women who anoint him in all four gospels (although only in John is the anointer named); the Syrophoenician or Canaanite woman who challenges Jesus in Mark (7.24–30) and Matthew (15.21–28); and women who ask him for healing, either for themselves or their families. Nevertheless, even healings are more likely to be of males: an average of three per gospel for females, and nine for males.

---

[6] Of course, this is an approximate figure, as it depends where you decide that the pieces of narrative begin and end, and some sections are much longer than others. Nevertheless, it is illustrative for showing how the gospels describe the respective involvement of men and women in Jesus' ministry.

[7] That is, women and men who encounter Jesus in a positive way (not Herod, Caiaphas, or Pilate).

In John's Gospel, with Mary Magdalene at the tomb, Martha at the raising of Lazarus, and the Samaritan woman at the well, women do seem to be represented more strongly than in the other gospels. Yet Adeline Fehribach, in her *The Women in the Life of the Bridegroom*, argues that the portrayal of women in John is necessary because, for the evangelist, Jesus is the Bridegroom, following the images of God as bridegroom in the Hebrew Scriptures. He encounters the women as the Bridegroom, and their function in the text is to convey this. She concludes that John is as male-centred as the other gospels.

It could be objected that the iterant nature of Jesus' ministry restricted it to males on practical grounds. Yet the gospels tell us that women accompanied Jesus and supported his ministry all the way from Galilee. However, we learn relatively little about them; Luke 8.2–3 mentions them briefly and then they reappear at the crucifixion. Compared to the information that we have about male disciples, and the conversations that Jesus has with them, this is minimal. He has very brief conversations with his mother in Luke 2, John 2, and John 19. There are few examples of women learning from Jesus in the way that the male disciples do: the obvious exceptions are Martha, who declares that Jesus is the Messiah and Son of God in John 11.20–28, and Mary in Luke 10.38–42, who is an exemplar of listening and learning.

Paul's letters give us an idea of the people who were active in the early Church. He names sixty Christian men (including James the brother of Jesus, Peter, and John) and sixteen Christian women in his letters, a ratio of 4:1 of men to women. Some of these people are also mentioned in Acts: fifteen men and one woman (Prisca). Additionally, Acts names thirty-one other Christian men not mentioned by Paul (which includes the other disciples in the list at Acts 1.13) and five women. The Acts of the Apostles, therefore, has a ratio of 8:1 of men to women. In Paul's letters, which reflect the ministry as it was experienced by him day to day, women are twice as prominent as in the narrated story of the same period. This corroborates the point that ancient texts may not always represent the reality as far as gender participation is concerned.

What we can conclude from this is that the absence of much information in the New Testament about Mary outside the key moments of Jesus' life – his birth and childhood (Luke), and at Cana and the cross (John) – does not imply that there was not much to be said about her. She, along with other women, suffers from a male-dominated silence which forces us to speculate to fill in the details. We know that there was more that could be said about Jesus and the male disciples; the last verse of John's Gospel (21.25) says that, 'But there are also many other things that Jesus did; if every one of them were written down, I suppose that the world itself could not contain the books that would be written.' That is even more the case for the women who followed Jesus and for his mother Mary.

To sum up, it is not at all far-fetched to imagine that women will have had a major input into the earliest Christian traditions as found in the New Testament in ways that can be glimpsed in the final textual versions of the stories but is not fully articulated in them. To say otherwise is to accept that the sacred origins of Christianity from which we derive the truth of Christ and the gospel message subsists on a narrative in which women were largely silent and men spoke on their behalf. While in the final versions of the gospels and Acts, this may appear to be the case, that does not mean that it is also true of the traditions that fed into them. The folk culture of early Christianity will have had a rich female component, just as extensive and diverse as that contributed by males. In principle, Mary is likely to have made a greater contribution to the formation of the earliest Church than the texts suggest.

Yet, despite this, the texts are the only place where we can find any clue as to what this contribution may have been.

Having clarified the groundwork for our investigation of Mary, we can now begin our research into specific texts. We will not be starting with the earliest documents, the epistles of Paul or Mark's Gospel, because they do not narrate the conception and birth of Jesus, which is the obvious place to begin. Instead, we turn to those gospels which do describe these events, the Gospels of Matthew and Luke.

3

The Conception and Birth of Jesus

The story of Jesus' birth is narrated in the gospels of Matthew and Luke. These accounts differ in many respects and concur in only a few important details: Mary was a virgin at the time of Jesus' conception and birth; the birth was in Bethlehem; Jesus was descended from David; the family lived in Nazareth *after* the birth. The differences are:

- MATTHEW 1–2: the story of the virgin conception is focused on Joseph, and it is he who sees an angel in a dream; the angel reassures him that he should marry Mary despite the irregularity of his not being the father of the baby; the family appear to live in Bethlehem already as there is no journey there; the visitors are magi who bring gifts; the family have to find refuge in Egypt for a time because of Herod's massacre of the young children; they then move to Nazareth.

- LUKE 1–2: Mary is the central character of Luke's version of the story; she receives a visit from the angel Gabriel to tell her about the coming birth which alarms her, because she is a virgin; when pregnant, she visits Elizabeth the mother of John the Baptist and proclaims the *Magnificat* hymn (drawing on the precedent of Hannah the mother of Samuel); the family are poor (reminiscent of David's humble origins); they move from Nazareth to Bethlehem because of a census and are forced to shelter among the animals; they are visited by shepherds; there is also detail about Jesus' circumcision a week after his birth, his presentation in the Temple after forty days, and his return there aged twelve.

THE PLACE AND TIME OF THE BIRTH OF JESUS

Jesus' birth in Bethlehem is one aspect of the story that the evangelists share. It was expected that the Messiah would be born in Bethlehem, as he was inheriting the mantle of David, the son of Jesse, a 'Bethlehemite' (1 Sam. 16.1). Bethlehem was the residence of David's great-grandparents Boaz and Ruth (Ruth 4.11). Micah 5.2 therefore prophesies that the new Messiah is to come from Bethlehem ('the house of bread'), also known as Ephrathah ('fruitful'). Matthew refers to this Messianic prophecy, quoting what is actually an amalgamation of the Micah 5.2 prophecy and 2 Samuel 5.2, which refers to David as the shepherd of Israel:[8]

'And you, Bethlehem, in the land of Judah,
    are by no means least among the rulers of Judah;

---

[8] There is the question as to whether the New Testament writers used the same version of the Greek Old Testament as the versions to which we have access now. This is explored by Margaret Barker in *Christmas: The Original Story*.

for from you shall come a ruler
who is to shepherd my people Israel.'

(Matt. 2.5–6)

We can conclude either that Jesus was born in Bethlehem, which would have strengthened his Messianic claim, or that he was not but the prophecy caused Christians to claim that he was. It is unlikely historically, however, that Joseph and Mary would have travelled to Bethlehem from Nazareth because of a census, as in Luke's Gospel, as there is no ancient record that suggests the necessity of this.[9] Matthew prefers to have them living in Bethlehem and only settling in Nazareth after the return from Egypt.

We do not know whether Jesus actually was a direct descendant of David, or whether this was a means of validating his right to be called the Messiah. It is more likely than the other details of the birth narratives of Matthew and Luke. There is the tradition that relatives of Jesus – notably Symeon the bishop of Jerusalem and the grandsons of Jude mentioned in Eusebius, *Church History* 3.20, 32 – claimed the Davidic inheritance some decades after Jesus' life and were persecuted for it. It is also difficult to see how Jesus could have been proclaimed as Messiah by some people during his lifetime if he did not have a Davidic claim. Paul refers to Jesus being 'descended from David according to the flesh' in Romans 1.3, which shows that the belief pre-dates the writing of the gospels of Matthew and Luke by some decades. Bartimaeus, a blind beggar, calls Jesus 'son of David' in the earliest gospel, Mark (10.46–48).

John's is the only gospel in which there is any doubt: some people, hearing that Jesus is claimed to be the Christ, ask:

---

[9] Among others, Raymond Brown, *The Birth of the Messiah*, discusses the historical problems arising from the birth narratives.

'Surely the Messiah does not come from Galilee, does he? Has not the scripture said that the Messiah is descended from David and comes from Bethlehem, the village where David lived?' (7.41–42). This taunt is left unanswered in the gospel. If we only knew John's Gospel, we might conclude that Jesus was neither descended from David nor born in Jerusalem. Yet John is clear at several points (for example, 20.31) that Jesus is the Messiah. What we can be reasonably sure of is that, at some point, the family of Jesus claimed the Davidic succession, and that was enough to convince people of the day.

Therefore, it may well be the case that Mary considered her son to be a descendant of David. It is notable that, despite Joseph not being considered to be Jesus' natural father in the birth narratives, the Davidic lineage passes through him in the gospel genealogies and not through Mary. We might wonder whether she was supposed to have been descended from Aaron like her relative Elizabeth (Luke 1.5), although this is not substantiated elsewhere, and it might have served Luke's purpose to suggest that Jesus was of the line of both David and Aaron, the archetypal king and priest of the Israelite heritage. The existence of a possible loophole in the Davidic claim of Jesus – because he was the son of Mary but not of Joseph, David's descendant according to the gospels – might have encouraged the tradition, emerging at the end of the first century, after the gospel period, that Mary was also of the lineage of David like her husband. It is just a hint in Ignatius of Antioch's *Epistle to the Ephesians* 18, but it is then expanded and established in tradition by the *Protevangelium* 10 and Tertullian's *On the Flesh of Christ* 21.

Is it even true that Jesus' birth occurred under Herod the Great? Matthew states this, although there is no historical record of Herod's massacre of the infants of Judea. Another problem is that Luke's census, under Quirinius as governor of Syria, occurred some ten years after the reign of Herod, who died in 4 BCE. Quirinius was not governor of Syria until 6 CE. But Luke also says that Elizabeth and Zechariah lived 'in the days of King Herod of Judea' (1.5). Perhaps he intended this to mean Herod's son, Herod Archelaus? It is certainly not Archelaus in Matthew's Gospel (see 2.22), but it is not clear in Luke. Yet Archelaus was deprived of his throne by the Romans at the same time as the census. We are left wondering whether the dates in these narratives might be rather loose. Certainly, the calculating of the years of what we now know as CE, the 'Common Era' (previously AD, the 'year of the Lord') is only approximate. The monk Dionysius Exiguus, in the fifth or sixth century, calculated this and ended up with a date that falls between the death of Herod and the census of Quirinius, satisfying none of the gospel descriptions. So perhaps, if we really want the Common Era to mark the length of time from the birth of Jesus, we should add a few extra to the number of our calendar years: 2000 becomes 2005, and so on!

Therefore, we cannot really be sure exactly when Jesus was born. If we assume that it is true that Jesus was Mary's firstborn, then probably she would have been about fourteen years older than him according to the customs of marriage of the time. Were Jesus to have been born late in Herod the Great's reign, this would suggest that her birthdate can be placed somewhere near 20 BCE.

Even Jesus' background in Nazareth has been questioned. It is fairly indisputable that he grew up in Galilee, but some writers have posited that the name 'Nazareth' is derived from the word 'Nazirite', which was a Hebrew term meaning a man who had consecrated himself to God by not cutting his hair, avoiding alcohol and any contact with the dead. We read about the process in Numbers 6: the Nazirite practices could be temporary, as an initiation into a state of consecration, or permanent. Samson was the prototypical Nazirite, and the practice continued from pre-exilic Israel into the early years of Christianity. Eusebius the fourth-century Church historian says that James the brother of Jesus was a Nazirite, which might imply that Jesus was too. However, for Jesus to have been a Nazirite for life, he could not have been the person accused of being 'a glutton and a drunkard' that we read about in Matthew 11.19 and Luke 7.34.

There is also the possibility that there was another group, known as 'Nazoreans' or 'Nazarenes'. Jesus is referred to as a Nazorean or Nazarene several times in the gospels, although this is usually translated 'of Nazareth', and Paul is called a Nazarene in Acts 24.5. The Hebrew verb *nzr* means 'to set oneself apart or consecrate', yielding the name Nazirite, and the similar *ntsr* is 'to watch over or preserve', suggesting a movement that regarded itself as guardians with the purpose of conserving Israel's traditions, which could be behind the words Nazorean or Nazarene. There is also a noun connected with *ntsr*, meaning 'branch' as used in Isaiah 11.1 for the branch of Jesse, that is, the line of David, also applicable to Jesus.

This is a complex question, and it is impossible to settle the question as to whether the claim that Jesus came from Nazareth is a fiction intended to cover up the fact that he was a Nazirite or Nazorean. Of course, it is possible that Jesus grew up in Nazareth and was *also* a Nazirite or Nazorean! We will never know for sure.

So there remain many questions that have provoked research, speculation, and controversy. Although the gospels of Matthew and Luke present the conception and birth stories in very different ways, it is very likely that the features common to both gospels belong to traditions, possibly oral, handed down before these gospels were written. They belonged to the folk culture of early Christianity. This could include material that has some historical basis along with much more in the way of embellishment that occurred in the growth of traditions about the life of Jesus. It is very difficult to distinguish which is which, but here we might venture that the Davidic ancestry of Jesus, at least as a claim by the family, and that he came from Galilee, belong to the actual history, but that the belief that he was born in Bethlehem might be better ascribed to early Christian legend based on readings of the prophetic books of the Hebrew Scriptures.

THE BIRTH AND INFANCY NARRATIVES AS THEOLOGY

The gospel narratives reflect the theological intentions of the evangelists, and this can be demonstrated for the birth and infancy stories. Matthew wants to present a Jesus who, while born in the Jewish tradition as a fulfilment of its prophecy, a new and greater Moses, is nevertheless presented as a Messiah to the whole world. Hence his magi come from afar; they are the wise ones of the world who recognize Jesus. Luke's Jesus is a Messiah with a mission to the poor, and the idea that he was born in a stable and visited by shepherds, the outsiders of Jewish society, relate to this overall theme. It was important to both evangelists that readers familiar with the Jewish tradition should understand how the coming of Jesus fulfilled its prophecies and traditions, hence the many quotes and allusions to them.

The narratives of Jesus' birth reflect the imaginative questions of those who accepted him as their Saviour: what would it have been like at the birth of Jesus? Again, the historical answer is that probably very little occurred apart from a family's delight at the coming into being of a firstborn child but, in the light of later events, a Christian picturing the scene might have imagined angels singing, and shepherds and wise men visiting the newborn in awe-inspired adoration. They would also have imagined the reaction of tyrants like Herod if he had known what was occurring.

Most biblical scholars agree that the birth and infancy narratives are legends or myths.[10] This does not mean that they are untruthful: far from it, as they present the story in a way that expresses *theological truth* (we will consider this in more detail in the next chapter). The original Greek word *mythos* meant a story that conveys truth. The birth and infancy narratives were never intended as history, and therefore they do not misrepresent the story. By the time of the writing of these gospels, the details of Jesus' birth were lost to history. Even the genealogies in Matthew and Luke differ substantially. If there were miraculous events, and they were remembered in the early Church, then it is unlikely that the gospels would have diverged so substantially, and that two of the gospels, Mark and John, would have omitted the details entirely.

According to Marcus Borg and John Dominic Crossan in *The First Christmas*, the writers of Matthew and Luke present the birth narratives as 'preludes' or 'overtures'; they prepare the reader for the material later on in their gospel by summarizing it in a symbolic way, in the form of long parables. The word 'parable' refers to Jesus' short, illustrative stories which are clearly meant to be allegorical and present a theological truth. Yet it can be extended to mean other passages which might at first sight describe historical events, but in fact are symbolic stories too. And so we learn from the conception, birth, and infancy narratives what is, from the point of view of the evangelists and their churches, theological truth. This is what they tell us:

---

[10] The words *myth* and *legend* can be distinguished as traditions about divine beings and human figures respectively, handed down in folk culture and/or written texts. In the gospels, the involvement of God in the stories of Jesus, Mary, and the disciples mean that the words myth and legend can be used as synonyms for New Testament stories that are not historical, but nevertheless express theological truth in symbolic forms.

- That Jesus is the Messiah prophesied throughout the Jewish Scriptures (and so these are referenced frequently in these texts);
- That God is intimately involved in the life of Jesus which has a very special divine and universally beneficial purpose;
- That the birth of Jesus occurred through the action of the Holy Spirit;
- That Jesus was born and raised in a believing and practising Jewish community.

With respect to Mary, both gospels state that she was the most important in the line of women who had furthered God's purposes for Israel through history: Matthew's genealogy and Luke's story of Mary's response to the angel both affirm this. Matthew's story of Mary in the birth and infancy narratives does not develop her character, but it does describe her being challenged by two major crises: the suspicion of impropriety in the conception of Jesus which could have led to Joseph abandoning her, and the need to flee Israel to seek refuge in Egypt because of Herod.

Luke has much more material than Matthew that reveals his idea of the personality of Mary. She is a young woman who, despite her surprise at the turn of events, accepts the mission with which she has been entrusted and reflects on the way that this unfolds. She interacts with the angel, a divine messenger, as do many predecessors in the Hebrew Scriptures (the women among them include Hagar and the mother of Samson). She articulates her response to this experience with a hymn of praise, the *Magnificat*, reminiscent of the song of Hannah, the mother of Samuel. She seeks the company of a relative, Elizabeth, and is prepared to travel to do so. She carries out the ritual requirements of the Jewish tradition with respect to the birth and circumcision of her son.

In literary terms, both gospels present Mary as a biblical heroine. This is implied in Matthew because of the challenges that she has to face, but in Luke, it is explicit: Mary is a believer in God with a strong faith, sensitive and receptive to God's presence. She cooperates with God's plan and helps to bring it to fruition. She is also an unusual person in whom a great miracle takes place: at the very beginning of her story is the conception of Jesus while she is still a virgin. The implication is that she was divinely chosen for this; she is 'blessed', as Elizabeth exclaims (Luke 1.42). The question we need to ask as we go forward in this book is: how much can we learn about Mary as an actual person in history from the ideal type that Luke portrays, if anything at all? We will start by discussing what it means to accept that there is symbolism and metaphor in the apparently historical passages in the Bible.

4

Symbolism and Metaphor
in the Bible

HISTORY OR THEOLOGICAL SYMBOLISM?

Few biblical scholars doubt that the gospels and Acts contain narratives that are written as if historical, but which are theological stories describing events in what could be called a poetic or symbolic mode of expression. Scholars are divided as to which of the events that are described in the gospels represent actual history, and which might be these parable-like passages that tell us what Jesus means to the Church in a symbolic way. This is highly relevant to the narratives that concern Mary.

The New Testament writers were more interested in confirming the faith of present and future generations than providing historical accuracy. They used theological symbolism to describe the realities of faith. This does not mean that the history of Jesus' ministry and the pre-gospel Church is impossible to recover, but historical research into the world behind the text is difficult, limited in what it can achieve, and requires careful sifting. To say this is not to go beyond what most of the mainstream Christian Churches themselves believe.

For many centuries, and into the early modern period, most Christians simply accepted the texts at face value. Unless it was absolutely clear that the text presented a story (as with Jesus' parables), then it happened in history, even if at the same time it expressed theological symbolism and/or it was intended to give moral guidance. It would not have been possible until relatively recently, except perhaps to a very few sophisticated thinkers, to believe that a narrative describing the actions of Jesus was a story created by the early Christians to present a theological view. However, even as far back as Origen in the third century, it was admitted that some events described in the Bible were impossible from a historical point of view.[11] Therefore, it was better to read these things allegorically or metaphorically. Eventually, from the eighteenth century, the time known as the Enlightenment, the stories of the Bible began to be subjected to a sustained critique that categorized certain parts of the Bible as legendary or mythological.

It would have to be conceded that the process of identifying myth in the Bible can lead to an unravelling in which everything is reduced to nothing but an enchanting story. For this reason, some Christians have responded defensively by arguing that the Bible has to be accepted in every detail as historical fact, and so there are the infamous calculations of the age of the Earth using the Bible, and the refusal to accept the theory of evolution and the existence of dinosaurs. This is what is known as 'fundamentalism', a term originally used

---

[11] For helpful overviews of the history of biblical interpretation with examples, see Stephen and Martin Westerholm, *Reading Sacred Scripture: Voices from the History of Biblical Interpretation*; Richard Soulen, *Sacred Scripture: A Short History of Interpretation*; and Michael J. Gorman, *Scripture: An Ecumenical Introduction to the Bible and its Interpretation*.

by Christians in the late nineteenth century who wanted to protect the Bible and their faith from doubt and critique. For many Christians, believing that everything narrated in the gospels actually happened in history is important to their faith. The belief that God is actively involved in human history, and entered the human world in the person of Jesus of Nazareth, goes along with the acceptance that many wonderful events occurred as a consequence.

However, other Christians continued to regard the Bible as God's word while at the same time accepting the findings of modern science; for them, certain stories could be seen as symbolic representations of the journey of faith rather than historical events. This has characterized what is known as the 'liberal' Christian tradition from the eighteenth century. Liberal Christians argue that people in the early Church *imagined* what Jesus might have said or did in the context of their faith and their experience of what they believed to be the Holy Spirit, sent by the risen Jesus into the Church. Consequently, in the New Testament, important truths of Christian theology are sometimes expressed in story form. The narratives of the gospels might also include experiences of the *risen* Jesus in apparitions or inspirations; these experiences would then be described in forms that make them appear as if they occurred in Jesus' earthly ministry.

For example: did Jesus walk on water (Matt. 14.22–33; Mark 6.45–52; John 6.16–21)? Clearly, this has theological meaning, in that Jesus is seen as having divine power; it recalls that God created the heavens and the Earth by controlling the 'waters' (Gen. 1.1–10) and then again parted the waters during the Exodus (Ex. 14). It could, of course, be symbolic and historical at the same time, as it could be argued that Jesus did this as a sign of his divine power as a real event in history. Jesus undertook symbolic acts to show us who he was, how we should relate to him, and how we should live. This has been the normal way of reading passages about miracles for many centuries.

Against this, some Christians in the modern age have felt that this contradicts the humanity of Jesus: humans cannot walk on water. According to Christian theology, Jesus was fully human and fully divine at the same time. Just as his humanity does not compromise or reduce his divinity, nor does his divinity call into question his humanity. As Paul wrote:

> Christ Jesus who, though he was in the form of God, did not regard equality with God as something to be exploited, but emptied himself, taking the form of a slave, being born in human likeness. And being found in human form, he humbled himself and became obedient to the point of death—even death on a cross.
>
> (Phil. 2.6–8)

As scholarship now better understands the ways in which gospel stories were used to describe symbolically what Christians believe, it is suggested that we can dispense with the difficulty of trying to believe impossible things. The very most that can be believed, according to this view, is that people after the resurrection saw the risen Christ walking on the water; it did not happen in his lifetime.

Conservative Christians might find this indigestible. They ask, quite justifiably, what happens if we unravel all the stories about Jesus and regard them as mere symbolism? What about the resurrection? Does this mean that Jesus was not really raised and that the resurrection was a story that helps us understand that Jesus' message will always be with us? Very few Christians would want to go this far. Clearly, there needs to be some limit to categorizing material in the New Testament as pure myth, even for Christians who embrace this approach. Paul also wrote: 'If Christ has not been raised, your faith is futile and you are still in your sins' (1 Cor. 15.17). There has to be an indisputable core of belief. It is probably best expressed in the Creed, in summary: it is objectively true that God exists as Trinity; that Jesus is the Incarnation of God, the second person of the Trinity; and that God raised Jesus from the dead and by doing so raised humanity from the state of sin and alienation from God. The details of *how* God exists as Trinity and raised Jesus might have to remain a mystery, only tentatively articulated in centuries of theology and doctrine in diverse forms. The fact that it *is* the case, however, is the core of Christian belief.

Symbolic stories such as Jesus walking on the water describe in narrative form the objective reality of the Incarnation. Limiting this to metaphor means we have to accept that, in history, Jesus of Nazareth *was unable to walk on water*. The advantage of seeing the story in this way is that Jesus, unable to walk on water, must have done other things that are symbolically described in the walking on water scene. His divine power was shown, not in walking on water, but in bringing hope to those who had lost it and building communities which included those previously excluded. This is a human Jesus that we can emulate: we can do those things too, but we cannot walk on water. After all, in John we read that: 'Very truly, I tell you, the one who believes in me will also do the works that I do and, in fact, will do greater works than these, because I am going to the Father' (John 14.12). Believers cannot do greater works than Jesus if walking on water is the standard.

We could extend this to other examples. Did Jesus raise the dead (Jairus' daughter, Mark 5.21–43; the widow's son at Nain, Luke 7.11–17; Lazarus, John 11)? Is this not a symbolic way of saying that Jesus saves us from the death that is sin and despair? It is not only Jesus but also the early disciples who have this power (for example, Peter's raising of Dorcas in Acts 9.36–43). In fact, Jesus instructs his disciples to raise the dead (Matt. 10.8). It is clear that Christians cannot do this now. Must we then assume that this power ebbed away from the Church at an early point? Or does it make more sense to suggest that bringing people to faith in resurrection is well described by saying that they have been 'raised from the dead'? Once again, this does not mean that we need to question the objective reality of resurrection as the final destination of human existence and its implication that our lives will not end in meaninglessness and nothingness.

FOLK TRADITION AND THE CHARACTERS OF THE NEW TESTAMENT

Most modern scholars assume that there was a middle stage between the events of Jesus' lifetime and the writing of the gospels. This was a period of *oral tradition*, handed down through the first generations of Christian believers. The question as to how far Christian oral tradition faithfully preserved real memories and how much it created new stories is open to the interpretation of biblical scholars and can never be fully resolved.

One the one hand, the conservative position is that: in a largely illiterate culture, handing down information orally is actually quite secure because people develop very good memories, and there will have been many people alive right from the death of Jesus to the writing of the gospels whose witness will have been regarded as very important. On the other hand, the more critical position suggests that: the rapid growth of the Church through a wide area in the Mediterranean region made it impossible to discern what was historical; competing and evolving beliefs and practices shaped the development of the traditions in quite diverse ways. Probably the best answer to this is somewhere between the two, to reject the two extremes, that is, it is neither all eyewitness memories nor is it all something that was made up later.

Oral tradition is akin to *folk culture*, in that sets of stories are circulated that define the beliefs and boundaries of a community. Despite presuppositions about it as being simplistic and non-intellectual, folk culture is often quite sophisticated; it expresses deeply held beliefs, guidelines, and other elements of folklore in traditional legends and myths that are profound and complex. Folk culture is full of fascinating stories which have meanings: they have been invented by highly intelligent thinkers rather than simple-minded people with a surfeit of imagination! The use of story to describe actual events and social forces is ancient, and it is very effective. Yet it can mislead the person who is inclined to be too literalist.

The development of folk tradition in early Christianity can lead us to ask questions about the history behind the traditions of the disciples such as: did Jesus really refer to Peter as 'Satan' because he refused to accept that Jesus needed to die, and did Peter deny Jesus? Was there someone called Judas Iscariot who betrayed him? We can identify two ways in which stories about biblical figures can be understood:

1. They are based on actual memories about a particular person who was regarded as a witness to the ministry, death, and resurrection of Jesus

It is difficult to establish the earliest traditions with certainty. Peter was certainly a historical figure in the Church, as is confirmed by mention of him as a missionary to the Jews by Paul in Galatians 2.7–8. It is supposed that he is the same person as Cephas given that John 1.42 states this; both names mean 'rock', the first in Greek, the second in Aramaic. (Despite this, the identification of the two has been disputed in both the early and modern Church but that is not something we can cover in this book.) Under one name or the other he appears in Paul's letters six times in Galatians 1–2 and four times in 1 Corinthians. But beyond the fact that Peter was a leader in the early Church and an important apostle, according to Paul the first to witness the resurrection (1 Cor. 15.5), it is only the gospels and Acts that contain details of what he did in the ministry of Jesus and afterwards. The gospels and Acts are unlike the epistles in that they contain narratives, which may in some cases include legendary material. So, we cannot be sure how much of this detail is historical.

As for Judas, there is no detail about him outside the gospels and Acts. We learn in Matthew 27.3–5 and Acts 1.15–20 that he took his life either shortly before or after the crucifixion. In the former, he hanged himself, in the latter, he fell to his death, but in both, the bribe that he received ('thirty pieces of silver' only in Matthew, unspecified elsewhere) was used to buy the 'Field of Blood'. The famous kiss by which he identified Jesus is mentioned in the synoptic gospels, but not in John. So we might suspect that the original tradition read something along these lines: Judas Iscariot betrayed Jesus in the garden of Gethsemane and received a bribe for doing so which was used to buy land which Christians referred to as the 'Field of Blood', but Judas died before he could enjoy the gains he had made. But this does not prove the historicity of this tradition.

2. The person is a representative figure who illustrates the actions or attitudes of people living before the writing of the gospels at the very beginning of the Church, and who acts as a role model for Christians reading the gospels in later generations

The traditions about Peter and Judas Iscariot can easily be understood in these terms, in which the stories about them are representational: they refer to Christians or potential Christians in the days of the early Church, those who found the idea of a crucified Messiah a 'stumbling block' (as Paul writes in 1 Cor. 1.23), or who denied Christ or betrayed other Christians at a time of persecution. Of course, in the gospel story, Peter eventually came to understand the truth and to follow Jesus without concern for his own safety, and so in that respect he is a positive role model, unlike Judas Iscariot. Judas' first name means 'Jew', and therefore perhaps he represented Jews who did not accept Christ and who, from a Christian point of view, betrayed the Messiah sent by the God whom they claimed to worship. Nevertheless, we should not overstate the connotations of this name, as there are other Judases in the New Testament who did not betray Jesus.

Other gospel characters – for example, 'doubting Thomas', the power-seeking sons of Zebedee, James and John, the woman who anointed Jesus and understood that he was destined to die, Martha and Mary with the one working and the other learning, Mary Magdalene who was healed of seven demons – all of these too were intended by the gospel writers as role models for Christians, and they have continued to fulfil this role. It is not easy to uncover the actual biographies behind this.

One way of seeing how biblical scholarship regards the gospels is to compare them to what we know in the modern world as the 'biopic', a life story dramatized on film. A good biopic will ensure that the main outlines of the biography are as accurate as possible in line with what can be documented historically. But the biopic has two other aspects: first, where facts are not known or unclear, the writer has the licence to fill in the pieces. Second, the biopic has to work *dramatically*, which might mean the rearranging of some events in the person's life or putting in dialogue where there is no record of what was actually said. We would evaluate a biopic by asking: does it present the person in such a way that we get a clear and accurate sense of what the person stood for, strove for, and meant to others? Does it inform the viewer in an educational way so that we know more about the life than when we started?

Of course, the gospels are more than biopics, as they are faith statements meant not just to represent who Jesus was but to bring new people into faith in him as the risen Messiah and Son of God, living still in the Church through the Holy Spirit. However, what can be said of biopics can also be applied to the gospels. They present the meaning of Christ and the summation of his mission for future generations, but they are not historically accurate except in the bare outlines: he was a Jew from Galilee, who attracted followers and preached about the Kingdom of God. He went to Jerusalem for festivals as any Jew would do and, on one of these occasions, he was crucified by the Roman garrison under the leadership of Pontius Pilate. His followers claimed that he rose from the dead and that he is therefore the Messiah and Son of God, indeed they came to believe that he *was* God. We will attempt to fill in more details as we go along. One of the facts we can be confident about, because it is so well attested, is that Jesus' mother was called Mary, or 'Mariam' in Aramaic, a name derived from the Hebrew original, 'Miriam'.[12]

THE CHURCHES AND FUNDAMENTALISM

Acceptance of the symbolic but not always historical nature of some biblical texts is not confined to the liberal Christian

---

[12] Or 'Maryam', as it is spelled in European translations of the Qur'an. Other ancient versions of this name include 'Mariamne', the name of the queen who was Herod the Great's wife.

tradition. It may be surprising to learn that this approach is also accepted to a considerable extent in the mainstream Churches, even the Roman Catholic and Orthodox. There too it is an established principle that we need to understand the *genre* of the biblical text and that, in some cases, texts were never intended to be read as historical facts. What is much more important for these Churches is that the Bible is understood as God's word, but they also accept that God's word was articulated by human beings writing in diverse historical contexts. Jewish cultural tradition, with its poetry and folklore, needs to be taken into account when interpreting a text. Scripture has also to be read as *canon*, in other words relating the various parts to the Bible as a whole and not taking passages out of context.

These principles were articulated in brief by the Roman Catholic Church at the Second Vatican Council in the 1960s in the document *Dei Verbum*. A more recent Roman Catholic document analysed biblical study at greater length. This was *The Interpretation of the Bible in the Church*, prepared by the Pontifical Biblical Commission in 1993 with a preface by Cardinal Joseph Ratzinger, the future Pope Benedict XVI. It explored various approaches to the Bible, including those by liberal Protestants, feminists, and liberation theologians. While, unsurprisingly, it provided a critique of these approaches, more unexpected was that its strongest attack was on fundamentalism:

> [Fundamentalism] refuses to admit that the inspired word of God has been expressed in human language and that this word has been expressed, under divine inspiration, by human authors possessed of limited capacities and resources. For this reason, it tends to treat the biblical text as if it had been dictated word for word by the Spirit. It fails to recognize that the word of God has

been formulated in language and expression conditioned by various periods. It pays no attention to the literary forms and to the human ways of thinking to be found in the biblical texts, many of which are the result of a process extending over long periods of time and bearing the mark of very diverse historical situations.

Fundamentalism also places undue stress upon the inerrancy of certain details in the biblical texts, especially in what concerns historical events or supposedly scientific truth. It often historicizes material which from the start never claimed to be historical. It considers historical everything that is reported or recounted with verbs in the past tense, failing to take the necessary account of the possibility of symbolic or figurative meaning.

(§I F)

The Catholic Church went on to reiterate that the literal sense of a text need not mean that it happened historically:

The literal sense is not to be confused with the 'literalist' sense to which fundamentalists are attached… When it is a question of a story, the literal sense does not necessarily imply belief that the facts recounted actually took place, for a story need not belong to the genre of history but be instead a work of imaginative fiction.

(§II B1)

This seems very reasonable guidance. The Roman Catholic, and Orthodox Churches too, accept that not everything in the Bible can be read as occurring exactly as it was written. Did God create vegetation before the sun? Could Eve have been created from Adam's rib? Was Methuselah really 969 when he died? Could the ark actually have taken on board two of each species? Did Joshua cause the sun to stand still? The Bible needs to be *interpreted*, and it contains metaphor, symbolism, and poetry as well as history. But, at the same time, the Churches would always insist that the Bible is nevertheless God's word and it therefore presents *truth*. The point is to know how to interpret that truth.

There will always be disagreement as to how much can be considered imaginative and symbolic instead of being historically factual. The Catholic Church, among others, would probably draw the line around certain texts (especially in the gospels which have pre-eminence in the Catholic Church) that more liberal interpreters would see as limited to the metaphorical or providing role models in narrative form. It is possible to regard the majority if not all of the gospels as having been constructed by people living decades after Christ, who did not know him and who wrote material that they felt would help the spread the gospel. Yet the Church bases doctrine on certain sections, and those passages therefore remain sacrosanct. Elsewhere in *The Interpretation of the Bible in the Church*, it is reported that scientific methods can cause concern among believers when they feel that interpreters have adopted 'positions contrary to the faith of the church on matters of great importance such as the virginal conception of Jesus and his miracles, and even his resurrection and divinity' (Introduction A).

MYTH AND TRUTH

This brings us to the question as to how *myth* – which can be defined as stories about the supernatural which are metaphorical but which should not be understood as historical – can also be *truth*. In terms of Christian theology, mythical elements are stories which convey the truth of the Christian understanding of God and the relationship between God and humanity in a metaphorical way. Symbols and stories tell the truth of God better than dogmatic theology ever could.

It is possible to find a middle place between reducing the Bible stories to complete fantasies, on the one hand, and insisting on them being history against all reason and evidence, on the other. It is not unreasonable to think that a gospel narrative is a mythical story (or legend), rather than history, but that what it says about Jesus and Mary tells us the truth in a symbolic form about who they were, what they did and, most importantly, what their lives mean for Christians today and for generations to come. Jesus really is the Saviour, whether or not he was tempted by Satan in the desert for forty days or walked on water. Mary really was the one who nurtured the Messiah and Son of God, whether or not there was an angel who told her that she would conceive while still a virgin.

We can ask whether myths and legends appropriately describe the person or situation they are describing. If I told you that, at the birth of Martin Luther King, the spirits of many African American slaves were heard singing spirituals, you would probably not think that actually happened, as no one at the time of his birth would have known that Martin Luther King would go on to be the inspirational leader that history remembers him for being. If I told you that he tore apart the chains of an unjustly condemned prisoner with his bare hands, you might doubt that too. However, you might think that these stories were fitting, as they describe in poetic form the aspirations of generations of African Americans for equality and freedom being partially realized in the Civil Rights Movement. Therefore, a criterion we can employ to evaluate material which is mythical and metaphorical is to ask whether it describes historical facts appropriately in poetic or symbolic forms.

Stories about important people within a religious belief system are *hagiographical*; they are texts which present someone in such a way as to demonstrate their holiness and to recommend them and their message to people in general. Hagiographical stories are understood on different levels, and some believers prefer to regard them as historical events so that they retain their force. For those who do not, believing that the content of the story represents a poetic but appropriate way of describing history means that it is quite possible to continue to derive meaning and inspiration from its retelling. In Christianity and other religions, retelling often occurs in a liturgical or worship setting. Symbolism and metaphor are, in other words, alternative ways of recounting history.

Therefore, a reading that understands the whole narrative as purely fictional and bearing no resemblance to history is not properly a Christian one. The meaning of the lives of Jesus and other prominent figures in the gospels, represented through story and parable, is for future generations of believers; this therefore represents *truth*, even if conveyed through the means of theologically based legends derived from prophetic fulfilment which may not be historically precise. Therefore, for example, the story of the Holy Family fleeing from Palestine into Egypt because of the murderous intentions of Herod (Matt. 2.3–18) does convey the danger that the fledgeling Church faced from antagonistic authorities, and it continues to inspire people to acts of hospitality for refugees and asylum seekers. The narrative in which we find the tax-gatherer Zacchaeus hiding in the tree, being prepared to pay back everything and more to those whom he has overcharged (Luke 19.1–10), does represent the spirit of the teaching of Jesus and it still provokes us to consider what we might owe to the poor in our society. Whether or not they represent historical events, these passages express the truth about who Jesus is and where we may find him in the world of today.

Jesus was a man, fully a human being. Some of the traditions about him suggest, as we have seen, someone who is superhuman, not confined to the usual boundaries of life as a human being. These are the stories that one suspects have much to tell us about what he meant to the early Church but do not establish anything historical. The most obvious examples are Jesus walking on water, calming the storm, feeding five thousand people with five loaves and two fish, and raising the dead back to life. These explain and encourage the Christian faith; they are true mythically as descriptions of what Jesus achieved and what he means to his believers, but not what he actually did in three-dimensional time and space. They suggest a post-resurrection, heavenly Jesus rather than a man among men. Other stories: his sermons, his advice to the disciples, his cleansing of the Temple, washing the disciples' feet, and sharing the Last Supper do not contradict what we know of human beings, particularly remarkable human beings. Like the biopic, they may be embellished as to the detail and timing, but these narratives might well be based on actual historical events.

The gospels represent an early stage of the process by which the human lives of Jesus Christ and his associates were mythologized, that is, established in eternity in order to become available to all believers after them. Thus Jesus, it could be said, is eternally feeding the five thousand, healing the diseased, and sharing the bread and wine of salvation; these occur through the actions of present-day Christians (hopefully!), but they are still the actions of Christ as the head of his body which is the Church. He is eternally present on the cross, offering his body to future generations. The Catholic crucifix captures this belief; it is not accepted as an image in Protestantism yet, there too, the cross remains important and the benefits of Christ's sacrifice remain eternally accessible. The early Church pictured a triumphant, risen Christ rather than an agonized figure on the cross; the crucifix that emerged in the medieval era was truer to historical reality. However, the original cross of Christ triumphant is closer to the process of mythologization that occurs with other aspects of the life of Christ as we read them in the gospels: Christ is larger than life in that he walks on water, raises Lazarus, and stills the storm. This is the heavenly Christ, the divine being, second person of the Trinity.

The Christian can connect to this Jesus across time and space. The Jesus in heaven and the Jesus during the Incarnation are one and the same person. Ways of describing the heavenly Jesus include mythical constructs which are accurate ways of articulating what the believer can expect to receive from Jesus. Jesus' real-life actions did not include walking on water, but they were nonetheless wonderful and expressed symbolically through this parable, which shows us that Jesus rises above, and takes the believer above, all those things which can drown and suffocate us in life.

As the early Christian tradition developed outside the writings of the New Testament, the description of Christ's mother included material which is unmistakeably mythology. The mother of Christ was described by the means of various theological associations in early Christian apocrypha,[13] such as Wisdom (*Odes of Solomon* 19, Davidson's translation), the Holy Spirit (*Gospel of the Hebrews* 3 quoted in Origen, *Commentary on John* 2.12.87), or an incarnation of the archangel Michael (as in the *Gospel of the Hebrews* 1, quoted in Cyril of Jerusalem, *Discourse on Mary Theotokos* 12).

Like Christ, Mary was regarded in Christian tradition as a historical person and mythological being at the same time. This was also the case with John the Baptist about whom it was asked whether he was a reincarnation of Elijah, Jeremiah, or one of the other prophets (Matt. 16.14; Mark 8.28; Luke

---

[13] The Christian apocrypha are those scripture-like Christian writings from the first few centuries of the Church which were not included in the New Testament.

9.19). In the second century, in the *Protevangelium* or *Infancy Gospel of James*, there is the image of Mary as a pure young child taken to the Temple, where she is fed by angels. Even later, there were many accounts of her death with all the apostles gathered followed by her assumption into heaven. An important question that arises about Mary in the birth and infancy narratives is whether the description of her as a virgin mother also belongs to this category of mythology in which truth is conveyed in parables, that is, in symbolic stories with a theological purpose.

5

Mary the Virgin in Ancient Texts

THE VIRGINAL CONCEPTION OF JESUS IN MATTHEW AND LUKE

The virgin conception is narrated by both Matthew and Luke but it is not easy for modern people to accept it literally, since we know that humans do not reproduce by parthenogenesis (birth from a female parent without male fertilization), and this view is supported by our relatively recent discovery of DNA and chromosomes. If Jesus had been born of an unfertilized embryo, he would not have been human in the normal sense of the word. This is problematic for the doctrine of the Incarnation, that is, God became a human being in every sense except sin. Another reason for not accepting the story literally is that there are many parallels in ancient literature which describe miraculous births that involve divine intervention. They are not historically true, either, but this shows that such stories were a common way of describing the birth of an important person in the ancient world. The early Christians had plenty of precedents in describing Jesus' birth in terms of miraculous and awe-inspiring events.

It has worried me in the past that denying the historical reality of the virgin conception might have the effect of damaging people's faith. Prospective parents often relate to Mary and bring their concerns to her because, as a virgin mother, she is a miraculous being in whom people can confide their worries about fertility and childbirth. Sarah Jane Boss makes this point in her book *Empress and Handmaid: On Nature and Gender in the Cult of the Virgin Mary*, giving several examples from Christian tradition. However, the recent publication of analysis by Elina Vuola, a Finnish scholar, *The Virgin Mary across Cultures: Devotion among Costa Rican Catholic and Finnish Orthodox Women*, reassured me considerably. Vuola interviewed female Marian devotees in both Costa Rica and Finland, and confirmed that Mary is indeed important in matters of fertility, childbirth, and child-rearing. However, in these two quite different contexts, the last thing that seems to concern Vuola's interviewees is that Mary was literally a virgin at the time of conceiving Jesus. Many of them disbelieved it, saying that it was an impossibility and the kind of thing that priests believe, but not ordinary people. The lack of belief in a literal understanding of the virgin birth did not harm their Catholic or Orthodox faith, or their recourse to Mary in prayer and devotion, at all.

Virgin conception is a theological metaphor, a very telling way of making the statement that Jesus was the Son of God in a special way (not the son of God in the sense that everyone is a child of God). The Christian claim that Jesus was the Son of God, as well as being theological, also stood out as a highly *political* one in its time. The Roman emperors from Julius Caesar onwards were regarded as divinities after their death and, when living, at least sons of gods. There was therefore an imperial cult that Christians and Jews refused to take part in, as it contradicted their monotheistic beliefs; it was difficult for Christians and Jews to enter the Roman military where participation in the emperor cult was a requirement. There were many legends about the miraculous births of emperors which reinforced their near-divine status. To claim that Jesus was the Son of God and born of a virgin stood in direct rivalry to these beliefs and made it clear where a person's allegiance lay. Therefore, it was not surprising that Christians suffered persecution in the Roman Empire.

Another reason why the virgin conception story arose naturally in the early Church is that the Hebrew Scriptures provide plenty of precedents for belief in miraculous conception. They abound with stories of births from women either past childbearing age or at least after many years of yearning: Sarah the wife of Abraham and mother of Isaac; Rebekah the mother of Jacob and Esau; Rachel the mother of Joseph and Benjamin; Hannah the mother of Samuel; all of these women fall into this category. The theme of waiting upon God's intervention is one that will have resonated with Jews at the time of the Exile, when the texts that included these characters were collected and edited into what eventually became the Hebrew Scriptures. The message is: be patient, God's purpose will be served eventually. Finally, centuries later, Luke added one more to this list of women who bore a child after years of waiting: Elizabeth, Mary's relative, the mother of John the Baptist. She is the representative of a nation that has been waiting for its deliverance.

Mary's virginity and youth are the polar opposite of late childbearing and there are no clear precedents for a virgin conception in the Hebrew Scriptures, but this story still reflects the theme of God's miraculous intervention in the history of the Jewish people. This time, in Mary, God is doing something extraordinary and creating something completely new. Faith in Jesus Christ relates to the *new* covenant. To reinforce the idea that the virgin conception is something rather different from the theme of late birth, the four women preceding Mary in the genealogy of Matthew (Matt. 1.1–17) do not include Sarah, Rebekah, Rachel, and Hannah, but instead Tamar, who conceived by Judah when pretending to be a prostitute; Rahab, the prostitute who helped Joshua invade Jericho; Ruth, the Moabite who became the great-grandmother of David by seducing Boaz; and Bathsheba, the wife of Uriah the Hittite who was desired by David and so became the mother of Solomon. Three of these women continued the line of Judah and one ensured that the Israelites captured the Promised Land, and so they are heroines in the Jewish tradition, but unlikely heroines in somewhat compromising situations. Mary is the fifth and last woman included in the genealogy.

It has been speculated that the genealogy and the four names of women of questionable reputation might imply that Mary's pregnancy was thought to have been controversial, perhaps the result of an illegitimate union; this was claimed in ancient anti-Christian polemical arguments which were scornful of the virgin conception. However, we do not need to speculate on whether there is hidden historical detail behind the story if we believe that all we have is a mythical story based on theological symbolism. Matthew only tells us that the conception occurred 'from the Holy Spirit' and that Joseph was persuaded of the fact by an angel.

A much better explanation that links these five women together is that they all brought very important new circumstances into being at crucial moments in the Davidic line. From Tamar comes the royal line of Judah through Perez, whose descendants were the kings in Jerusalem, including David; Rahab facilitated Israel's entry into the Promised Land under Joshua; Ruth was the great-grandmother of David and the one close Davidic ancestor of whom readers of the

Jewish Scriptures knew the life details; Bathsheba gave birth to Solomon, who built the Temple and continued David's line. Finally, Mary brought into being Jesus, the one who represents all these things in himself: he is the new David and Joshua, the foundation of the new community of salvation, the King of the kingdom of heaven who brings it into being, and the High Priest of the new Temple. Mary then is the natural fifth in the list of women because of whom she brings into being, and not because of the potentially scandalous circumstances by which this occurs.

The virgin conception was thought to have been foreshadowed in Isaiah 7.14: 'Therefore the Lord himself will give you a sign. Look, the young woman is with child and shall bear a son, and shall name him Immanuel.' This is the English translation of the Hebrew, but Matthew 1.23 quotes the Greek version which includes the word 'virgin', *parthenos*. Translated into English, it reads: 'Look, the virgin shall conceive and bear a son, and they shall name him Emmanuel, which means "God is with us".' This was the proof text which Matthew used to show that the virgin conception was prophesied in the Jewish tradition.

The original context of Isaiah's prophecy is rather different to the way it is understood in the New Testament. Isaiah was telling King Ahaz that the Assyrians would destroy Judah's enemies, Syria and the northern tribes of Israel, in the very near future, and also threaten Judah itself before the child of the prophecy was old enough to tell between good and evil. The son's name is Immanuel because this prophetic sign is to announce God's action in punishing both Israel and Judah, although Judah eventually survived the successive Assyrian invasions when Jerusalem stood firm under Ahaz's son Hezekiah, who was also advised by Isaiah. The boy is a prophetic metaphor, like other such symbolic allusions in the prophetic books (for example, the basket of fruit in Amos

8.1–2 or Hosea's prostitute wife in Hosea 1.2). Who the boy was or whether he lived at all is insignificant. The theme of a boy being born who will not grow very old before Assyria invades the lands of Israel is repeated in Isaiah 8; this child is the fruit of a meeting between Isaiah and a prophetess.

In actual fact, the coming of Christ is much better pre-figured by the prophecy of Isaiah 9.6 which promises peace for the Davidic kingdom: 'For a child has been born for us, a son given to us; authority rests upon his shoulders; and he is named Wonderful Counsellor, Mighty God, Everlasting Father, Prince of Peace.' This is a message of hope made very familiar thanks to Handel's setting in the *Messiah*. In its original context, this probably reflected the new reign of King Hezekiah, Ahaz's son, regarded much more favourably than Ahaz in the Hebrew tradition. However, Matthew chose Isaiah 7.14 because it acted as a proof text for the virgin conception. *Parthenos* can also mean 'betrothed person' as in 1 Corinthians 7, and thus serves a double purpose, as Mary was betrothed to Joseph but had not 'known' him at the birth of Jesus, as Matthew 1.25 states. Therefore, Matthew gave the Isaiah 7.14 text an interpretation which has endured in Christianity.

For all these reasons: the competition with miraculous claims for the Roman emperors, and their deified lineage; the context in which early Christian culture expressed theological and religious ideas through symbolic forms; the way in which miraculous births have precedents in the Hebrew Scriptures; and taking into account all these along with scientific advance in knowledge of human reproduction, we can conclude that there are very good historical and literary arguments that should lead us to regard the virgin conception as presenting a theological truth in the form of a symbolic story that suited the context but not historical fact. The title 'Virgin' might be a fitting way of describing Mary, but it did not relate to her permanent physical state.

Who then was Jesus' actual father? There is no reason to think that it was anyone other than Joseph. If the virgin conception narratives are mythical, then the detail about Joseph's concern because of Mary's premature pregnancy is not historical, and in the absence of other information we are left with the fact that Jesus was described as Joseph's son (Luke 4.22; John 6.42). Second-century opponents of Christianity claimed that it was a Roman soldier named Panthera, but that was an obvious way of pouring doubt on belief in the virgin birth which was established in the Church by then. Any suggestion other than Joseph the husband of Mary is unfounded speculation.

THE VIRGINAL CONCEPTION IN ANCIENT LITERATURE

What would the original readers of the gospels have understood when they read about the virgin conception? Mary Foskett asks this question in her book *A Virgin Conceived: Mary and Classical Representations of Virginity*. In both ancient Greco-Roman and Jewish culture, the word 'virgin' applied to a young woman evoked an interconnected set of ideas:

- It referred to the state between one stage of life – childhood – and another – adulthood;
- It was therefore an indication of the purity and innocence of a person at the very beginning of their adult life;
- It was also an indication of honour and spiritual power, but also vulnerability;
- Virginity referred more to social status than to the state of the physical body (it was only regarded as being compromised when there were clear reasons to doubt it).

Virginity was a *liminal* or in-between state: it represented the point when females were no longer girls, but not yet fully married women. The state of betrothal was an intermediate period when the young woman had not yet moved to her husband's house (despite this, Luke refers to Mary as betrothed rather than wife even though she travels with Joseph to Bethlehem). 'Liminal' is a word which refers to the borderline between places, seasons, or periods of life, and these boundaries are regarded across the world as having the quality of an openness to divine or supernatural forces. In the life cycle, it principally relates to birth, adulthood, conversion, marriage, and death. These present opportunities for members of a community to gather and come into contact with their tradition and its deities, representing all this in ritual drama. Liminality is both sacred and dangerous, hence the need for ritual observances and taboos.

The spiritual dangers of liminality, such as the threat of pollution by incorrect observance of traditional customs, go along with practical dangers. In the case of female virginity, there is the possibility of sex being forced on the young woman before she is ready through marriage, or her seeking it. This has the potential to cause parents much stress; in traditional patriarchal cultures, the virgin is an important asset, a person with financial and social value, a commodity. This is clearly described in the Wisdom of Jesus ben Sirach (42.9–14);[14] the passage has a misogynistic conclusion, but it illustrates the concern over virgin daughters in the ancient world!

A daughter is a secret anxiety to her father,
  and worry over her robs him of sleep;
when she is young, for fear she may not marry,

---

[14] Better known as Ecclesiasticus; in the Protestant canon, this book is placed among the apocrypha.

or if married, for fear she may be disliked;
while a virgin, for fear she may be seduced
  and become pregnant in her father's house;
or having a husband, for fear she may go astray,
  or, though married, for fear she may be barren.
Keep strict watch over a headstrong daughter,
  or she may make you a laughingstock to your enemies,
a byword in the city and the assembly of the people,
  and put you to shame in public gatherings.
See that there is no lattice in her room,
  no spot that overlooks the approaches to the house.
Do not let her parade her beauty before any man,
  or spend her time among married women;
for from garments comes the moth,
  and from a woman comes woman's wickedness.
Better is the wickedness of a man than a woman who
    does good;
  it is woman who brings shame and disgrace.

Mary as *parthenos* is pictured in Matthew and Luke as being in this liminal period between girlhood and marriage, just after the onset of puberty. She is the ideal virgin, honourable and attentive to the moral customs, but an unexpected pregnancy would certainly have caused consternation both with her fiancé, as we see in the story of Joseph's reaction, Matt. 1.18–25, and with her parents, whose reaction we do not read about in the gospels nor in the second-century *Protevangelium of James* where they feature. Matthew rather than Luke is alert to the social questions that describing Mary as a virgin at the time of conception would have raised; Luke simply states Mary's own concern: 'How can this be?', but she is quickly reassured by Gabriel.

Readers of Matthew and Luke who knew the Hebrew Scriptures would have been aware of the many references to a female who is a virgin, *betulah* in Hebrew. The Greek version of the Jewish texts (Septuagint) was in wide circulation at the time of the writing of the gospels, so it is important to consider also the instances of the Greek word for virgin, *parthenos*, in the Septuagint. See Appendix 3 for the details of the biblical occurrences of these words.

What is unanimous in all these references is that the idea of 'virgin' relates to the liminal state between childhood and womanhood. It never refers to the idea of a virgin as an adult female. The one possible exception is Joel 1.8 which concerns a lamentation over the ruin of Israel: 'Lament like a virgin dressed in sackcloth for the husband of her youth.' Here the unfortunate woman indicated in the simile is like Dickens' Miss Havisham: she remains in the virgin state because the husband she was expecting to marry has been killed. She is not a model for virginity as an adult vocation.

THE VIRGIN DAUGHTERS OF GOD

The virgin in the Hebrew Scriptures is either a specific person (Rebekah; the daughter of the host in Gibeah; Jephthah's daughter; Abishag; Esther) or figurative, describing a situation (future good or bad outcomes, 'it will be a time when virgins...', etc.), or legal, indicating what is to be done in a particular situation ('if a virgin...' etc.). In thirteen cases, the word 'virgin' describes not a person, but a nation or community. Israel is a virgin daughter four times, Jerusalem or Zion three times, Judah twice, and Samaria, Sidon, Babylon, Egypt once each. In these passages, God is imaged as the anxious and angry father of the wayward daughter intending to impose punishment, except in Jeremiah 31, where virgin Israel is restored. It is interesting to note that the natural enemies of ancient Israel, the Egyptians and Babylonians, are also regarded as

God's failing daughters, a reminder of the way that Israel's texts present a God who is a father to all peoples.

For the Hebrew prophets, God is both a concerned father of Israel and her prospective bridegroom. References of both types occur in Isaiah, Jeremiah and Lamentations, Ezekiel, and Amos. Hosea's famous image is of Israel as a whore (in Hosea 5.3, the male symbolic figure Ephraim is also used for the whoring metaphor). The prostitute metaphor is also used in Isaiah, Jeremiah, and Ezekiel in referring to Israel, Judah, Jerusalem, Samaria, and Sodom. Overall, the prophetic message is that the perfect daughter or wife as the community or nation is the one who listens only to her father or husband, preserving her virginity for marriage and whose attention does not waver towards false gods. In the New Testament, the symbol of the divine bridegroom passes to Christ.

In the apocryphal books, those not in the Hebrew canon but part of the Septuagint, once again a virgin is a young female in the liminal period between the stages of childhood and adulthood. There is one interesting reference to Wisdom as a virgin bride, in Sirach 15.2.

What is clear, therefore, is that Mary as a virgin will have been understood in the light of these passages in the Hebrew and Greek Scriptures of the Jewish people. She is a young woman having just entered puberty and a symbol of Israel or Jerusalem, the 'Daughter of Zion'. The association made between the virginity of Mary and scriptural metaphors about the virgin daughters of God cannot have been lost on any reader in the early Church familiar with the Jewish Scriptures in either Greek or Hebrew. Mary's *Magnificat* (Luke 1.46–55) makes this abundantly clear:

My soul magnifies the Lord,
  and my spirit rejoices in God my Saviour,

for he has looked with favour on the lowliness of his
    servant.
  Surely, from now on all generations will call me blessed;
for the Mighty One has done great things for me,
  and holy is his name.
His mercy is for those who fear him
  from generation to generation.
He has shown strength with his arm;
  he has scattered the proud in the thoughts of their hearts.
He has brought down the powerful from their thrones,
  and lifted up the lowly;
he has filled the hungry with good things,
  and sent the rich away empty.
He has helped his servant Israel,
  in remembrance of his mercy,
according to the promise he made to our ancestors,
  to Abraham and to his descendants forever.

Mary is God's servant in this hymn but so is Israel (although different Greek words are used, *doulē*, slave or servant in the first instance, and *pais*, child, which can be translated 'servant', in the second). Mary has suffered lowliness but will now be called blessed; God has helped Israel and made good all the promises made to the nation. Israel has suffered from powerlessness and, when Luke was writing his gospel, had suffered over one hundred years of Roman rule which, after the Hasmonean period, had returned Israel to the state they were in before it, as vassals to a dominant and tyrannical foreign empire (imaged as a destructive beast in the book of Daniel). We do not need to speculate, as many have, as to why Mary as an individual is lowly; we do not know very much about her background in Luke. She is rather the representative of Israel, particularly its believers loyal to the monotheistic tradition who are the *anawim* of Jewish culture, that is, the poor, both economically and politically. These are the ones who understand the importance of waiting on God.

According to Luke's *Magnificat*, that part of Israel which has been lifted up are those who believe in Christ as the risen Son of God. For the rest, the nation was still under the Roman Empire and, by the time of the writing of Luke's Gospel, had been defeated in a disastrous war against Rome and the Temple destroyed. Therefore, Mary is at the same time Israel and the Church. While the association of Mary as a type (that is, a representative image) of the Church is not made explicit until Ambrose in the late fourth century, it is clearly implicit in the New Testament itself, nowhere more obviously than in the first two chapters of Luke. Like Mary, the Church in the apostolic period was in a liminal place where the outcomes were not clear. It too faced dangers and temptations which had the potential to take it away from faithfulness to the original message of Christ. These concerns are expressed in the epistles of Paul and John.

The metaphor in which the Church is likened to a virgin was employed at an early point. Paul's epistles portray the Church as Christ's bride, 'holy and without blemish' (Eph. 5.27), and liken the Corinthian church to a 'chaste virgin', with the danger of being led astray like Eve with the serpent (2 Cor. 11.2–3). In Revelation, chapters 19 and 21, the Bride of the Lamb is the new Jerusalem with clear associations with the Church. The fourth-century Christian historian Eusebius recorded the second-century writer Hegesippus as comparing the very earliest church with a virgin: 'They used to call the Church a virgin for this reason, that she had not yet been seduced by listening to nonsense', in other words, before the coming of what were, in his view, various heresies which attracted many Christians. He was referring to the time during which James was the 'bishop' in Jerusalem (*Church History* IV.22, see also III.32.7). Here the metaphor emphasizes the innocence but also potential corruptibility of the virgin, yet Mary is the Virgin who cannot be corrupted. At the end of the second century, Clement of Alexandria likewise spoke of the Church as a Virgin Mother (*Pedagogy* 1.6), and this symbolic image is established by the time of Ambrose and Augustine in the fourth to fifth centuries.

Therefore, the fourfold association between Israel – Church – Virgin – Mary is implied at an early stage in Christian tradition.

In the Greco-Roman world, virginity was likewise a metaphor for a community in some aspect, for example, a city or nation that had not been conquered, as in the virgin goddess Athene/Minerva, the patroness of Athens, the deity of culture and the arts, including the art of war. Other goddesses associated with virginity were Artemis/Diana, the deity of the natural world, hunting and blood, and therefore the patroness of childbirth and female puberty, including the beginning of menstruation; Hestia/Vesta, patroness of the family, the home, and the state; and (in some accounts) Hecate, the goddess of witchcraft, dogs, the dead, crossroads, and doorways. These virgins represented powerful forces in human experience, either civic or social (Athene and Hestia), natural (Artemis), or the liminal, those aspects of life on the boundaries of social organization (Hecate). The recognition that the state or family could not control everything was reflected in the importance of the wild goddesses Artemis and Hecate in the female life cycle and reproduction. There was also the poetic idea of a virgin understood as Justice bringing in a new age of peace represented by her boy child, in Virgil's *Fourth Eclogue*, written a few years before the birth of Jesus. This was so strikingly similar to the story of the birth of the bringer of peace by a virgin that Christians claimed that Virgil had been inspired as a prophet.

THE EXALTATION OF THE VIRGINAL STATE

The exaltation of virginity as a permanent, desirable adult state for females is not derived from the Hebrew Scriptures. It is associated with the Greco-Roman world. While, generally, virginity was not a virtue in Greek society and its prolongation not regarded as particularly healthy, nevertheless, sexual activity was devalued in the philosophical traditions of Pythagoras and Plato and, in some prominent cults, lifelong virgins were regarded as especially holy and mediators with the divine in classical Greece and Rome. For example, it was believed that the steadfast chastity of the Vestal Virgins and the continuity of their flame preserved Rome (and the diminishing of either threatened it). Virginity was also important in the Greek cultic traditions of the priestesses at Delphi, where the priestess was possessed by Apollo in the course of prophecy, thereby reflecting the relationship with the divine as an alternative to human marriage. The idea of marriage to divinity became a feature of future Christian female religious orders, nuns as 'brides' of Christ.

Virgin priestesses were unknown in the Jewish tradition. Luke and Matthew would not have wanted their readers to view Mary as equivalent to the Greco-Roman female deities or classical poetic concepts, or to see her conception by the Holy Spirit as having any parallel with the intercourse between gods and nymphs in Greek or Roman myth. However, because of the associations, their Gentile audience will have understood the story as being in direct competition with these ideas, and to represent a superior version of the relationship between God and faithful human communities. Gentile converts to Christianity were replacing their inherited traditions of classical mythology with the biblical theology of the Jewish tradition, as it was understood to be realized in Jesus Christ. The narrative of the virgin conception will have struck a chord with a Gentile Christian readership in a different way than with a Jewish Christian one, although the process by which Gentile Christians learned and elevated the Jewish scriptural traditions will have meant that their interpretations soon merged. However, the continuation of the tradition of virginity suggests that the Greco-Roman inheritance did have considerable influence.

Female adult virginity as a vocation may have made its way into Jewish communities in some isolated cases. The Jewish philosopher Philo refers to a Jewish sect near Alexandria, the 'Therapeutrides', as being ascetic and including elderly 'virgins'. So virginity out of choice may not have been unknown to the Jewish tradition at the time of the writing of the gospels, although the Therapeutrides were not in mainstream Jewish culture, and their sources seem to have been eclectic (in addition, the actual existence of the Therapeutrides has been questioned in scholarship).

Abstinence from sexual relations was adopted by *males* in some sections of Jewish culture at the time of Christ, for example, the Essenes at Qumran. Jesus' remark about people becoming eunuchs for the sake of the kingdom (Matt. 19.10–12) suggests that it might have applied to some of his followers, but this is hardly evidence for a general acceptance of the importance of sexual abstinence for both males and females in Jesus' movement. Paul suggests not marrying simply because of the imminence of the Parousia, the return of Christ, and the primacy of the task of spreading the gospel, but he is certainly not against marriage per se, nor does he hold up female celibacy as a virtue (1 Cor. 7.1–16, 25–40).

Celibacy became important in Christianity as Roman and Greek culture influenced the early Church over many decades, and the virtue of celibacy emerged much later in Christianity in its religious orders and eventually its priesthood; in this context, Mary's physical state came to be of interest and she was believed to have been a virgin before, during, and after the birth of Jesus, then for the whole of her life; her hymen remained unchanged. She was the 'Ever Virgin'. Yet this is a long way from the intentions of Matthew, Luke, and the early Church traditions which preceded them. In the gospels, the virgin conception is symbolic of a new divine action that has no precedent and no human cause. Virginity in the gospels is a statement about what God was doing in the birth of Jesus, rather than referring to the physical condition of Mary.

While the New Testament does not show any interest in the physical state of Mary's body, it can be conceded that the process of literalization – the move from seeing something as metaphor to regarding it as historical fact – has already been initiated in the gospel narratives, because Luke and Matthew wanted to answer the reader's questions: 'How could a virgin conceive a child' and 'what would happen socially if a virgin conceived?' The first question is placed on the lips of Mary by Luke, and the second is answered in Matthew by Joseph's dilemma resolved by his dream, both referring to the action of the Holy Spirit.

More explicit concern for Mary's physical condition appeared in the second-century Christian apocryphal gospel, the *Protevangelium*, when a woman called Salome inspects Mary's womb to check that the virgin really has given birth. Here we see the process by which the original metaphor evolved to become a doctrine about Mary's Perpetual Virginity. The *Protevangelium* states that the siblings of Jesus are step-brothers and sisters by a previous marriage of Joseph, who is widowed when he takes on the responsibility of the young virgin Mary. This establishes the lack of sexual contact between them.

6

Mary the Virgin:
Symbolism and Theology

MARY'S VIRGINITY AS THEOLOGICAL METAPHOR

T he word 'virgin' had metaphorical connotations in the ancient world just as it continues to do today. It denotes innocence and youth, the promise of a new life that is uncharted and full of potential. Originally, it also meant unspoiled, incorrupt, intact. While we might want to be cautious about this aspect of the metaphor today if we do not regard loving, consensual, and non-abusive sex as something that spoils or corrupts, nevertheless, we can understand the connotations of the word in its original context.

Mary's virginity conveys the message that, in the Incarnation of the Son of God, God enacts *renewal*. Israel in the person of Mary was returning to the opportunities present in the liminal virginal state and this time fulfilling its true divine vocation. The original newness of God's creation was bursting forth once again in the life, ministry, and death of Jesus, something that was not dependent on anything or anyone that had gone before: it did not rely on Jewish history but *fulfilled* it. This is summed up in John 1.17: 'The law indeed was given through Moses; grace and truth came through Jesus Christ.' The virgin conception captures this idea in the simple but wonderful story of the one who came into being through the Holy Spirit and not because of the initiative of human beings.

John's prologue (John 1.1–18) is very different from Matthew's and Luke's birth narratives. It identifies Jesus as the Word of God existent from all eternity and has clear echoes of Genesis 1 in which the world is created through God's speech. Despite this very different approach, John's prologue is in many ways equivalent to the story of Matthew's and Luke's virgin becoming pregnant by the action of the Holy Spirit. Both stress the divine initiative, speak about the origins of Jesus, and proclaim the advent of new things for the benefit of humanity. One does this with a theological hymn and the others with a story. The birth narratives of Matthew and Luke are prologues of their gospels in the same way as John's.

In the Christian story, Mary, the young woman between girlhood and marriage, is taken up into cosmic eternity: for each successive generation, she continues to hear the words of the angel and respond with her 'Let it be'. In this sense, she is the 'Ever Virgin'. That liminal moment in which the young woman becomes pregnant with the Messiah is forever available to us. She, like Eve, stands in the garden of eternity and makes a decision which is with humanity for all time. Mary is accessed through mythical language and ideas in which she is larger than life: the 'Ever Virgin' and 'New Eve'.

The other moment in which Mary is especially and eternally present is the crucifixion. Christian theology does not make a distinction between the virgin as a young woman and the older woman who now stands as a mother lamenting the execution of her son. The mythical language of eternity does not need to take account of such discontinuities; in its language, she can be virgin and mother, young and old, all at the same time. All aspects of her life present themselves together.

Those two states of Mary, the young virgin and the ageing, sorrowful mother, are not necessarily opposites. The crucifixion as a painful but necessary process – a transition into salvation and the emergence of the Church – was imagined as a birth that moved from pain to joy, a metaphor used in both the Gospel of John (16.21–22) and the book of Revelation, which we will shortly consider further. The image of Mary giving birth to Jesus not only applied to his actual birth from her, but also to the crucifixion and resurrection. It has been suggested that Luke saw it this way too, as the swaddling clothes and the manger in the nativity story (2.7) prefigure the burial shroud and the tomb. We can also wonder whether John regarded the presence of the mother of Jesus at the crucifixion (19.25–27) as indicative of the new birth that the cross represented. Certainly, later artists and sculptors understood this association, using images of the man Jesus with his arms outstretched as they would be on the cross while an infant on Mary's lap, or images of the Pietà where the dead Jesus in Mary's arms is only the size of an infant.

Perhaps, then, the virgin is an appropriate metaphor for the older mother in whose presence Christ was raised from the dead, just as it was for the young woman who represented new beginnings. Both are Mary, but also Israel, the virgin daughter of God. From this Mother Israel, the resurrection comes forth as a new birth, to give salvation to all nations.

The virgin metaphor has another important dimension. This is related to the association of the young woman who remains uncompromised with the 'garden locked' and 'fountain sealed' in Song of Songs 4.12. It also had ancient connotations with virgin goddesses like Athene who represented an unconquered city. We know in everyday life that gardens, fountains, and cities are not unbreachable, and that nobody is immune to abuse, disaster, or disease. However, Christianity teaches that, on the spiritual level, Christ is unconquered and unconquerable and that souls who commit to him are equally so (as described in the image of the Church firm against the gates of hell in Matthew 16.18). The virgin metaphor can refer to the soul itself. Whatever disaster may prevail upon the body and the social position of a person, the soul remains intact and cannot be destroyed. This is an extremely important aspect of the Christian faith. It is far more crucial than the question as to whether God really did create a miracle in making a virgin conceive, or whether she remained a virgin for all of her life. That is transferring the things of eternity to concerns over sexuality, as is the problem when metaphors become literalized so far that they lose their original force.

Therefore, the virgin conception, in the same way as choirs of angels, visiting shepherds and wise men, or the inn at Bethlehem, was an appropriate metaphorical way of describing the beginning of Jesus' life, which is at the same time the beginning of Christianity and the Church as the community of salvation. Mary in the annunciation, visitation, and birth narratives, above all the other characters in the gospels, has been inspirational as a role model for Christians, both male and female, throughout Christian history. In Luke 1–2, she is the archetype for the Christian who accepts the Word of God and brings Christ into being through living the gospel. This is reinforced by Elizabeth's words in Luke 1.45: 'And blessed is she who believed that there would be a fulfilment of what was spoken to her by the Lord.' As a virgin and mother, she has also been an important exemplar for people in both religious and family life.

The birth narratives create a picture of a woman who is a representative of believing Israel, an important witness to the birth and infancy of Jesus, and a role model for future Christians. She is also portrayed as the Church in prototype, representing people who lived before the time of the gospels at the very beginning of the Church, that is, Christians who accepted Jesus and thus heard the Word and said, like Mary, 'Let it be to me according to your Word' (Luke 1.38). Mark 3.35, which we will discuss in a later chapter, shows us that the idea of being Jesus' mother or brother was related to 'whoever does the will of God', which could be any disciple. The difference between Luke 1–2 and Mark 3.31–35 is that Luke portrays Mary as the role model for Christians, but Mark thinks that looking to Mary the mother of Jesus to provide this example is unnecessary. These opposing tendencies continue today in Catholicism and Protestantism. But, for Luke, Mary was understood as a type or image of the Church itself from the very beginning. He makes it clear that she was a poor Jewish woman who was responsive to the ways in which God spoke to the Jewish people and promised them a better future. In doing this and understanding that Jesus was the promised Messiah, she helped to bring that future into being. She was the archetypal and prototypical Christian in the Jewish origins of the Church.

However, the critical reader will ask: while Mary provides an exemplary image for Christians who 'give birth to Christ in their lives', are the stories about her appropriate, however metaphorical and legendary, to the mother of Jesus who actually existed as a historical person? So far all we have discovered about her as a historical rather than mythical figure is the surprising fact that, despite the usual way of describing her as the 'Virgin Mary', she was not a virgin in the physical sense, that is, not someone who did not 'know' her husband at the time of the conception of Jesus, nor someone who never 'knew' him at any time. This will only be a shock if we think that sexuality must always be polluted, even when it is practised between loving and mutually responsive persons. In saying that Mary was not literally a virgin, we do not need to surrender any of our cherished ideas that she was a wonderful woman who, like her son, is remembered for her service to humanity and with whom we do not associate any selfish or abusive act. It does *not* mean that we should desist from describing her as the Queen of Heaven or Mother of God. Indeed, if the title Virgin is detached from its physical and sexual meaning, perhaps it is an appropriate word to describe such a person.

The Catholic theologian Karl Rahner, in accepting the probability of the metaphorical rather than historical nature of Mary's virginity, wrote that he was:

> ...convinced in faith that Mary was incorporated with her whole body-soul existence into the historical salv-ific mission of Jesus. Have we not then jointly a basic understanding of what her 'virginity' means for all of us, even though we do not think that we all know with equal certainty and clarity what exactly this integrated-ness means 'biologically', particularly since we are all sure that this absolute integratedness must also include Mary's participation in the ordinariness and lowliness of Jesus' human existence?
>
> (*Theological Investigations* 19, p. 228)

Yet is there any basis for thinking that Mary was involved in Christ's mission, in the way that Rahner suggests, and an extraordinary woman who served humanity? If the birth and infancy narratives are legends, do we learn from them anything about the actual person Mary the mother of Jesus? In later chapters, we tackle the question as to how much we can know about the Mary of history as opposed to the Mary of mythology and metaphor.

THE WOMAN CLOTHED WITH THE SUN IN REVELATION 12

Apart from the gospels of Luke and Matthew, there is another passage where the birth of the Messiah is described. This can be found in the book of Revelation. It is a famous image, a visionary picture which was never intended to be anything other than metaphorical:

> A great portent appeared in heaven: a woman clothed with the sun, with the moon under her feet, and on her head a crown of twelve stars. She was pregnant and was crying out in birth pangs, in the agony of giving birth. Then another portent appeared in heaven: a great red dragon, with seven heads and ten horns, and seven diadems on his heads. His tail swept down a third of the stars of heaven and threw them to the earth. Then the dragon stood before the woman who was about to bear a child, so that he might devour her child as soon as it was born. And she gave birth to a son, a male child, who is to rule all the nations with a rod of iron. But her child was snatched away and taken to God and to his throne; and the woman fled into the wilderness, where she has a place prepared by God, so that there she can be nourished for one thousand two hundred and sixty days.
>
> (Revelation 12.1–6)

The image of the woman in Revelation 12 is clearly a mythical one; while there can be debate about the historicity of the birth stories in Luke and Matthew, no one has ever disputed the fact that the woman in Revelation 12 is a symbolic creation, even if regarded as a divinely inspired vision. She was interpreted, first, as the image of the Church and, later, as a symbol of Mary, because the woman clothed with the sun bore the male child who is clearly meant to represent Christ. It is strange that the connection with Mary was not made earlier; one obstacle to it might have been the belief that Mary's childbirth was painless, which appeared quite early in Christian tradition. This clearly contradicts the picture of the agonizing delivery that we find in Revelation. The birth pangs are very reminiscent of the images of the crucifixion as a painful birth in the Gospel of John, not by the same author but for centuries thought to be so.

The myth in Revelation 12 is a pictorial way of describing the events of the early Church: the context is the persecution of the early Church at the hands of the Roman and Jewish authorities. The woman, the Church, gives birth to Christ; she will continue to suffer from the enmity of the threatening dragon and so has to flee into the wilderness. She is also Israel, as signified by the twelve stars. The painful birth is the crucifixion, and the taking away of the child into heaven represents the resurrection and ascension. The child will return to judge the world; this is narrated in Revelation chapter 19. The birth story in Revelation has a parallel in Matthew, with the story of Herod's slaughter of the innocents which, as far as can be known, is not historical. Herod, of course, was a local ruler established by the Roman system. Therefore, there are several points of correspondence between the birth narratives of Matthew and Luke, and the Revelation myth:

REVELATION 12	MATTHEW 1–2	LUKE 1–2
Birth of the Messiah	Birth of Jesus	Birth of Jesus
Painful delivery		Mary told by Simeon to anticipate sorrow; she wraps the child in a way that brings burial to mind
The dragon, a metaphor for those who are trying to destroy Christianity	Herod's massacre	

This might suggest that all the metaphors involved here are telling us one story:

- That Jesus' being crucified, buried, and raised is integral to his being the Messiah;
- That the crucifixion of the Messiah is like a painful birth (a metaphor also found in John's Gospel);
- That the Church is the faithful remnant of Israel which knows that its Messiah has come;
- That the Church by its proclamation of the resurrection is like a mother bringing the child Jesus into the world and thereby giving birth to a new age;
- That the Church is vulnerable to persecution, particularly by the Roman system which promotes emperor worship and for whom the claim that Jesus is the Son of God and God Incarnate is a threat.

The book of Revelation, like the gospels of Matthew and Luke, narrates a birth which precedes the consummation of marriage. Revelation chapters 19–21 narrate the marriage of the Lamb to the Bride, the new Jerusalem. If Matthew's and Luke's Mary represents the Church and Israel at the same time, then in all three texts we have the image of a Church as a new Israel or Jerusalem who gives birth as a mother, and then anticipates her marriage. In Revelation, her bridegroom is at the same time her son. The consummation is, of course, spiritual and metaphorical like the images of God as bridegroom to Israel in the Hebrew Scriptures. Matthew and Luke, unlike Revelation, set this story in historical narrative, which brings more mundane matters into play, in particular, the presence of a human bridegroom (Joseph), and the need to answer questions concerning the social awkwardness of a virgin who is pregnant. But the resemblances might make us wonder whether a common template lies behind them both or indeed whether Revelation's images might be the original basis from which the gospel nativity stories were constructed.

It might be objected that the sequence of birth before marriage does not occur in Matthew. Joseph took Mary 'as his wife...' (Matt. 1.24) as soon as he has seen the angel in a dream, and before the birth of Jesus: '...but had no marital relations with her [Greek: did not know her] until she had borne a son [in some texts, firstborn son]; and he named him Jesus' (1.25). This appears at first sight to differ from Luke, where 2.5 tells us that Joseph travelled to Bethlehem 'with Mary, to whom he was engaged, and who was expecting a child'. Some ancient manuscripts have in Luke 2.5 'Mary his wife', but this is not the normally accepted reading. Nevertheless, Luke is not disagreeing with Matthew; a betrothed woman is already a 'wife', as the betrothal was a binding contract, and so the two words 'betrothed' and 'wife' are not necessarily mutually exclusive.

However, the marriage is not complete in either Luke or Matthew. Matthew quotes from the Greek/Septuagint version of Isaiah 7.14 in 1.23: 'Look, the virgin shall conceive and bear a son...' The sense of the word *parthenos* pertains to the marital state of the person as well as to the question of their physical virginity. You could not be a *parthenos* and have had your marriage consummated all at the same time. It is not surprising then that Luke, whose sources presumably also included Isaiah 7.14, referred to Mary as being 'betrothed' at the time of the birth.

To conclude, the theme of a woman giving birth before the consummation of marriage is present in all three traditions: Matthew, Luke, and Revelation. It is a mythical story which depicts the crucifixion of Christ as a painful birth preceding the consummation of the marriage of Christ with the New Jerusalem, the Church. Christ has died, is risen, and will come again. The metaphorical and mythological nature of this narrative means that there is no problem with the idea that Christ's mother becomes his wife, because both represent the Church.

The beauty and power of the images of Mary the mother of Jesus in Luke's Gospel, associated with the mythology of Revelation 12, make it easy to understand why she has been described as the Church, or 'Mother of the Church', the prototype and archetype for all of those who have followed Christ after her, and the one who works to bring them into close communion with him. Mary in Luke is a human being in history who has been taken up into an eternal space, the place where she says yes to God to bring the Incarnation into birth. This is a wonderful story which has inspired Christians in all centuries. It is only a small step from John's new understanding of Genesis, in which Jesus is the Word through whom all things were made, superimposed upon Luke's Mary as heroine of salvation history, to suggest that Mary is the New Eve, as she was described in the second century by Justin Martyr and Irenaeus and then by the generations that succeeded them. She came to be regarded as the one whose answer to a supernatural figure made right what had been made wrong by a previous answer from the first Eve, encountering the anti-archangel, Satan. Mary the mother of Jesus is historical, because she had a human life, and also mythical, a figure of cosmic drama taken up into eternal space. Encountering Mary means encountering both these aspects of her being.

Mary in Luke's Gospel is an ideal mother type. Like mothers before her in Israel's patriarchal history, she was regarded as important because of the person that she bears. Edward Sri, in *Rethinking Mary*, devotes a chapter to the concept of the queen mother, the *gebirah*, in ancient Israel. During the monarchy period, a widowed queen mother, the mother of the new king, was more important than the king's wives. This is clear from the books in the Hebrew Scriptures (especially 1 and 2 Kings) that deal with the history of the monarchy. With this in the background, Mary is honoured by Elizabeth in Luke 1.43 as 'the mother of my Lord'.

So, in that cultural context, it will have been assumed that the mother of Jesus was someone deserving of prestige. But we return to the question: what can we know of the historical Mary who lived as a flesh and blood woman in ancient Israel, and never knew the trappings of a royal court? In order to begin to answer this, we turn to the earliest gospel, that of Mark.

7

The Family in Nazareth

MARK 6.3

We have discussed how Mary in the virgin birth narratives is a figure on the cosmic stage helping to bring in a new relationship between God and Israel, a paradigm, exemplar, and representative of disciples, past and present. However, this does not necessarily establish anything about the historical Mary. We could argue that the New Testament would not present Mary as this kind of representative unless she was a fitting one, in other words, that in reality she *was* someone who heard the Word of God and responded to it. That is a reasonable conclusion to make, but it is not a strong basis for establishing history. To try and dig further into the Mary of history, we need to tackle the text that seems least promising, as it says the least about Mary. That is the earliest gospel, the Gospel of Mark.[15]

---

[15] The hypothesis of Matthew Larsen, published in *Gospels Before the Book* and based upon research into ancient literature, is that Mark was never a book in the modern sense at all, more a series of notes and traditions that other gospels built upon by filling in the gaps and expanding on the narrative.

There is so little on Mary in the Gospel of Mark, one could say that, were it to have been the only gospel to have survived, then a biblically-based Mariology would scarcely exist. Given that Mark is regarded as the earliest gospel by biblical scholars and the source for much that is in Matthew and Luke, probably some of the material in John as well, this might present a major problem. Our other primary sources for earliest Christianity, the letters of Paul, do not mention Mary at all. Does this mean that the picture of Mary that we find in Matthew, Luke, and John was a late construction, in other words, a great 'myth' of Mary overlaid on an earlier tradition in which she was not important at all?

Fortunately, the situation is not quite as bad as this. Mark's Gospel does at least say something about Mary. The writer or compiler of Mark shows little interest in promoting her as the heroine of salvation history in the same way as Luke's Gospel, nor does he present the mysterious figure of John's Gospel who is intimately present at the crucial moments of Jesus' life, the wedding at Cana and the crucifixion. Mark's apparent disinterest in Mary suggests that the verses which speak of her in this gospel belong to a tradition that the writer of Mark has used. Therefore, it is our best hope for finding biographical information present in the earliest decades of the Church.

Mark 6.1–6 is a story that tells us how Jesus was regarded by the residents of Nazareth:

He left that place and came to his home town, and his disciples followed him. On the sabbath he began to teach in the synagogue, and many who heard him were astounded. They said, 'Where did this man get all this? What is this wisdom that has been given to him? What deeds of power are being done by his hands! Is not this the carpenter, the son of Mary and brother of

James and Joses and Judas and Simon, and are not his sisters here with us?' And they took offence at him. Then Jesus said to them, 'Prophets are not without honour, except in their home town, and among their own kin, and in their own house.' And he could do no deed of power there, except that he laid his hands on a few sick people and cured them. And he was amazed at their unbelief.

Mark's Gospel tells us that Jesus was the Son of God, but that it was a struggle for anyone in his lifetime to recognize this. Jesus looks for faith, but he does not find it very often. The family of Jesus and the disciples in Mark are not paragons of belief: they doubt, misunderstand, deny, and even betray Jesus. In Mark, people who believe in Jesus and gain his praise are remarkable because they are so few. These include people who receive healing because they believe: the woman with haemorrhages (5.34), the Syrophoenician woman (7.29), and Bartimaeus, a blind beggar (10.52). There are those who seem to understand what Jesus is trying to tell them: the scribe for his answer (12.34), and the anointing woman (14.6). Finally, he praises the poor widow because of her generosity (12.43). But that is the full extent of the list. Overall, Mark's Gospel invites the reader to understand the implications of Jesus' Messianic status while suggesting that many people who met him in his lifetime did not.

The residents of Nazareth are a classic example of this. In Mark's account, they think that Jesus is an ordinary man without any outstanding qualities because he grew up among them. This is a common experience for anyone who becomes famous. Those who knew them before they were regarded as celebrities will register surprise: 'She was just a quiet little lass who played along with the other children'; 'I remember him delivering groceries to earn some extra money.' Jesus had been a carpenter, a relatively unremarkable worker in Jewish society and the crowd are well aware of this. 'Carpenter', *tekton*, could easily be translated as 'construction worker'; while a very important function in any society, it does not suggest much in the way of social status. Therefore, Mark is drawing on an experience to which the reader can relate, that people who know someone and their family well, along with their humble origins, might be reluctant to accept them as having anything important to say, particularly if this presents challenges to them. Jesus refers this common occurrence to the mission of the prophets: like him, their honour often derived from people who enjoyed the objectivity of distance.

What the residents of Nazareth fail to understand is that Jesus is the Son of God, the Messiah. Mark recounts in 6.3 that they think he is rather 'the son of Mary, and brother of James and Joses and Judas and Simon', as well as having some unnamed sisters. There is a clear contrast between the two. Mark, unlike Luke, does not want to link the two facts that Jesus is both the Son of God *and* the son of Mary. For Mark, he is the Son of God, and very little else about his background before the ministry is important; the fact that he is the son of Mary is only for the unbelievers. This reflects Paul's description of Jesus in Galatians 4.4: 'But when the fullness of time had come, God sent his Son, born of a woman, born under the law...' Paul accepts that, despite his divine origin, Jesus was born of a woman like everyone else, and that he was a Jew. However, he is not really interested in the detail because the important facts are theological, not historical.

Mark helps us more than Paul with respect to Mary because he does provide a small amount of information about Jesus' family. We find out the names of his mother, Mary, and his brothers. The description 'son of Mary' is odd, as Jewish men were usually known by their father's name. To find out that Jesus is the son of Joseph, we need to read the other gospels, as Joseph is nowhere mentioned in Mark. Unfortunately, the sisters are not named, although there was a tradition that they were called Salome and Mary (Epiphanius, *Panarion* 78.8–9 from the fourth century; the *Gospel of Philip* 59.6–11 from possibly the third century). It has been speculated as to whether Salome the sister is the same woman as the one who observed the crucifixion and attended the tomb in Mark 15.40 and 16.1. We do not know this from the gospel, although it would make sense in the social context for a female in the family to be involved in the burial rites. However, the point of Mark 6.1–6 is that the people of Nazareth declare that Jesus was a member of a known family, and this prevents them from seeing Jesus as they really should: as the Son of God, the Christ or Messiah, the one who brings into being the kingdom of God (1.1, 11, 15).

The story is reproduced in other gospels in different forms but none of them refer to Jesus as the 'son of Mary'. Matthew 13.55–56 is close to Mark 6.3 but with important differences: 'Is not this the carpenter's son? Is not his mother called Mary? And are not his brothers James and Joseph and Simon and Judas? And are not all his sisters here with us?' So, for Matthew, Jesus' father was the carpenter rather than Jesus as specified in Mark (these are the only instances of the word 'carpenter' in the New Testament). Matthew also avoids the awkward 'son of Mary'. The name of one of the brothers, Joses, is replaced with Joseph; Joses seems to have been a familiar form of Joseph. In all these respects, Matthew seems to be tidying up the language of Mark's account and clarifying some of the questions that might arise from it. Luke 4.22 tells the story with a straightforward question by the residents of Nazareth: 'Is not this Joseph's son?' In John 6.42, the questioners are Jews from the region of the Sea of Galilee and say: 'Is not this Jesus, the son of Joseph, whose father and mother we know?'

There are two approaches from very different perspectives that one could take to the question as to why Mark describes Jesus as the 'son of Mary', but neither are satisfying. The first is held by those who want to preserve the integrity of the gospels and their interconnection. They claim that the writer of this section of Mark's Gospel knew that Jesus had been born from a virgin and that Joseph was not his father in the usual sense. This then concurs with Luke's statement in 3.23 that Jesus 'was the son (as was thought) of Joseph son of Heli': Jesus born of a virgin is, strictly speaking, the 'son of Mary' as in Mark 6.3. The problem with this view is that Mark's Gospel nowhere shows any knowledge of something as sensational as the virgin birth of Jesus.

There is a second possible answer: that the crowd were voicing doubts about Jesus' legitimacy. As sons were normally named after their father, 'son of Mary' suggests that he is the product of an extramarital relationship, which would have been scandalous and a reason for denouncing him. This has a possible parallel in John 8.41, where Jesus' protagonists, simply referred to as 'the Jews', say: '*We* are not illegitimate children...'; the stress on the *we* might suggest that they are claiming that Jesus *is* an illegitimate child. This answer would strengthen the case for those who argue that there was a very early tradition of the illegitimacy of Jesus, something that appears later in anti-Christian polemic as a counter to the belief in the virgin birth.

These two approaches involve two hypotheses that cannot be proved: either that the writer of Mark knew about the virgin birth, or that he was aware of a controversy concerning Jesus' legitimacy. A third answer is much more straightforward. Mark is simply including information about the family that has been passed down. Mary, along with the brothers and unnamed sisters, was known to the pre-gospel tradition in a way that Joseph was not. That Mary and the brothers were known in the early Church is confirmed by their appearances together elsewhere: in John 2.12, after the wedding in Cana, and Acts 1.14, after the Ascension and before Pentecost (sadly, the sisters are not mentioned in either of these verses). In placing this biographical detail in a story about people who misunderstand Jesus and underestimate his importance, the passage in Mark 6 achieves two objectives at once:

1. It includes information about Jesus' family; given that Mark was written with no previous gospels as sources, then it is not surprising that it briefly describes the background to the story of Jesus' life and ministry.
2. It suggests that this biographical information is not particularly important in contradiction to those who think that it is. Jesus is the Son of God and being the son of Mary or the brother of James is not determinative for his identity.

THE MOTHER AND BROTHERS OF JESUS

Mark 3.21 tells us that Jesus' family 'went out to restrain him [Jesus], for people were saying, "He has gone out of his mind"'. It is difficult to know which members of the family are meant, as people in first-century Jewish society lived in extended families, but the overall intent is clear: Mark wants to create a sense of distance between Jesus' ministry and his relatives. In 3.31–35, the mother and brothers of Jesus are given less priority than the disciples:

Then his mother and his brothers came; and standing outside, they sent to him and called him. A crowd was sitting around him; and they said to him, 'Your mother and your brothers and sisters are outside, asking for you.' And he replied, 'Who are my mother and my brothers?' And looking at those who sat around him, he said, 'Here are my mother and my brothers! Whoever does the will of God is my brother and sister and mother.'

When a text argues against something, it is normally a sign that many people held the opposite view. This passage suggests that, for some people in the early Church, the mother and brothers did have authority, and that this has been included to counter that claim. If Mark had simply wanted to stress that Jesus regarded his disciples as a family, then he could have stated that without the part of the story which distanced the natural family.

A version of this story is included in Matthew 12.46–50 and Luke 8.19–21 although, in those gospels, there seems to be a softening of the negative view of Jesus' family. Matthew and Luke omit the passage about the family trying to restrain Jesus, and in Matthew 13.54–58, the parallel to Mark 6.1–6, 'own kin' is not included in the list of people who reject the prophets and Jesus. Luke 8.19–21 states that 'my mother and my brothers are those who hear the word of God and do it', which does not necessarily rule out the possibility that Jesus' natural mother and brothers qualify. Luke does have another passage along these lines:

While he was saying this, a woman in the crowd raised her voice and said to him, 'Blessed is the womb that bore you and the breasts that nursed you!' But he said, 'Blessed rather are those who hear the word of God and obey it!'

(Luke 11.27–28)

This could be included as another instance of Jesus distancing himself from his mother but the context of the whole gospel suggests something else. Luke 1.38 has described Mary as someone who did hear the word of God: 'Let it be to me according to your word.' Therefore, Luke does not necessarily diminish Mary here but suggests that her honour is due to her actions rather than the bare fact of her being the mother of Jesus.

John 2.12 describes the companionship of Jesus with his mother, brothers, and disciples after the marriage in Cana. However, John 7.5 tells us that 'not even his brothers believed in him'. What is confusing is that the family in Mark attempt to restrain Jesus from his ministry, whereas the brothers in John 7.3–4 encourage him; they tell Jesus to 'leave here and go to Judea so that your disciples also may see the works you are doing; for no one who wants to be widely known acts in secret. If you do these things, show yourself to the world.' So, while Mark and John agree that Jesus' family misunderstood his mission, they give different interpretations of how that problem presented itself.

We can conclude from these passages that there was a memory of the involvement of the mother and brothers of Jesus in the early Church, even though some of the gospels question the appropriateness of it. There is other biblical evidence: as we have seen, the mother and brothers appear in Acts 1.14 which, chronologically, is the last mention of Mary's role. But the brothers were travellers to various Christian communities and known to Paul, as we read in 1 Corinthians 9.5. Two of them, James and Jude or Judas, are identified as the writers of the epistles of those names; whether they actually wrote them or not, the claim that they authored these epistles is enough to show their importance in the early Church.

The question as to whether Mary was the natural birth mother of James, Joses, Judas, and Simon is not something with which Mark's Gospel is concerned. The belief that Mary remained a virgin after the birth of Jesus is something that grew in the centuries after the apostolic and gospel forming age of the first century. To believe this requires an answer as to who these brothers might be, and why they would be called brothers. The Roman Catholic Church, following Jerome (*On the Perpetual Virginity of Blessed Mary* 13–18), says that they were cousins in an extended family, which was the normal mode of family life in ancient Israel. The Eastern Orthodox Churches draw on *Protevangelium* 9.2 and Epiphanius (*Panarion: Against the Antidicomarianites* 78.7–10) and regard them as stepbrothers, children of Joseph by a previous marriage. Both these interpretations are possible.

However, Paul, our earliest testimony to the post-resurrection period, calls James 'the Lord's brother' (Gal. 1.19), and his distrust of James (see Gal. 2.12) meant that he would have had plenty of reason not to do this if he knew any different. Throughout the New Testament, the words 'brother' and 'sister' can refer to fellow Christians, but James, Joses, Judas, and Simon are brothers in a special sense, as is obvious from 1 Cor. 9.5 ('the other apostles and the brothers of the Lord and Cephas'). There was a Greek word for cousin, *anepsios*, and for relative, *suggeneus* (which is used in Mark 6.4 and Luke 1.36). Jerome's solution identified James and the rest as relatives of Jesus in an extended family, with the Mary mentioned at the cross as 'mother of James the younger and of Joses' (Mark 15.40) being their mother. This would create a strange scenario in which this other Mary was notable enough to be remembered as involved in the ministry and following Jesus to the cross, yet her children were identified as belonging to a family unit with Mary the mother of Jesus at Mark 6.3, a passage where this other Mary is not mentioned.

Suggestions that the brothers were not born from Mary were based on a determination to preserve the Catholic and

Orthodox doctrine of her perpetual virginity. Of course, it is possible that Mary was a mother figure in a large extended family to people not born to her and related or adopted in some way. However, it is easier to accept the text at face value.

It is reasonable to suggest that Mark 6.3 is based on the memory of the mother, brothers, and sisters of Jesus as a family unit, influential in the early Church, especially when we relate this passage to other gospels which refer to them in this way. Mark does not mention Jesus' father Joseph. In the other gospels, Joseph does not feature in any story about Jesus after his visit to Jerusalem at the age of twelve, in Luke 2.41–51. For this reason, it has often been assumed that he died before Jesus reached adulthood, leaving Mary a widow. If that is the case, there is no evidence that she married again, and the probability that she remained in the households of adult sons is completely consonant with both Jewish and Greco-Roman social norms. But she need not have been subservient to her sons; she would have been entitled to property left by the husband, and widows, as we have seen, could be women of means and authority in a household.

Summing up, given that Mark's Gospel does not promote the memory of the mother of Jesus in the same way as Luke and John for whom Mary is a key figure in the gospel story, then the information we find there is the most likely to have some historical validity. Mark's Gospel draws on an early Christian tradition, one that found its way into other gospels. Therefore, we know that:

1. The mother and brothers of Jesus were known in the early Church and were described as a family unit. This unit also features in the other gospels and Acts.
2. The description 'son of Mary' in Mark 6.3 need not derive from either belief in the virgin birth or the memory of a charge of illegitimacy, but from the simple fact that

Mark's information includes only the surviving family unit of Jesus which was influential in the early Church, that is, his mother and brothers (and unnamed sisters).

3. Jesus' four brothers had names common to the period in Jewish culture: James (which is Jacob in Hebrew), Joses or Joseph, Judas, and Simon. As we have already dismissed any historical basis for the belief that Mary was always a virgin, in the absence of any information to the contrary we can accept the most obvious reading of the text that Mary was the natural mother of these men.

The traditions behind Mark therefore knew that Jesus' mother and brothers comprised a known and influential family unit, before and after the crucifixion of Jesus. Presumably, the sense of purpose that came with the belief that Jesus was the Messiah would have strengthened the bonds between them. Given the prominence of the eldest brother, James, in the early Church (which is evident in Galatians 1–2 and Acts 15), scholars agree that Jesus' brothers had considerable authority in the Church: they were Jesus' *heirs* and, if the New Testament is historically accurate in stating that Jesus claimed to be a descendant of David, then they would have shared this with him. As Mark was writing in a patriarchal world, the sisters' names are not given; presumably, the writer did not inherit any record of their importance in the Church community or, if he did, he failed to acknowledge it.

Yet this leads us to ask: why are James and the other brothers of Jesus treated with suspicion in both Mark and John? Why did they not have a more prominent place in the gospel memory generally? The answer to this question lies in the developing rift between the Christian churches and Jewish culture, the soil in which they had grown originally. It is that which we need to investigate to get to the bottom of what happened to the family of Jesus in the New Testament tradition.

8

Jews and Judaism

THE ALIENATION OF JUDAISM AND CHRISTIANITY

Biblical scholars since the Holocaust have tried to tackle the difficult question as to how far the horrors of antisemitism have their origins in the New Testament. Throughout Christian history, Jews were blamed for the death of Jesus; they were regarded as the ones who rejected and killed their own Messiah. While the New Testament texts include many inspirational passages and the gospel message of salvation in Christ, they have also left an unintended and unfortunate legacy which modern interpreters cannot ignore.

The New Testament texts were probably written by Jews but at the very least Gentiles with an extremely good knowledge of the Jewish tradition and its scriptures. There is little evidence, despite the language chosen being Greek, of substantial Hellenistic or Roman cultural legacies. Nor are the gospels pro-Roman, as has been suggested. Yet, while antisemitism is perhaps an anachronistic term to use about the New Testament in its origins, it has certainly been read in ways that have encouraged antisemitism through the centuries. The gospels and Acts were written in a time when Christians were suffering rejection and banishment by the Jewish authorities, and they reflect this sense of alienation.

This is particularly true of the Gospel of John which, unlike the synoptic gospels, refers to Jesus' enemies as 'the Jews' (except at 4.22, when Jesus identifies himself as a Jew, and where Jews are followers of Jesus at 11.31–45 and 12.11). John 16.2 has Jesus telling the disciples that 'they will put you out of the synagogues'. It has been mooted that the Greek word *Judaioi* could mean Judeans rather than Jews in general, and that John's Gospel has its origin in a time when the Judeans in general were seen as opponents of Jesus' Galilean movement. This theory is unproven, however. It cannot be denied that the result of the negative impression of the portrayal of the 'Jews' in John's Gospel has not helped the cause of protecting Jews from Christian persecution through the centuries.

In terms of the origins of the relationship between Christianity and Judaism, the answer is simple: Jesus was an observant Jew. This fact is not challenged in the New Testament. Jesus' critical attacks were not made upon Jews in general, but on particular parties. Therefore, biblical interpretation needs to separate the ministry of Jesus from later contexts in which there was antagonism between Jews and Christians in general.

Most crucially in the argument for the anti-Jewish nature of the gospel narratives, many scholars have pointed out that the shift of blame for the crucifixion passes from the Romans, whose method of execution it was, to the Jews. All four gospels include the story of Jesus' condemnation by the Jews who tell Pilate to crucify Jesus; they choose the criminal

Barabbas to be released in his place, despite the fact that Pilate finds no fault in Jesus. This does not seem to conform to Pilate's reputation as a ruler unafraid to mete out harsh punishment (recorded by Philo and Josephus but also in evidence at Luke 13.1). In Matthew, Pilate washes his hands of the responsibility for Jesus' death and the people take it on themselves: 'Then the people as a whole answered, "His blood be on us and on our children!"' (27.25). This has been a proof text for antisemitism.

Nevertheless, critical readings of the New Testament's portrayal of events can run the risk of being antisemitic by overlooking the fact that the Christian message which has changed the world and inspired millions is Jewish at its very core. A typical modern argument goes like this: Jesus was unyielding in his zeal for the *Torah* and probably a Nazirite, maybe a Zealot revolutionary; the New Testament downplays this aspect and presents Jesus in an inaccurate way as a peaceful man who was critical of Jewish practices and accepting of Rome. There are several problems with this. First, it overlooks the several subtle references in the gospels that show the early Christian traditions to have been critical of Rome. The very fact that Jesus was proclaimed divine Son of God was itself a challenge to the imperial cult. Second, it presumes that a non-violent stance could not have emerged from the Jewish people of the period. Third, it misses the point that other groups, such as the Essenes, were likewise critical of the Temple and its priesthood without thereby being anti-Jewish. Fourth, the prophetic tradition in the Hebrew Scriptures shows that Jews were not afraid to speak out against their leaders when they seemed to be taking the nation in the wrong direction. Fifth, there was a variety of Jewish interpretations of the *Torah*, some of which were close to Jesus' own. Sixth, a critique of religious hypocrisy and manipulation is a universal phenomenon; while Jesus' opponents were Jewish, a critique of religious leaders is not anti-Jewish per se and one can see the references to them in the New Testament as caricatures which apply well to many religious functionaries, including Christian ones.

The image of a man who stands up to the misuse of religion and for a faith that is centred upon love of God and neighbour, the central tenets of the Jewish tradition, is inspiring across different cultures and religions, including Judaism. Of all religions, one could not accuse the Jewish people in particular of blind and unthinking observance. And that is the point: it was Jesus *the Jew* who presented this great vision of a God for whom social justice, the spirit and not the letter of the law, and love and forgiveness of others were central to faith. At no time in the gospels does Jesus decry circumcision, the synagogue, Jewish prayers or scriptures, but he does – like the prophets before him – denounce a misuse of faith that is self-serving and results in the oppression of people rather than their liberation.

E.P. Sanders' work (as in *The Historical Figure of Jesus*) demonstrates that the popular image of Jews as particularly fastidious and obsessed with purity is inaccurate. While this view is derived from certain passages in the New Testament, historical research shows that Jews were not particularly unusual in the ancient world in the mode of their adherence to rules and customs. Jewish lay people, the Pharisees in particular, were involved in interpreting the Law and debating it from different perspectives. The Pharisees were an influential Jewish group founded in the second century BCE; they interpreted the spirit rather than the letter of the Jewish Law, the *Torah*, and respected oral as well as written traditions. Thus, it is not unreasonable to regard Jesus' approach to Jewish tradition as aligning with that of the Pharisees. This makes unlikely that any disagreement with Jesus' understanding, for example, of food laws and the Sabbath, would lead for demands from the Pharisees for him to be executed as the New Testament suggests.

A similar characterization of the Jews to that in John's Gospel can be found in the Acts narrative after the point where Paul is converted; here Jews are often referred to collectively as the enemies of the Church, although occasionally also as converts (and Paul, like Jesus in John, identifies himself as a Jew). Paul's letters also contain a couple of references where Jews are treated collectively as enemies: 2 Corinthians 11.24 and 1 Thessalonians 2.14. So clearly, the idea that the Jews in general were opponents of Christianity evolved in the earliest Church, but it is not evident everywhere in the New Testament. In the synoptic gospels, the word 'Jews' appears mainly in terms of Jesus being called 'King of the Jews'. The opponents in the synoptics are more specifically described: scribes (the religious lawyers of the period), Pharisees, chief priests, and Sadducees (a priestly faction, usually wealthy and aristocratic, with a conservative view of Jewish Scripture). The 'scribes and Pharisees' are denounced throughout Matthew 23 and in Luke 11.42–44 and 20.45–47. It could be said that these are also generalizations; they act as foils so that Christian arguments can be expressed through the mouth of Jesus.

There are exceptions where such figures were presented positively. In Acts, Paul identifies himself as 'a Pharisee, a son of Pharisees' (23.6; see also 26.5) and enjoys some support among the Pharisees (23.9). Nicodemus (John 3.1) and Gamaliel (Acts 5.43) were also Pharisees. Nicodemus and Joseph of Arimathea come together as members of the Sanhedrin to bury Jesus (John 19.38–42); John's Gospel has already told us that his supporters included members of the authorities (12.42–43), although these as well as Joseph and Nicodemus were concerned for their safety and not prepared to confess Jesus openly. Jesus himself praises a scribe in Mark 12.34 and there are scribes who follow Jesus in Matthew 8.19

and 13.52. However, there is one group for whom there are no exceptions: the gospels always present Jesus in opposition to the priests.

Overall, we can deduce that the gospels and Acts were written in a time when the Pharisees and scribes no longer had any standing among Christians, probably because in general they would have rejected any movement that integrated with Gentiles so freely, and so they are caricatured in the texts as self-seeking hypocrites, but there is a memory that some among them were supportive of the early Christian tradition. There is also plenty of material that cuts against generalizations and confirms that Jews, including some members of the authoritative and scribal classes, were among the original supporters of Jesus. Therefore, the generalized terms 'Jews', 'Pharisees', 'scribes', and so on, in the gospels and Acts should be read as *representatives* of the influential people within Judaism who rejected the Christian faith. There may have also been many who rejected it but after a dalliance, represented by the unproductive seeds in the parable of the sower (Mark's version is in 4.1–20). The hostility to those Jews who had been supportive but then changed their minds can be illustrated in John 8.31–59: the group of Jews to whom Jesus is talking seem to have been followers, but this segues into their being people out to kill him.

THE MISSION TO THE GENTILES

In his lifetime, it is reasonable to suppose that Jesus saw his ministry as primarily reaching out to his fellow Jews. This can be concluded on the basis of Matthew 10.5–6: 'These twelve Jesus sent out with the following instructions: "Go nowhere among the Gentiles, and enter no town of the Samaritans, but go rather to the lost sheep of the house of Israel."' In

Matthew 15.24, Jesus says to the Canaanite woman with the possessed daughter, 'I was sent only to the lost sheep of the house of Israel.' On the other hand, the overall impression the gospels give is that the Gentiles were more responsive to Jesus' mission than his own fellow Jews. So perhaps these little hints in Matthew, which seem to contradict the general trend, go back to Jesus himself and indicate that Jesus was more exclusive to the Jewish community than the gospels suggest, and that this continued into the very earliest Church. This possibility is supported by Paul's statement in Galatians 2.7–9, where we learn that:

> when they [the Christian leaders in Jerusalem] saw that I had been entrusted with the gospel for the uncircumcised, just as Peter had been entrusted with the gospel for the circumcised ... they gave to Barnabas and me the right hand of fellowship, agreeing that we should go to the Gentiles and they to the circumcised.

Therefore, Paul was instrumental in taking the new faith to the Gentiles. Evidence for the growth of Gentiles participating in Christianity can be found in Acts 10.28, when Peter's vision of creatures that he is now permitted to eat leads him to say: 'You yourselves know that it is unlawful for a Jew to associate with or to visit a Gentile; but God has shown me that I should not call anyone profane or unclean.' It would be difficult to conclude that Jesus had already established a ministry to the Gentiles based on these passages. It seems that the mission to the Gentiles began with Paul and not with Jesus. So, at the very least, we can conclude that Jesus' ministry, while it may have encountered Gentiles, was not ready to approach them in earnest.

However, in the New Testament, the story of Jesus is associated with an opening up to the faith of the Gentiles, which reflects the journey of the Church in its initial decades. Gentile converts receive special praise from Jesus and obtain favour in contrast to Jews in the gospels. Jesus is amazed at Gentile faith in his healing power, for example, the faith of a centurion:

> 'Truly I tell you, in no one in Israel have I found such faith. I tell you, many will come from east and west and will eat with Abraham and Isaac and Jacob in the kingdom of heaven, while the heirs of the kingdom will be thrown into the outer darkness, where there will be weeping and gnashing of teeth.'
>
> (Matt. 8.10–12; see also Luke 7.9)

It will have been hard for Jews to read an account in which a centurion of the occupying Roman army gets special attention from Jesus. This centurion does not appear in the earlier gospel, Mark, but there a centurion at the cross recognizes Jesus as God's Son (15.39). The Syrophoenician or Canaanite woman, too, is praised (Mark 7.29; Matt. 15.28) for her asking for Jesus' help despite him telling her that the Jews should come first.

The gospels are critical of the Jews' lack of response to Jesus and so they are very quick to identify not only Gentiles but also Samaritans (the remnants of the Israelite tradition who retained local shrines against the Jewish mainstream tradition with its emphasis on the Jerusalem Temple) as paragons of faith and response to Jesus. This was polemical: it would have annoyed Jews to think that Roman centurions and Samaritans, of all people, are praised in the gospels as having greater faith than them.

All this is not to deny the possibility that Jesus did attract some Gentiles into his movement, even if he did not actively seek to do so. While the identification of genuine faith among Gentiles in the gospels probably reflects the development of the early Church, it may have some basis in Jesus himself. These stories may have had origins in experiences of actual Samaritan and Gentile converts, both during the ministry of Jesus and afterward. However, the likely conclusion is that, during Jesus' lifetime, they were exceptions.

EARLY JEWISH CHRISTIANITY AND JAMES, THE BROTHER OF JESUS

Most of the New Testament emerged from certain strands of the early Church, those in which the numbers of Gentiles had overtaken those of Jews, and the members of which followed Paul in not expecting Christians to adhere to the Jewish *Torah* in practices such as circumcision and table fellowship. Many Jews were included in this strand of the Church, indeed they initiated it, but there were also other Jewish Christians who continued to follow their age-old traditions, and a minority Jewish Christian Church survived for some centuries. We can identify at least three distinct and divergent groups emerging from Jewish society in the time before and after the Jewish War: 1. Christians (Gentiles and Jews), who did not follow the *Torah*; 2. Jewish Christians (some of whom may have been Gentile converts) who recognized Jesus as Messiah but did follow the *Torah*; 3. Jews who did not recognize Jesus as the Messiah. The provenance of most of the New Testament is the first of these three, and therefore the Jewish Christians were gradually marginalized. The possible exceptions where Jewish Christian perspectives are more faithfully preserved are the epistles of James and Jude, attributed to the brothers of Jesus, and the book of Revelation.

The importance of this for our purpose is that the family of Jesus were prominent in the Church before the period of the gospels and they belonged to the second group, the Jews who continued to adhere to the *Torah*. James, the brother of Jesus (as identified in Gal. 1.19), is associated with those Christians who want to keep to the *Torah*, although he accepted Paul's mission to the Gentiles (Gal. 2.9). James was a dominant figure in the early Church, as is confirmed by Galatians 1–2 and Acts 15, and is traditionally known as the first bishop of Jerusalem. Recent scholarship generally accepts the theory that the leadership of the very earliest Church was dynastic, that is, passed on from Jesus to his brother James after the crucifixion. This is not made explicit in the New Testament which for the most part followed Paul, but it is stated clearly in one of the earliest non-canonical Christian writings, the Gospel of Thomas.

In Galatians 2.11–12, we read about Paul's indignation that Cephas had been talked out of a more liberal stance towards table fellowship with Gentiles:

> But when Cephas came to Antioch, I opposed him to his face, because he stood self-condemned; for until certain people came from James, he used to eat with the Gentiles. But after they came, he drew back and kept himself separate for fear of the circumcision faction.

Acts 15.1–35 describes a harmonious compromise between James, Peter, and Paul on the question of the obligations of Gentiles becoming Christians. The epistles of Paul, particularly Galatians and Romans, suggests that this was a much harder-fought argument. The disagreement between James and Paul on the question as to how much a Christian needed to live by the *Torah* was remembered in the Jewish Christian tradition: Paul is rather surprisingly described as the 'enemy' of James in the fourth-century *Pseudo-Clementines*.

It is not clear how strict James was in relation to the *Torah*. In Galatians 2.11–12, cited above, he appears to be associated with the 'circumcision faction'. However, in the same chapter, verses 7–10, he agrees that Paul can evangelize the 'uncircumcised'. In Acts 15.19–29, he asks that Christians 'abstain only from things polluted by idols and from fornication and from whatever has been strangled and from blood'. This would be a lighter requirement than the full range of Jewish table customs and food laws. Raymond Brown and John Meier, in the introduction to *Antioch and Rome*, suggest that Jewish Christians followed a range of approaches to conversion, from insisting on circumcision, to asking that food laws be maintained, to a more liberal position on these practices, to abandoning the Jewish cult altogether. While James would not have been in the last of these camps, considering Galatians and Acts together does not fully clarify his exact position. What we can infer from Galatians 2.6 is that Paul did not respect the authority of James in his letters quite as much as Acts 15.1–35 and 21.17–26 suggest that he did publicly when visiting Jerusalem.

To reconstruct a history of James, we also have the historical record compiled by Flavius Josephus.[16] Josephus was a Jewish commander against the Romans, but after the defeat of the Jews in Galilee in 67 CE, Josephus accepted the inevitability of Roman victory and defected, becoming a Roman citizen and advisor to the Roman general and future emperor Titus who stormed Jerusalem and destroyed the Temple. He wrote a history of the Jewish people in two works, the *Antiquities of the Jews*, narrating the whole history of Israel until the beginning of the Jewish War (66 CE), and *The Jewish War*, covering the period between the conquest of Jerusalem by Antiochus IV Epiphanes provoking the successful Maccabean revolt (167–160 BCE) to the end of the Jewish War (73 CE).

---

[16] For more detail, see the article by Nicholas Allen in *Journal of Early Christian History* 7.1.

Josephus describes the martyrdom of James with detail which gives us the possible date of 62 CE. He tells us more than we know about James from the New Testament. He writes (*Antiquities of the Jews*, Book XX: 9.1) about the decision made by Ananus the high priest to execute 'the brother of Jesus who was called Christ, whose name was James, and some others'. This act angered those Jews who disliked injustice and unlawfulness. This account is controversial, as some scholars argue that it was inserted by Origen in the third century to add a Christian element to Josephus' history, or at the very least the reference to James being the brother of Jesus might have been added to the original text.

The fourth-century Church historian Eusebius adds more information about James in his *History of the Church* (Book 2: 1, 23; Book 7: 19). Eusebius quotes Clement of Alexandria, *Outlines*, Book 8 (the *Outlines* did not survive) in saying that James had been 'thrown down from the parapet and beaten to death with a fuller's club'. He also refers to Hegesippus' fifth book (no works of Hegesippus have survived) in saying that James was a Nazirite who was allowed to enter the Sanctuary of the Temple (normally reserved for high priests alone). He was executed by being clubbed to death after being stoned first. After his death, the fall of Jerusalem was believed to have occurred as a result; here Eusebius quotes Josephus but it is not in surviving manuscripts, although Origen quotes it too and so it must have existed in one version. Eusebius then refers to the letter of James, although he says that 'admittedly, its authenticity is doubted, since few early writers refer to it', which shows us that biblical criticism was not unknown in the early Church while the canon was still being formed. Finally, Eusebius tells us that the episcopal throne of James in Jerusalem was still preserved and venerated there.

The testimony of the writers in the early centuries of the Church confirm that James was unanimously acknowledged as the first Christian leader in Jerusalem and referred to as 'James the Just'. But the gospels lack anything more than a passing reference to James, containing only critical passages about the role of Jesus' brothers in general. This suggests that the gospels downplayed the brothers' importance in the early Church. The lists of twelve disciples do not include the brothers, that is, James, Joses or Joseph, Judas, and Simon (Mark 6.3; Matt. 13.55), at least not explicitly: there is a second James, Simon, and Judas in them but no mention of them being Jesus' brothers. Mention of the most important disciples does not include James the Lord's brother, but the central group of three in the synoptic gospels are Peter, James the son of Zebedee, and his brother John. Eusebius (quoting Clement, *Outlines*, Book 6) says that these disciples 'did not claim pre-eminence because the Saviour has specially honoured them, but instead chose James the Righteous (or Just) as Bishop of Jerusalem'. This led to the belief that Jesus' brothers were late converts to belief in Jesus, something that appears to be corroborated by Paul's list of the resurrection witnesses in 1 Corinthians 15, in which James comes after the twelve disciples and more than five hundred other believers. However, recent scholarship[17] has concluded that James and the other brothers were determined to retain adherence to the Jewish *Torah* among Christians, and this led to them being sidelined in the gospel tradition, which followed Paul in seeking freedom from these obligations. If this is true, then we have to read the gospel references to the family of Jesus with that in mind.

It is not necessary to regard this acknowledgement of the bias against Jesus' brothers as implying condemnation of the gospel writers. We can simply accept that, following Paul, they

---

[17] This includes Pierre-Antoine Bernheim, *James the Brother of Jesus*; Bruce Chilton and Jacob Neusner, *The Brother of Jesus*; and Patrick Hartin, *James of Jerusalem*.

felt that the spread of the gospel message among the Gentiles required a strategy of challenging any overestimation by new Christians of the brothers of Jesus as the primary heirs to his heritage. In this respect, the evangelists are echoing Paul's complaint about hero worship of the apostles:

> What I mean is that each of you says, 'I belong to Paul', or 'I belong to Apollos', or 'I belong to Cephas', or 'I belong to Christ.' Has Christ been divided? Was Paul crucified for you? Or were you baptized in the name of Paul?
>
> (1 Cor. 1.12)

In other words, Christians should not look to mediators of the message but to the one to whom the message points: the Lord Jesus Christ, Son of God. Nevertheless, we can see the tendency to downplay the Jewish Christians in the context of a general negativity in the New Testament towards Jews who do not accept Jesus, but also against Jews who insisted that being a Christian means following the *Torah* in the same way as any Jew. The most prominent of these were members of Jesus' own family. Mary was the senior member of this family, and so reservations about the authority of the family, and what that meant in terms of the Christian understanding of the *Torah*, will have affected how she was viewed in the period of the writing of the gospels. We now return to her story as it is recounted in the Gospel of John.

9

Mary in the Gospel of John

MARY AT CANA

In John's Gospel, like Luke's, the mother of Jesus has a special role to play in the story of salvation. Here there are no birth narratives; she appears just twice in the life of Jesus as an adult, but they are the pivotal moments of John's Gospel. She is not named, which is something of a mystery for the biblical interpreter. Why is this so? The first time we meet the mother of Jesus in John is at the wedding in Cana at the beginning of Jesus' ministry, the occasion of his first miracle:

> On the third day there was a wedding in Cana of Galilee, and the mother of Jesus was there. Jesus and his disciples had also been invited to the wedding. When the wine gave out, the mother of Jesus said to him, 'They have no wine.' And Jesus said to her, 'Woman, what concern is that to you and to me? My hour has not yet come.' His mother said to the servants, 'Do whatever he tells

you.' Now standing there were six stone water jars for the Jewish rites of purification, each holding twenty or thirty gallons. Jesus said to them, 'Fill the jars with water.' And they filled them up to the brim. He said to them, 'Now draw some out, and take it to the chief steward.' So they took it. When the steward tasted the water that had become wine, and did not know where it came from (though the servants who had drawn the water knew), the steward called the bridegroom and said to him, 'Everyone serves the good wine first, and then the inferior wine after the guests have become drunk. But you have kept the good wine until now.' Jesus did this, the first of his signs, in Cana of Galilee, and revealed his glory; and his disciples believed in him. After this he went down to Capernaum with his mother, his brothers, and his disciples; and they remained there a few days.

(John 2.1–12)

What do we find out from this passage? First, we notice that Jesus is somewhat reluctant to respond to Mary's prompting. 'Woman, what concern is that to you and to me' is from a Hebrew idiom which could be translated, 'Woman, what has that got to do with us?' His attention is focused on looking forward to his 'hour', a word related to the hour of a painful birth, which in the Gospel of John is a metaphor for the crucifixion. John's Gospel refers several times to Christian life as being 'born again' in the Spirit, especially in the dialogue with Nicodemus in chapter 3. John 16.21 likens the death of Jesus to a painful birth after which there is joy. Therefore, at Cana Jesus sounds surprised that he is being asked to do this miracle well in advance of the crucifixion.

Perhaps his question could be interpreted as something along these lines: 'Do you realize that if my ministry begins

here, we will have set foot on the road that leads to the cross?'
Jesus' response in changing the water into wine is an anticipation of his suffering on the cross which will turn into the
victory of the resurrection. The miracle anticipates the joyous
feast that will occur at the resurrection, which will be like a
wedding; another common theme in John's Gospel is the identification of Jesus as the Bridegroom (refer also to Revelation
19.9: 'the marriage supper of the Lamb'). The wine also has
eucharistic connotations, in the same way as the miracle of
the bread and fish in John 6.1–14. Jesus is both the 'Bread of
Life' (6.25–35) and the 'True Vine' (15.1–8), the source of the
elements of the Eucharist.

The wedding at Cana stands at the beginning of the ministry, but it is also a symbolic image of its end: it occurs 'on
the third day'. Is the evangelist simply referring to Tuesday
here, the third day of the Jewish week? Nowhere in the
New Testament is the day of the week mentioned in a setting for a story, except for the Sabbath and the first day of
the week; in those cases, the day of the week is relevant
to the story. All other instances of 'on the third day' in the
New Testament refer to the resurrection, although none of
these are in John. It has been suggested that the use of the
expression is quite mundane, as it follows on from John's
previous reference to the 'next day' in the first chapter (John
1.29, 35, 43), but it is not easy to see why the third day is
mentioned here when it seems to be the fifth in the sequence.
Therefore, it is likely that 'on the third day' refers forward to
the resurrection.

The drinking of wine is a symbol of resurrection and the
coming of the Messianic Kingdom, as in the synoptic traditions of the Last Supper, where Jesus says that he will not
drink wine again until these events (Matt. 26.29; Mark 14.25;
Luke 22.18). Isaiah 25.6–8 speaks of God's feast of deliverance
on the mountain of Zion:

On this mountain the LORD of hosts will make for all
peoples
  a feast of rich food, a feast of well-aged wines,
  of rich food filled with marrow, of well-aged wines
    strained clear.
And he will destroy on this mountain
  the shroud that is cast over all peoples,
  the sheet that is spread over all nations;
He will swallow up death forever.
Then the Lord GOD will wipe away the tears from all faces,
  and the disgrace of his people he will take away from all
    the earth,
  for the LORD has spoken.

Jesus' reply to Mary's request is one of the most debated verses
in the New Testament; it is enigmatic and invites a variety
of responses. First, it seems to align with the reservations
in Mark's Gospel about the importance of Mary, and early
Church commentators saw it as keeping Mary in her place
(for example, Irenaeus, *Against Heresies* 3.16.7). Yet, this was
a somewhat misogynistic and unnecessary interpretation:
the only clear fact that we can draw from the passage is that
Jesus' mother is associated with this 'hour', as she appears
both here and at the cross. As the mother of Jesus, she will
experience the painful but joyful birth that is the crucifixion
and resurrection, and she is portrayed as the person who
initiates the journey to the cross.

Second, we notice that Jesus addresses his mother 'Woman',
which sounds odd in English; it does not necessarily suggest a
dismissive tone, however, and Jesus uses the expression again,
to his mother at the cross (19.26) and to Mary Magdalene in
the garden of the resurrection (20.15). Great tenderness is
implied as both Mary and Mary Magdalene are struggling
with the terrible events of his execution and death. It has

been suggested that, in both cases, 'Woman' may be a reference back to the archetypal 'woman' of the Bible: Eve. John's Gospel is the story of rebirth, not just of individuals but of the whole of creation. The prologue relates to Genesis, and so it is not unreasonable to see this theme reflected elsewhere in John. Thus, the later theological speculation that Mary is the new Eve of a renewed creation, a concept introduced by Justin Martyr and Irenaeus in the second century, might be seen to have a foundation in John's Gospel, although we can only infer the relationship of Mary to Eve as it is not explicit there. One could say the same thing about Mary Magdalene, as she meets the risen Jesus in a garden, reminding us of the original garden in Eden. Perhaps we should beware of making too much of John's use of 'Woman', as it is also used by Jesus to address the Samaritan woman in John 4.21 and the woman taken in adultery in 8.10. Yet, with exception of the woman taken in adultery (who was probably not included in the original version of John's Gospel as the passage does not appear in the oldest versions), we have three remarkable women addressed in this way, as the Samaritan woman was an important evangelist in her own community.

Third, we note that Jesus carries out the miracle instigated by his mother and she tells the servants to obey him. This has also become the basis of later theology: the belief that Mary is an intercessor. In other words, if we pray to her, she will ask Jesus to listen to our prayers and respond to them, just as she represented the wedding host when he had no wine. The idea that we have recourse to an intercessor with Jesus is generally unacceptable to Protestants, but Mary and other saints fulfilling this role is a traditional theme in both Catholicism and Orthodoxy. It is not possible to ascribe the theology of intercession to the writer of John, but what he has given us is the image of Jesus listening to his mother and responding to her, despite what can be read as his initial reservations.

It is noteworthy that two very prominent people in John's Gospel – the mother of Jesus and the disciple whom Jesus loved – appear to remain anonymous in this gospel. It is not possible for us to ever fully know why this was the case. A popular answer is that they are symbolic characters, more important for what they represented than for the way in which they were named. However, there is a second possibility which may be added to the first. This is that their names and identities had become complicated in the traditions that fed into the final version of John's Gospel. As we will see, there may have been more than one way of describing Mary. There may also have been one or more candidate for the beloved disciple, or a preferred beloved disciple may have been replaced by another in the tradition. John's Gospel could have avoided any confusion or controversy on these questions by leaving the names out and allowing their symbolic function to be emphasized.

Finally, we see again the mother and the brothers of Jesus mentioned as a group. In John 2.12, they accompany Jesus and the disciples from Cana to Capernaum.

MARY AT THE CROSS

John's Passion narrative diverges from those in the synoptic gospels. In John, the crucifixion occurs on the day of the Passover feast rather than the day after it. The people observing the crucifixion now come closer, near enough to be in communication with Jesus (John 19.25–27). The only named follower of Jesus observing the crucifixion who can also be found in the synoptic accounts would appear to be Mary Magdalene. The passage narrating the presence of Mary at the cross in John 19.25–27 reads:

> Meanwhile, standing near the cross of Jesus were his mother, and his mother's sister, Mary the wife of Clopas, and Mary Magdalene. When Jesus saw his mother and the disciple whom he loved standing beside her, he said to his mother, 'Woman, here is your son.' Then he said to the disciple, 'Here is your mother.' And from that hour the disciple took her into his own home.

Jesus has arrived at his 'hour' and his mother is present. He speaks from the cross in order to bring the beloved disciple and his mother together into a new relationship. This is quite intriguing, and there has been much debate about the meaning of this. Surely if Jesus had brothers who were also the children of Mary, he would have had no need to place his mother in the care of another person. This point was made by those early Church fathers who argued for the perpetual virginity of Mary, such as Origen (*Commentary on John* 1.6) and Jerome (*On the Perpetual Virginity of Blessed Mary* 15).

Yet of course the scene goes far beyond Jesus pragmatically making provision for his mother. It is full of theological significance. And so Church tradition has viewed this as a symbolic depiction of the new family of the Church brought into being by the cross. The beloved disciple is the ideal witness in John's gospel and his relationship with Jesus' mother means that he now has a kinship relationship with Jesus. We are reminded again of Mark 3.35 and its relationship with Luke 1–2:

> Mark 3.35: The disciples are Jesus' family because they 'do the will of God' – in Mark's version Mary is not important in her own right;
> Luke 1–2: Mary is the forerunner and prototype of all those who hear God's word and bring Christ into the world;
> John 19.26–27: The beloved disciple is drawn into a family relationship with Jesus by becoming the son of Mary.

Therefore, in Luke and John, Mary's role has greater significance than it does in Mark.

To say that Church tradition regards John 19.25–27 as having symbolic significance does not mean that it has been viewed as unhistorical by the Churches, as Christian tradition generally sees symbol and history as coming together in the New Testament story of Jesus. However, modern biblical scholarship has been less inclined to accept this as history, but rather to stress its theological basis and to explore what kind of symbols might be involved. After all, in the synoptic gospels, this scene is absent, the beloved disciple does not appear anywhere, and the women who observe the crucifixion are far off and unable to hear Jesus' words. John's version, therefore, must be in the form that it is for a reason. The Gospel of John abounds with theological ideas and it describes Christ as the spiritual centre of Christianity with many metaphors such as Christ as the Way, the Truth, and the Life; the True Vine; the Bread of Life; the Living Water, and so the crucifixion scene is probably also symbolic. This is not to say that John's Gospel contains no history; this is a popular contention that has been challenged in recent decades. However, it does suggest that this Gospel is concerned even more so than the synoptic gospels with telling us who Jesus is for Christians rather than with the biographical details of his life.

The relationship between Mary and the beloved disciple has led the Catholic Church to expand on its view of her as the type and forerunner of the Church, to say that she is also the 'Mother of the Church'. This was declared during the Second Vatican Council by Pope Paul VI in 1964 (although it is an ancient title, not a new one). The Church of believers, the beloved disciples through history, find their kinship with Jesus through Mary as their mother just as the original beloved disciple did. It is important not to forget, however, that the beloved disciple has a *special privilege* as the witness who has handed down the truth of Jesus' life, death, and resurrection; he is not just 'every disciple'. Nevertheless, one can see him as the prototype of believers in the same way as Mary is for Luke. This then leads to the Catholic understanding of Mary as Mother of the Church. It can be contrasted to Mark's Gospel, in which disciples are Jesus' kin through their believing and doing the will of God and need no connection to Mary. However, the writer of John's Gospel sees the mother of Jesus as crucial to the family relationship of believers which is forged at the cross. Perhaps Mark wrote what he did in opposition to the view already widespread that Mary and the brothers were somehow central to faith in Jesus, which survives in John's Gospel only with respect to Mary.

Given that the author of John's Gospel does not name the mother of Jesus as Mary, does he regard her as a real human being at all? We saw in an earlier chapter that some apocryphal gospels equated the mother of Christ with Wisdom, or an incarnation of the Archangel Michael, or the Holy Spirit. Could she be here in John's Gospel a depiction of the Holy Spirit inspiring Jesus and the beloved disciple? This seems unlikely, as the Holy Spirit is described elsewhere in John 14.15–31 as the 'Advocate' with no mention of the mother of Jesus. Nevertheless, these other metaphorical allusions have led some people to ask whether John's 'mother of Jesus' is meant to be the historical Mary or purely a symbolic figure. She may be a symbolic construct in the same way as she appears to be in the birth narratives in Luke. However, even there we found some basic details that stand behind the legendary material: that Mary really was the mother of Jesus, that she was based in Nazareth during his childhood, and that she understood her son to have a claim to the line of David. Can we, in the same way, assume that the writer of John's Gospel inherited a tradition that she was present at the crucifixion, which he may have embellished?

MARY OF CLOPAS

One of the women at the cross in John 19.25–27 has been tra-ditionally referred to as 'Mary the wife of Clopas'. The original Greek is 'Mary of Clopas' and so it could be translated as the mother, wife, or daughter of Clopas. The best translation is probably 'Clopas' Mary', or even 'Mary of Clopas' household', although that does not establish their exact relationship.

Who was Mary of Clopas? What we can reject at the outset is the idea that she has simply been inserted because someone somewhere passed on a memory that she was present in the same way as the women mentioned in just one of the synoptic gospels, Salome (in Mark), the mother of the sons of Zebedee (in Matthew), or Joanna (in Luke). The names of the women at the cross in all four gospels are not there by accident; they serve a purpose. After all, the gospels attest that there were more women than those named in the texts. Mary of Clopas has earned her place.

There are two things that Church tradition remembered about Clopas. We find them in Eusebius (*History of the Church* 3.11 and 4.22), who quotes the second-century writer known as Hegesippus, of whom no works survive. They are that (1) Clopas was the brother of Joseph, which means that Mary wife of Clopas was Mary's sister-in-law; (2) Clopas was also the father of Symeon, the leader of the Jerusalem Church after James. Symeon (the same name as Simon, but nearer to the Hebrew original) would therefore have been a cousin of Jesus.

The first of these traditions makes sense when we consider what early Christian interpreters would have made of John's description of the presence of the mother of Jesus at the cross with her sister. Given that we know that Jesus' mother was named Mary, then how could her sister also be called Mary? Even in ancient families, this was unlikely. Therefore, it was concluded that she must have been her sister-in-law, a logical deduction to make although it may not have been the intention of the writer of John's Gospel.

The second of these traditions, that Clopas was the father of Symeon, the second leader at Jerusalem, is more illuminating as it provides an answer to what might strike the modern reader as mysterious, just as much as it could have done to an ancient one. Why is a previously unknown person, Mary of Clopas, placed at such an important position in this gospel? Why is she named among all the possible women when she has no place in the synoptic accounts? Clopas is not mentioned until this point in John and there were so many other people more important in the ministry of Jesus.

This question can also be asked of Luke's Gospel, where someone called Cleopas (24.18) is the first person to be credited with seeing the risen Jesus in that gospel, but this is the first and only time we ever hear of him. He is almost certainly the same person as Clopas: Cleopas is probably the Greek equivalent of the Aramaic Clopas. There are parallel traditions behind Luke and John (which both include, for example, the sisters Mary and Martha; a Lazarus associated with resurrection; Peter at the tomb). Why is Cleopas in Luke given the privilege of a resurrection appearance, rather than Peter/Cephas, whom we know from 1 Corinthians 15.5 was regarded as the first apostle to see the risen Christ (this is also implied in Mark 16.7 and Luke 24.34)?

However, thanks to Hegesippus and Eusebius, there is an answer to this mystery: Cleopas or Clopas (we will refer to him as Clopas from now on) was the father of the Jerusalem Church's second leader (and long-time leader, according to Eusebius 3.22), at a time when the gospels of Luke and John were being compiled. This does explain his importance and his appearance in the texts.

It would be reasonable to assume that Symeon, bishop of Jerusalem apparently from about 62 CE to the end of the century (the reign of Trajan), was either not born or very young at the time of the crucifixion. Eusebius explains that his status as the cousin of Jesus led to him receiving the honour of being Jerusalem's second bishop, the successor to James the brother of Jesus. Presumably, for him to be given such an important position, he needed to have a true apostle as a father, one that could confirm his right to it. This is a good reason for Clopas appearing in gospels written well after the time of the change of leadership. This should not imply that Clopas' status as a witness to the resurrection was invented; we know from 1 Corinthians 15 that there were many such witnesses, and there is every likelihood that he was one. But the choosing of his son Symeon as Jerusalem Church leader explains why Clopas was singled out among the many to feature in the gospel accounts.

The answer that Hegesippus provides is the best answer to the riddle of the appearance of Clopas at such important points in the gospels; indeed, it is the only one we have.

In John's Gospel we have identified that:

- The mother of Jesus is identified as a key person at the beginning of Jesus' ministry; Jesus' brothers too encourage him to show his power (see Chapter 7);
- The mother of Jesus is intimately associated with Jesus' 'hour', that is, the crucifixion seen as a new birth which is painful but, because of the resurrection, ultimately joyful, and the basis and inspiration for new births of Christians in the Spirit;
- The mother of Jesus is the pivotal member of a new family of believers for whom the 'beloved disciple', the ideal witness to Jesus' truth, is a prototype; therefore, taking the mother of Jesus into one's home seems to be the equivalent of entering the kinship of Jesus;
- The sudden appearance of Clopas in the narrative at the cross was based on the rising to prominence of his son,

Symeon, as the second leader (or bishop) of the Jerusalem Church.

Yet, the text does not say that Mary was Clopas' wife; this is only inferred from it. In a later chapter, we will investigate further the identity of this Mary, who is apparently one of three Marys at the cross in John's Gospel: Mary the mother of Jesus, Mary Magdalene, and Mary of Clopas.

10

The Cross and Tomb

THE SYNOPTIC ACCOUNTS

Compared to John's Gospel, the crucifixion in the synoptic gospels is a stark affair; the onlookers observe the events from a distance. Jesus dies alone and quotes Psalm 22, 'My God, my God, why have you forsaken me?'[18] (Mark 15.34, also in Matt. 27.45 but not in Luke). This is not as desperate as is sometimes thought: Psalm 22 has a happy conclusion, for example, verse 24 says that 'For he did not despise or abhor the affliction of the afflicted; he did not hide his face from me but heard when I cried to him.' But it does enhance the sense of the desolation of the cross. Jesus could have asked the same question, 'Why have you forsaken me?' of the disciples, who have run away or denied him as he faces his trial and execution. However, it is the women who follow

---

[18] Psalm 22 in the Hebrew numbering adopted after the Reformation and now most commonly used; Psalm 21 in the traditional Catholic and Orthodox Bibles.

him to the cross, even if they cannot get near. Mark 15.40–41 has this detail:

> There were also women looking on from a distance; among them were Mary Magdalene, and Mary the mother of James the younger and of Joses, and Salome. These used to follow him and provided for him when he was in Galilee; and there were many other women who had come up with him to Jerusalem.

What will strike the reader at first sight is that there is another Mary here with sons called James and Joses. This will recall Mark 6.3, where the brothers of Jesus are called James, Joses, Judas, and Simon. Could the Mary at the cross be the same person as Mary the mother of Jesus given that she is described as having sons with the same names? Matthew follows Mark closely at these points but changes the name Joses to Joseph, both in Nazareth at 13.55 and at the crucifixion in 27.56. We might have expected Mark or Matthew to distinguish between the two families in a clearer way if they were not the same.

However, there is the problem that the Mary observing the cross is not referred to as the mother of Jesus: if she is, why doesn't Mark's Gospel say so? Another factor is that only two of the brothers are mentioned this time, and not Simon and Judas. Weighing it up, it is not clear whether this is Mary the mother of Jesus. She is not usually regarded as being the same person, but there are some notable exceptions to this view. We will come back to this question after a little more information.

Mark's Gospel refers to this woman again as she observes the burial of Jesus at 15.46–47, or at least we assume that he does, as he refers to her here simply as 'Mary of Joses' in the original Greek, translated in most versions of the Bible as 'Mary the mother of Joses':

Then Joseph bought a linen cloth, and taking down the body, wrapped it in the linen cloth, and laid it in a tomb that had been hewn out of the rock. He then rolled a stone against the door of the tomb. Mary Magdalene and Mary the mother of Joses saw where the body was laid.

She is again accompanied by Mary Magdalene but not by Salome. Someone being described as 'Mary of Joses' could be Joses' mother, wife, or daughter, as it simply means that she is of the household of Joses. Given that we have already been introduced to Mary the mother of James and Joses a few verses earlier, it is reasonable to conclude that she is his mother and that this is the same person.

She appears again visiting the empty tomb on Easter Sunday at Mark 16.1–2, this time as 'Mary of James' along with Mary Magdalene and Salome:

When the sabbath was over, Mary Magdalene, and Mary the mother of James, and Salome bought spices, so that they might go and anoint him. And very early on the first day of the week, when the sun had risen, they went to the tomb.

Mark's use of three different ways to refer to the same person is a little confusing, and it is not surprising, perhaps, that Matthew's version simply refers to her as 'the other Mary' on both occasions at the tomb (27.61 and 28.1). Again, the writer of Matthew is tidying up Mark's original version. His other change is to leave out Salome in the list of women at the crucifixion and insert instead 'the mother of the sons of Zebedee', although this woman is not included at either the burial or empty tomb in his account.

In Luke, the women are named only at the empty tomb on Easter Sunday; at the cross, they are simply referred to as 'the women who had followed him from Galilee' (Luke 23.49). At the tomb, they are 'Mary Magdalene, Joanna, Mary the mother of James [again, the Greek text gives 'Mary of James'], and the other women' (24.10). In Luke, these names do not come out of the blue as they do in Mark and Matthew, as we have been introduced to Mary Magdalene and Joanna (along with someone called Susanna) in Luke 8.2–3. These are the women that, as Mark 15.41 says, 'provided for him when he was in Galilee' and followed him to Jerusalem. Luke reproduces this memory, and adds a little more detail, including the fact that some of the women 'had been cured of evil spirits and infirmities', including Mary Magdalene from 'seven demons'. Overall, the synoptic gospels make it clear that the named women are the most prominent of a number of female followers. Among them, only Mary Magdalene and Mary of James appear in all three synoptic gospels; the others are peculiar to just one of the gospels, and it is interesting that Matthew and Luke do not follow Mark in every detail at this point.

Any attempt to analyse why the evangelists Matthew and Luke have made these small changes can only be speculative. Mark's Salome is not regarded as important by Matthew unless, as some have suggested, Salome was also the mother of the sons of Zebedee, but then why not name her? The mother of James and John, the sons of Zebedee, has been encountered before at Matthew 20.20–28, when she attempts to gain her sons special favour at the right and left hand of Jesus in the coming Kingdom, but Jesus replies that instead they need to be servants. Matthew seems to want to improve the readers' view of the disciples gained in Mark; for example, Peter is referred to as 'Satan' in Matthew 16.23 as in Mark but, unlike Mark, Matthew adds the section on Peter being the rock on which Jesus will build his Church (16.13–20). In Mark 10.35–45, James and John ask for privileges themselves, but Matthew has displaced this inappropriate request onto their mother.

Matthew then places this same woman at the cross. He therefore has two mothers at the cross, both of whom have two sons named, and seems to want to balance James and Joseph (and he removes the adjective 'younger' from James) with the two that he regards as equally important: James and John. Despite this, he does not seem to know their mother's name.

Luke has two good reasons to include someone new: first, Matthew and Mark are not in agreement. Second and perhaps more important, Joanna is described at Luke 8.3 as 'the wife of Herod's steward Chuza', so it serves Luke's purpose to give as a role model a woman who deserted the court for the ministry of Jesus and its commitment to the poor, following him all the way to the tomb. He follows Mark in placing 'Mary of James' at the tomb but decides to forego the complexity of Mark's and Matthew's accounts by not including the names of the women at the cross and burial.

Briefly, we move to John's Gospel, which we discussed in the last chapter. In John's Gospel, the mother of Jesus is in attendance at the crucifixion. So, returning to our discussion as to whether Mary the mother of James the younger and of Joses at the cross and tomb is to be identified as Mary the mother of Jesus, supporting this possibility we have the fact that John's tradition explicitly places the mother of Jesus in the crucifixion scene.

However, we still need to deal with the problem as to why Mark does not state that she is in fact the mother of Jesus. There is an obvious answer. It arises from the way we have interpreted Mark 6.3 in a previous chapter: the only people who think that Jesus' family ties are important are the unbelievers of Nazareth. Jesus is the Son *of God*; nowhere is this more evident than in the way that he lays down his life on the cross, and it is declared by the centurion at 15.39 just before the women are mentioned. The letters attributed to James and Judas/Jude in the New Testament include the authors' own self-identification as the *servants* of the Lord Jesus Christ, not his brothers, despite the fact that Paul in the Epistle to the Galatians attests that James is the Lord's brother. Jude says that he is 'a servant of Jesus Christ and brother of James'. Jesus is the Son of God who now sits at the right hand of the Father and will come again to judge the world. Therefore, despite the fact that being his brothers gave James and Jude prominence in the early Church, the New Testament tradition preferred not to stress their sibling relationship to Jesus.

Therefore, there is no incentive for the writer of Mark at this point to add that it was Jesus' mother observing the crucifixion from afar. Nevertheless, his sources have given him the names of the women, and so he has included them. As we saw in an earlier chapter, after the death of Jesus, Mary and the brothers continued to be a known force in the formation of the Church. We do not know how long Mary was alive after this. However, the fact is that, after the death of Jesus, she would have been known as Mary, the mother of James, Joses, Judas, and Simon.

Why would Mark describe Mary as the mother of James the younger and of Joses, and not of James, Joses, Judas, and Simon? This is not answerable, but there are places where one brother is named rather than two: Mark 15.47, 16.1, and Luke 24.10. The possibility that the list was shortened for convenience is not improbable.

Why is James known as James the younger? It has also been translated 'James the lesser' or James the less' and it could even be 'James the small'. Of these, the New Revised Standard Version has selected the 'younger'. We might ask: younger, lesser, and smaller than whom? The obvious answer is James the son of Zebedee. Throughout Mark's Gospel, James and John the sons of Zebedee along with Peter form Jesus' inner circle of three disciples. They are the ones who witness the Transfiguration. Having spoken of James son of

Zebedee repeatedly in the gospel, Mark may have wanted to distinguish this other James, son of Mary, as being younger, or lesser, or smaller. If this James is the brother of Jesus, the adjective may help him to further diminish James who, as we have seen, was associated with a conservative view in relation to eating with Gentiles and observing the *Torah*.

The possibility that Mary the mother of James and Joses is the same person as Mary the mother of Jesus was mooted as long ago as the fourth century. A certain Helvidius in Rome argued that the Mary at the cross and tomb in the synoptic accounts was also the mother of Jesus. He was refuted by Jerome, but Jerome's intention was to uphold the teaching that Mary was always a virgin, so calling her the mother of James and Joses was problematic for him; he had an agenda in disagreeing with Helvidius. In the Eastern churches, this was not so problematic, as it was declared by Epiphanius, who drew on the text of the *Protevangelium*, that Mary was the *stepmother* of James and Joses. Some of the greatest theologians of the Eastern tradition agreed that Mary mother of James and Joses at the crucifixion and tomb in the synoptic tradition was at the same time the mother of Jesus, in works attributed to Gregory of Nyssa (*Oration on the Resurrection of Christ* 2) and John Chrysostom (*Homily on Matthew* 88) in the fourth century, and Gregory Palamas (*Homily for the Sunday of the Myrrhbearing Women*) in the fourteenth. In the modern period, several writers and scholars have also come to this conclusion. It would not be unreasonable to suggest that it is the best answer to an age-old riddle.

We will argue here that Mary the mother of James and Joses in Mark (or Mary the mother of James and Joseph in Matthew, or Mary the mother of James in Luke) is at the same time the mother of Jesus. This is more plausible as believing that she is not, as it is the plain reading of the texts in Mark 6.3 and 15.40 or Matthew 13.55 and 27.56 by anyone unfamiliar with them. For Mary to be called the mother of James rather than the mother of Jesus would not have been unusual in a Church in which James was a leader, probably the highest authority, as is suggested in Acts 15. This does not mean that it was forgotten that she was also the mother of the Lord, but Mark had reasons for distancing Jesus from his family at the cross, and this was inherited by Matthew and Luke. Mary is also called the mother of Joses in Mark's Gospel, but we have no other information about Joses; only the brothers James and Judas/Jude are remembered in the tradition. It is possible that some of Jesus' brothers, living in a precarious age, may not have survived long enough to make the same impact that James and Jude did.

Therefore, *Mary the mother of Jesus* was associated not only with the cross but also the empty tomb narrative at an early point in the life of the Church, and this tradition made its way into the synoptic gospels. However, only Mary Magdalene is named at the tomb in John's Gospel, although the 'we' in John 20.2 suggests that other women had visited the tomb with her. John narrowed the story of the women's visit to the tomb down to the meeting of the risen Jesus and Mary Magdalene alone.

Yet, in Matthew's Gospel, the 'other Mary' at the crucifixion and tomb, who we are suggesting is also the mother of Jesus, saw the risen Jesus while visiting the tomb with Mary Magdalene:

So they [Mary Magdalene and the other Mary] left the tomb quickly with fear and great joy, and ran to tell his disciples. Suddenly Jesus met them and said, 'Greetings!' And they came to him, took hold of his feet, and worshipped him. Then Jesus said to them, 'Do not be afraid; go and tell my brothers to go to Galilee; there they will see me.'

(Matt. 28.8–10)

This encounter with the risen Jesus is not recorded in Mark or Luke. Later in tradition, with the growth of Marian devotion, many Christians were keen on including a meeting between the risen Jesus and his mother, adding descriptions of it in apocryphal gospels and other writings narrating the life of Mary. Yet, the New Testament itself may describe this encounter, although only in Matthew.

However, why does Matthew refer to the mother of Jesus as 'the other Mary'; does this not belittle her? Perhaps he had Mark's account in front of him as well as a tradition that the women at the empty tomb saw the risen Jesus, and so he may not have known that 'Mary the mother of James and Joses' was also the mother of Jesus. Perhaps he did not think that abbreviating the description of Mary to a more manageable 'the other Mary' was problematic. Or perhaps he was content to obscure the fact that Jesus' mother was associated with the tomb and resurrection. We will never know. As far as Mary is concerned, Matthew follows Mark and says very little.

Luke, too, only refers to the Mary at the tomb as '(the mother) of James'. This is despite the fact that he has told us all about Mary in the conception and birth narratives, and also in Acts 1.14 that she and the brothers were present in the gatherings of the very earliest Church. So perhaps that is more difficult to explain than Matthew's omission. It is something of a mystery as to why Luke just does not state that this same woman, whom he has featured more than any other gospel, was the one at the tomb. On the other hand, he has made nothing of her role in the ministry, and so, in this respect, he too follows Mark.

However, there is no mystery as to why Luke includes Mary the mother of James (and of Jesus, we would argue) in the list at 24.10 but not at 8.2–3. The women in Luke 8 are described as being healed, presumably by Jesus. Clearly, Mary the mother of James was not in that category. This is another argument for the case that she preceded the other women and therefore had no need to be called as a disciple, or referred to as being healed or invited to join the ministry in Galilee; she was the mother of Jesus, not a disciple, and already present.

It seems that the cross and tomb traditions about the women were too important and well known to be omitted from the gospel accounts. The Markan tradition of the two Marys at the cross became established, in such a way that the other evangelists had to record their version of it. All in all, we can be reasonably sure that Mary's motherhood of James (and possibly other brothers) was an important feature of the original crucifixion and tomb stories and was recorded in the synoptic gospels, although omitting any explicit reference to her maternal relationship to Jesus.

THE HISTORICITY OF THE EMPTY TOMB

We have suggested that the virgin birth narratives are based on theological symbolism and not on history; is this not also true of the empty tomb? The empty tomb is attested to in all four gospels, showing that it was accepted in the Church by the time of the writing of Mark, but it is not mentioned in Paul's testimony to the resurrection in 1 Corinthians 15.

It has been suggested that Jesus' body was lost to his relatives and followers because of what we know about the Roman Empire at the time of Christ. This would mean that the empty tomb never existed. However, there is evidence to show that Romans did allow crucified criminals to be buried, although an executed criminal was not afforded the proper funerary rites under Jewish custom. These would have included burial in the family tomb, and so the fact that Jesus was laid in a new tomb actually suggests that he was denied an honourable burial in accordance with Jewish norms concerning a man that they had condemned.[19] The presence of the women and their return on the third day shows that there was an attempt to fulfil the proper rites, but there is no record of their having conducted the usual mourning, which is loud lamenting. The desire that a proper anointing should have been carried out for someone like Jesus yields a context for the story of the anointing at Bethany in Mark 14.3–9 and Matthew 26.6–13, which Jesus suggests is an anticipation of burial, difficult to undertake properly under the circumstances of crucifixion. In John's Gospel, the anointing of the body *does* take place after the crucifixion, carried out by Nicodemus and Joseph of Arimathea (John 19.38–42).

The gospels anticipate and refute the claim that Jesus' body would not have been available to his followers by telling us about the intervention of Joseph of Arimathea, a member of the Sanhedrin. He asks Pilate for the body of Jesus. All four gospels include this detail and so it is as near to an early canonical tradition about the events after the crucifixion as we have. It is entirely plausible, as all societies in all periods are familiar with the idea that people of wealth and status can get around the usual constraints of the social world. It is true that the association of Jesus' death with a rich man has the function of fulfilling Isaiah 53.9 in the Suffering Servant passage. This might suggest that it is an embellishment of the story or that Joseph may never have existed. Yet it is also entirely plausible that Jesus' movement attracted Jews of importance, or at least that they had some sympathy with him.

It is not clear from the earliest account, Mark's, that Joseph of Arimathea was a follower of Jesus. He was 'a respected member of the council, who was also himself waiting expectantly for

---

[19] For more detail, see the articles by InHee Berg in *Biblical Theology Bulletin* 47.4; Petra Dijkhuizen in *Neotestamentica* 45.1; Craig Evans in *Journal for the Study of the Historical Jesus* 3.2; and Byron McCane in *Authenticating the Activities of Jesus*, edited by Chilton & Evans.

the kingdom of God' (15.43). Mark has already told us that all the council condemned Jesus (14.64), which would include Joseph. From Mark's account, we could infer that perhaps he was someone who agreed with reluctance that Jesus had to die but took pity on the family by having him buried. The fact that the women, who should have been the ones to carry out the funerary rites, observe the burial but do not participate, might suggest that they had been tipped off where the burial was to take place so that they could return later when it was safe. These details cannot be established historically; they are simply implied by Mark's version of the narrative.

Mark's empty tomb story lacks the details that the other gospels include which stress its wondrous nature. There is a young man rather than angels; there are no witnesses other than the women, not the guards as in Matthew, nor Peter, as in Luke, nor Peter and the beloved disciple, as in John; no embalming, as in John; the women say nothing and do not pass on the good news, unlike all three other gospels. There is no appearance of Jesus in the original first eight verses.[20] If we did not have the promise of the resurrection in Mark 16.6–7, we could be left with a quite depressing account of execution, a dishonourable death without family burial, and no witnesses. For Mark 16.1–8, the ending of the original version of this gospel, the glory of the resurrection is only anticipated rather than narrated, as Jesus' appearances are not included; we have to experience the resurrection for ourselves.

The problem of the lack of veneration at the tomb has been raised by scholars: if it existed, why would the tomb not have become a shrine to the resurrection as with Helena's foundation of the Church of the Holy Sepulchre on the site, as it was believed to be, in the fourth century? Against this, the argument would be that the tomb itself was not important,

---

[20] The most ancient full manuscripts of Mark end with 16.8.

rather the devotional emphasis is on Christ who was raised from it: 'He is not here' (Luke 24.5). Tombs were places of dishonour and not where Jesus would be glorified; he was not a ghost, haunting the place. Even the most graphic depiction of Jesus' appearance at the tomb, to Mary Magdalene in John 20, includes the words 'Do not hold on to me, because I have not yet ascended to the Father' (20.17), indicating that, for the evangelists, the tomb was liminal, a place in which Jesus is not tarrying but leaving to ascend to heavenly glory.

Christians will *either* see the empty tomb as a metaphor for resurrection because they have already accepted the existence of plentiful legendary material in the New Testament *or* they will think that the tomb really was empty, as Jesus' human body was the basis for his glorified body and could not be left corrupting in the darkness. In Britain, David Jenkins, the new Bishop of Durham in 1984, caused a stir by stating that the resurrection 'was not a conjuring trick with bones'. What he meant by that was that arguments over the historicity of the empty tomb were not really a priority in Christian life: the point was that Christians should live the resurrection by understanding that Christ's risen existence was at work in them, however the resurrection occurred. By moving the attention from the tomb in history to Christian life in the contemporary world, Jenkins was echoing the words of the angelic beings in Luke 24.5: 'Why do you look for the living among the dead? He is not here, but has risen.'

The empty tomb is central to the Christian proclamation because it tells us in a pictorial way that the needless destruction of lives through oppression, violence, neglect or simply because of disease or old age is not the last word from God's perspective. The Romans could not end Christ's existence through tyranny. Christ's empty tomb is everyone's empty tomb: we are not there, we have risen. Life's end in Christian belief, whenever it occurs – the tragic death of a tiny infant to the final breath of a long eventful life – is a taking up into God, not a sudden and meaningless cessation of being. Crucifixion as conceived by the authorities was the opposite of this, a statement of the lack of value and worthlessness of the victim and the pointlessness of their life and death, portrayed in a vicious, agonizing public display. This is negated and wholly reversed by the understanding of the cross in Christianity. The empty tomb may or may not be a legend from the point of view of what happened to Jesus' body, but the good news it declares is that God's raising of the dead is an objective and absolute truth.

Yet even if the empty tomb were to be a legend conveying theological metaphor, the names of the women are nevertheless of historical interest. The fact that they are confusing and vary from gospel to gospel shows that this aspect of the tomb story does not belong to the creation and transmission of a smooth story and its rewriting. They were handed down because of the memory of the women's involvement with the very beginnings of the Christian faith.

WOMEN MINISTERING TO JESUS

In Mark 15.41, we read:

> These [Mary Magdalene, Mary the mother of James and Joses, and Salome] used to follow him and provided for him when he was in Galilee; and there were many other women who had come up with him to Jerusalem.

Matthew 27.55 has an equivalent statement. Luke 23.55 just gives 'all his acquaintances, including the women who had followed him from Galilee, stood at a distance, watching these things'; however, he has already introduced them in 8.2–3 with the observation that, all the way from the ministry in Galilee, there were Mary Magdalene, Joanna, and Susanna, 'and many others, who provided for them [Jesus and the twelve] out of their resources'. The fact that they came from Galilee and learned from Jesus is reinforced by the angelic men's words in the empty tomb: 'Remember how he told you, while he was still in Galilee, that the Son of Man must be handed over to sinners, and be crucified, and on the third day rise again' (Luke 24.6–7).

These passages show that Mary was associated with the women who followed Jesus as well as with his brothers. The several references to her in the gospels suggest that she is likely to have been a prominent person among them. The synoptic gospels state that the group of women was quite extensive. They were central to the growing understanding that Jesus had risen, a belief initiated through a series of appearances, for which the gospels suggest female priority as opposed to Paul, in 1 Corinthians 15.3–7, who asserts male precedence in the list of witnesses to the resurrection (although one can posit women among the 'more than five hundred brothers', as the male noun includes both genders). This is expressed through the stories of the empty tomb.

All four gospels place the first news of the resurrection on the lips of women. In Mark 16.6–7 the angelic figure says to the women:

'Do not be alarmed; you are looking for Jesus of Nazareth, who was crucified. He has been raised; he is not here. Look, there is the place they laid him. But go, tell his disciples and Peter that he is going ahead of you to Galilee; there you will see him, just as he told you.'

Matthew 28.7 is similar and here, as we noted above, the women see the risen Jesus (28.9–10). Luke does not include a resurrection appearance to women, but his narrative does have an emphasis on the women being the first believers. They find the empty tomb, but the apostles do not believe them (24.11). In 24.22–25, on the road to Emmaus, Cleopas and his companion say, with a sense of disappointment:

> 'Moreover, some women of our group astounded us. They were at the tomb early this morning, and when they did not find his body there, they came back and told us that they had indeed seen a vision of angels who said that he was alive. Some of those who were with us went to the tomb and found it just as the women had said; but they did not see him.'

However, Jesus chides them for not believing the women: 'Oh, how foolish you are, and how slow of heart to believe all that the prophets have declared!'

John's account of Mary Magdalene includes Jesus saying to her (20.17): 'But go to my brothers and say to them, "I am ascending to my Father and your Father, to my God and your God."' This famous passage led to Mary Magdalene being referred to as the 'apostle to the apostles'. Therefore, there is a constant gospel witness to the primacy of the women in the initial revelation of the resurrection.

Summing up, Mark 15.40–41, 15.47, and 16.1 are just as unlikely to have been invented by the compiler of this material as Mark 6.3. The names are complex and have been handed down to him. This tradition then fed into Matthew and Luke. So, we can deduce that:

1. In an early tradition, Mary travelled with other women from Galilee who, between them, supported the ministry of Jesus.
2. Mary (referred to as the mother of James and Joses) was associated with narratives describing the death of

Jesus, and these most probably pre-date the gospels, at least in an oral form.

In Mark, followed by Matthew and Luke, Mary observes the crucifixion from a distance, and then sees where he is buried. She returns on the third day at dawn to find the tomb empty. There would be nothing remarkable about a mother being involved in the death rites of her son, albeit in difficult circumstances after a crucifixion; the family was customarily involved, particularly the women. So, there could be a historical kernel behind these stories, even if the gospel versions have been shaped and embellished both in the oral tradition and by the evangelists themselves. But we can note that Mary's relationship to James (and to Joses/Joseph in two of the gospels) is a very important feature of her role at the tomb.

Yet we are left with the query: having cleared up the question of the identity of Mary mother of James and Joses, who is the other Mary at the crucifixion in John's Gospel, the one called Mary of Clopas?

11

Mary of Clopas and
Mary the Mother of Jesus

IS MARY OF CLOPAS ALSO MARY THE MOTHER
OF JESUS?

Now we return to the account of the cross in John's
Gospel introduced in Chapter 9. Who was Mary of
Clopas? The evangelists had their reasons for including the material that they did; the names of the women are
not simply mentioned in passing.

To start with, it is not absolutely clear whether Mary
of Clopas was Clopas' wife as it is usually translated (see
Appendix 4 for an explanation of familial relationships in
Greek). Neither is it certain whether there are three women
in John's crucifixion narrative (19.25–27) as is normally supposed. It could be two, three, or four. These possibilities have
all been considered in biblical scholarship. The commas would
not have been present in the original Greek documents: 'standing near the cross of Jesus were his mother and his mother's
sister Mary of Clopas and Mary Magdalene'.

(a) This could refer to two women only: the mother of Jesus and her sister, who are then named as Mary of Clopas and Mary Magdalene. If so, Mary of Clopas is another name for the mother of Jesus, and her sister is Mary Magdalene. This is usually rejected as being an unusual and improbable option.

(b) The traditional position is that three women are referred to in John 19.25: the mother of Jesus (who we know is called Mary, but John does not name her); his mother's sister who is called Mary of Clopas; Mary Magdalene, thus, three Marys in all.

(c) If four, then they constitute the mother of Jesus and her sister, neither of whom are named, and two other women called Mary of Clopas and Mary Magdalene. Some scholars prefer (c) to the usual option (b).

Despite the fact that option (a) is the least popular in traditional scholarship, it makes sense in light of the discussion in the previous chapter, where we saw that Mary was not always described simply as the mother of Jesus. I am going to argue that the Mary described as 'Mary of Clopas' was originally Mary the mother of Jesus, in the same way as Mary mother of James and Joses in Mark's Gospel.[21] The arguments for this are more intricate than those in the last chapter concerning

---

[21] Other writers have concluded that Mary of Clopas is actually Mary the mother of Jesus, for example, Robert Eisenman, in *James, the Brother of Jesus* and Peter Cresswell, *The Invention of Jesus*. This means that I am not alone in reaching this conclusion, suggesting that it might have some basis. However, I first mooted the idea in December 1996 in an article in *The Month*, and so it is not derived from these writers. They approach the New Testament in a very different way to the one that I do, and they come to this answer for reasons which contrast with my own. For the most part, they reject the foundations of New Testament belief in ways that I do not, as discussed in Chapter 1. James D. Tabor, *The Jesus Dynasty*, also identified Mary of Clopas as the mother of Jesus, but in his recent book, *Marie*, he now suggests that Mary of Clopas was Mary's daughter and Jesus' sister.

Mary mother of James and Joses/Joseph. Jerome in the fourth century suggested that Mary the mother of James and Joses and Mary of Clopas might be the same person although, as we have seen, he strongly disagreed that this was also Mary the mother of Jesus (*On the Perpetual Virginity of Blessed Mary* 15–16).

The first argument for this is quite simple: the presence of two Marys observing the cross, one of whom is Mary Magdalene and the other Mary the mother of Jesus, can be found in the synoptic gospels, Mark, Matthew, and Luke, and this seems to have been passed down from the pre-gospel Passion tradition. Therefore, it would be no surprise to find it in John.

If we are right, then the description of Mary at the cross changed from 'Mary of James' (as in Mark 16.1 and Luke 23.49) to 'Mary of Clopas' in John 19.25. This will remind us of the succession in the Jerusalem Church, which passed from James to Symeon, son of Clopas. This is the second argument. For some reason, Mary was associated with the leadership of the Church at Jerusalem, as belonging to the household of the leader: first, with her son James (and his brother Joses/Joseph), and then Clopas, the father of the second leader.

It is quite possible that 'Mary of James, etc.,' was reformulated (in an oral or written tradition) as 'Mary of Clopas' sometime after the succession of Symeon, when it was important to establish Symeon's credentials. Clopas' name will then have been inserted into an older naming of the witnesses at the cross, that is, 'Mary of James and Mary Magdalene' (the other way round in the synoptic gospels) became 'Mary of Clopas and Mary Magdalene'.

This can be summarized in this table:

LEADERSHIP OF JERUSALEM CHURCH	DESCRIPTION OF MARY THE MOTHER OF JESUS AT THE CROSS
James (from sometime after the crucifixion to c. 62 CE)	She is referred to as Mary mother of James the younger and Joses (Mark), or Mary mother of James and Joseph (Matthew)
Symeon son of Clopas (from c. 62 to the reign of Trajan, 98–117 CE, according to Hegesippus)	She is referred to as Mary of Clopas, who goes to the home of the 'disciple whom [Jesus] loved' (John)

Mary the mother of Jesus was not the mother, wife, or daughter of Clopas as far as we know.[22] After all, were she to have been one of these, the writer of John's Gospel had words available in Greek. Why would you refer to a person as Clopas' Mary without identifying the precise relation?

The answer might not be far away. It could emerge from a reading of the next verse which refers to the beloved disciple: 'And from that hour the disciple took her into his own home.' This describes a relationship where a woman who is not the mother, wife, or daughter of a man yet moves into his home. By means of these verses, John's Gospel tells us that the first-century Christian tradition included the notion that the mother of Jesus could be regarded in a symbolic sense as the mother of a man who was not her son. This will be very important as we consider the role of Mary in relation to leading apostles.

This would mean that Clopas is a candidate in the identification of the 'disciple whom Jesus loved'. Mary is 'Clopas'

---

[22] She was traditionally his sister-in-law, as he was thought to be the brother of Joseph by Hegesippus (see chapter 9), but that might simply have been derived from the belief that she was Mary of Clopas' sister. Even if it were true, it doesn't change our overall argument.

Mary' because she has been taken into his home, at least metaphorically. Therefore, we have a rationale for option (a): there are two women at the cross in John, one of whom is Mary Magdalene and the other is the mother of Jesus = Mary of Clopas. If this is the case, then the mother of Jesus and the beloved disciple are not anonymous after all.

There is another reason to suggest that the Mary at the cross with Mary Magdalene in the four gospels is the same woman, the mother of Jesus. The assumption that the evangelists simply included various women who were remembered as being there makes it statistically unlikely that so many different Marys were the prominent witnesses that the gospel writers had to hand (unless they had a particular reason for naming a Mary rather than anyone else). If Mary the mother of Jesus, Mary the mother of James and Joses, and Mary of Clopas are all different people, as is usually believed, then of the six named women at the cross and tomb across the gospels (these plus Mary Magdalene, Salome, and Joanna), four are called Mary. The fact that about one in four women in the Jewish community were called Mary does not make this occurrence particularly likely. The chance of any four of six women being called Mary are about 1 in 30. If two of the Marys are the same person (the mother of Jesus and the mother of James and Joses, but not Mary of Clopas), there are five women and three Marys; the likelihood drops to about 1 in 11. If, however, three of the Marys are the same person, there are four women and two Marys, yielding a likelihood of about 1 in 5, thus being six times more likely than the traditional view.

Here is a summary of the arguments for Mary of Clopas being Mary the mother of Jesus:

- There are two Marys at the cross and tomb in the gospels of Matthew, Mark, and Luke, Mary the mother of James and Joses (that is, Mary the mother of Jesus), and Mary Magdalene. It makes sense that John too followed this template, which must have been an early tradition.

- Clopas' son was the successor to James in Jerusalem; therefore, in John's Gospel, Clopas has replaced James (and Joses) in the description of Mary at the cross.

- The theory that Mary was linked in early Christian tradition using the metaphor of adoption to important apostles who were not her actual sons is confirmed by the fact that John's Gospel describes her as being taken into the household of the beloved disciple.

- It is unlikely, even given that one in four women in that society were called Mary, that so many different women called Mary would be remembered in the cross traditions.

However, there are also arguments against. The first problem is that the mother of Jesus is unnamed in John 2, at the marriage of Cana, so why would she be named now, as 'Mary of Clopas'? Surely, the traditional interpretation, that she is unnamed in John 19 as well, is the more likely? To try and answer this objection, one can only suggest that the name 'Mary of Clopas' was in John's source for the crucifixion (as with 'Mary of James, etc.,' in the synoptic gospels), and so he faithfully reproduced it.

The second problem with our argument is that the beloved disciple was identified as John and not Clopas at a reasonably early point in the Church. The second-century bishop Polycrates of Ephesus (according to Eusebius, *Church History* III.31.3) wrote that the gospel was written by 'John, who was both a witness and a teacher, who reclined upon the bosom of the Lord, and being a priest wore the sacerdotal plate. He also sleeps at Ephesus.' This John has been traditionally reckoned to be John the son of Zebedee, the disciple who was one of the twelve, but there has been an argument that a second John, known as 'the Elder' (as he calls himself in the opening of the second and third epistles of John), is a better solution. To account for the second-century understanding that John was the beloved disciple, we would have to assume that the tradition in which Clopas was regarded as the beloved disciple was eventually supplanted by one naming John.

To explain that, we can point out the likelihood, given the Gospel of John's view of Jesus' brothers as non-believers in John 7.5, that the community in which the gospel was compiled had become alienated from the Jerusalem leadership. Therefore, James and Symeon son of Clopas were no longer figures held in reverence by the Johannine community. While John does mention Clopas, he does not expand on the importance of this figure. Like Mark, he felt constrained to include what had been handed down to him but without providing further detail.

A third problem is that, if there are only two women at the cross in John's Gospel, we now have Mary the mother of Jesus and Mary Magdalene described as sisters, something that occurs nowhere else. We will explore this further in the final section of this chapter.

Finally, it might be objected that we have fallen into the same trap as many interpreters, starting as far back as the early centuries of the Church, in trying to conflate two or more figures from different gospels into being just one person for convenience, because it is uncomfortable having so many distinct characters with which to deal. This certainly happened in the Western Church with Mary Magdalene, Mary of Bethany, and the anointing woman in Luke 7. While remaining aware of that danger, we could argue that Mary's case is an exception. We can make a case for the divergent ways in which she is described: because of her importance to the crucifixion narrative and its meaning for authoritative witness in the

Church, she attracted a variety of qualifying relationships: she is related to Jesus, to James and Joses, Jesus' brothers and heirs, and now to Clopas, the father of the heir to James.

Here summarized are the arguments against:

- The mother of Jesus is not named in John 2, so it is reasonable to think that she was likewise anonymous in John 19.
- The beloved disciple has always been associated with the name John, and not with Clopas.
- There is no tradition that Mary the mother of Jesus and Mary Magdalene were sisters.
- It is dangerous to assume that characters in the New Testament are the same person in order to simplify the problem of the gospels being different.

On balance, I think that we can proceed with the assumption that Mary of Clopas was another way of describing Mary the mother of Jesus. This solution would have three people in the tradition being reduced to just one: Mary the mother of Jesus, Mary the mother of James and Joses, and Mary of Clopas are all the same person. They are all ways of describing Mary.

Therefore, it is best to conclude that two women are named in all four gospels as being observers at the crucifixion: Mary Magdalene and Mary the mother of Jesus described in various ways. Given that there is interdependence between the gospels, and that Mary Magdalene is consistently identified as being present, it should not surprise us that Mary the mother of Jesus (and of James, etc.) is there in each one as well. It is only the different ways of referring to her that have obscured this.

Our argument is supported by the fact that Mark uses the Greek version of the name Mary, which is *Maria*, at the cross and tomb. The other evangelists, when mentioning the Marys at the cross in all four gospels, and at the tomb in the synoptic gospels, stay with the Markan *Maria*. However, when the other evangelists developed various stories about women called Mary that are not in Mark (Mary the mother of Jesus in the birth narratives in Matthew and Luke; Mary of Bethany in Luke and John; Mary Magdalene at the tomb in John), they generally use the Aramaic name *Mariam* (the manuscript variants are complex – see Appendix 5.)

From this, we can conclude that '*Maria* mother of (or just "of") X and *Maria* Magdalene' constituted a traditional formula in the gospel tradition that could not be overlooked or ignored in relation to the cross and tomb list. As it happens, the expression 'X the mother of Y' is a rare expression in the New Testament and it only occurs when the mother's name is Mary.

It is therefore not unreasonable to suggest that all the Marys at the cross and tomb except for Mary Magdalene were derived from the same person, a mother figure for certain prominent apostles in the very earliest Church. Otherwise, we would have to assume that being called Mary was a qualification for several otherwise insignificant women to get a special mention in the early Christian tradition!

MARY AND JERUSALEM

Our conclusion is that Mary of Clopas is Mary the mother of Jesus, and that this identification arises from her association with the Jerusalem Church leadership. Like other theories about the origin of John's Gospel, concluding that the description of Mary at the cross is based on the succession in the Jerusalem Church from James to Symeon cannot be proven beyond doubt, but it is certainly plausible and, I would argue, the best solution to the enigma of the Marys. It suggests that the idea of the beloved disciple, the pre-eminent witness, derives *originally* from an honour bestowed on the Jerusalem leadership. The original 'beloved disciple' was James, who actually was the son of Mary, and so this would not have needed an adoption scene by the cross, but then the honour passed to Clopas and maybe others. Eventually, the beloved disciple was identified as John the son of Zebedee.

This theory corroborates two conclusions that scholars have arrived at with respect to John's Gospel: that its sources are very much earlier than the writing of the gospel, and that the gospel shows evidence of an intimate knowledge of Jerusalem.

In the earliest Church tradition, therefore, a relationship to *Mary* was crucial in the Church at Jerusalem. James was the son of Mary and the brother of Jesus. The succession from brother to brother is an obvious one. If we did not have John's story of the beloved disciple, we could leave it there. But that text establishes a relationship with Mary as a key aspect of apostolic authority in the Jerusalem Church even when the leader was not her son. Given that the Jerusalem Church was originally dedicated to maintaining the Jewish tradition in Christianity, this explains why Mark (in 3.31–35, see Chapter 7) was keen to say that Christians could be taken into the family of Jesus without needing to refer to the mother and brothers of Jesus.

This might also help to explain the mysterious reference in Acts 12.12 to the 'house of Mary, the mother of John whose other name was Mark, where many had gathered and were praying'. Another Mary and another key apostle as a son! John Mark is important in Acts chapters 12 to 15 as a companion of Paul and his co-missionary Barnabas, of whom John Mark was possibly a cousin (Col. 4.10).[23] Acts 12.12 is the first mention of John Mark, and so the reference to his mother's

---

[23] He may or may not be the Mark referred to in the epistles (2 Tim. 4.11; Philemon 1.24; 1 Pet. 5.13).

house serves as an introduction to this character. That is why the house of Mary is not associated in this instance with any other of the Jerusalem apostles.

Acts goes on to relate that he was the cause of the separation of Paul and Barnabas, as Paul did not want him on their mission, thinking of him as unreliable. Barnabas disagreed and sailed to his native Cyprus with John Mark. This is one of the few places in Acts where we see dissension among the apostles. Yet the reference in Acts 12.12 establishes John Mark as an important Christian in Jerusalem and Paul had his opponents there, so the argument may have been linked to viewpoints on Christians observing the *Torah*; Galatians 2.13 shows that there was disagreement between Paul and Barnabas on the question of table fellowship.

It seems reasonable to ask: was Mary regarded as a mother to the Jerusalem community as a whole? Did she adopt in some spiritual sense the leading apostles, such as Clopas and John Mark, and regard them as sons along with James, Joses, Judas, and Simon? Is this the origin of the idea of her adopting the beloved disciple in John 19.26–27? Throughout the New Testament, Christians are called brothers and sisters; 'Father' refers to God. Mothers, on the other hand, nearly always seem to have the name Mary. Paul does not speak of Mary the mother of Jesus, but he does write just once about a spiritual mother. He contrasts the mothers of Abraham's children, Hagar the slave and Sarah the free woman, relating these to the Law and freedom in Christ: 'Now Hagar is Mount Sinai in Arabia and corresponds to the present Jerusalem, for she is in slavery with her children. But the other woman corresponds to the Jerusalem above; she is free, and she is our mother' (Gal. 4.25–26). This idea of spiritual motherhood links to Jerusalem and corresponds to the heavenly Jerusalem spoken of in Revelation. Yet the mother Church may have had at one time a human mother figure.

In conclusion, the argument that Mary of Clopas is at the same time Mary the mother of Jesus depends on whether we accept that John's Gospel incorporates an older tradition into the heart of the gospel in the crucifixion narrative in the same way as Mark's does. The confusion surrounding the lists of women make this likely.

SISTERS?

Our theory leaves just two Marys at the cross in each of the gospels and, if we are right about John 19.25, in John's Gospel they were described as sisters. Could Mary the mother of Jesus and Mary Magdalene have been sisters in some sense? It would not be surprising if Mary Magdalene were to have been a relative of Jesus, given her role in the burial (it is fashionable for people to think of her as the wife of Jesus, but we have no evidence in the New Testament for that). Mary and Mary Magdalene being birth sisters runs into the same problem as Mary and Mary of Clopas being sisters: they would not have had the same first name. Therefore, this sister relationship, if it existed, was the sisterhood of either relatives or close friends.

Both women feature at very important moments in John's Gospel: the ministry begins with the mother of Jesus' initiative at the marriage at Cana, and the tomb stories end with the appearance of the risen Jesus to Mary Magdalene. In John, Mary Magdalene has the garden scene alone where Matthew's version includes both women seeing the risen Jesus. It is true that, several times, John uses the dramatic effect of Jesus relating to an individual rather than a group (for example, Nicodemus, the Samaritan woman, Martha). In his gospel, both the Marys experience one important moment of the story alone with Jesus: the mother of Jesus at the wedding at Cana and Mary Magdalene at the garden tomb. They experience one together (the crucifixion).

There is a powerful symmetry here: the cross scene through its female characters points back, first, through the mother of Jesus, to the beginning of the ministry and the first of the signs of Jesus which made the crucifixion inevitable and, second, through Mary Magdalene, forward to the garden and its tomb, which is inevitable because of the crucifixion. There is a logic in supposing that the mother of Jesus takes us from Cana to the cross, and Mary Magdalene from the cross to the resurrection, so that these two women stand together at the central point of the crucifixion.

Martha and Mary of Bethany, who appear at another crucial moment in the gospel, the raising of Lazarus (chapters 11 and 12), are also sisters. This is the only passage in John's Gospel, apart from 19.25, where the word 'sister' is included. The raising of Lazarus is one of the events which are the 'signs', so important to John's Gospel. There are seven such signs (if we do not include the resurrection itself): Cana, three healings, the feeding of the crowd, the walking on water, and the raising of Lazarus. Mary and Martha therefore appear at the seventh and last sign. The raising of Lazarus in John's Gospel is the event which caused the critical tension with the authorities leading to the execution of Jesus; it is another pivotal moment on the journey to the garden tomb. It is followed by Mary of Bethany's anointing of Jesus.

John's Gospel could be said to rest on a fulcrum of sister relationships which includes two pairs: Martha and Mary; Mary the mother of Jesus and Mary Magdalene. A possible clue to the importance of sisters lies in the short second epistle of John, written by the same person as the gospel. It begins: 'The elder to the elect lady and her children, whom I love in the truth, and not only I but also all who know the truth, because of the truth that abides in us and will be with us forever' and concludes: 'The children of your elect sister send you their greetings'.[24] 1 Peter 5.13 corroborates this: 'your sister church in Babylon [= Rome]', literally 'she who is at Babylon'.

This table illustrates the theme of sisters in the writings of the author of the Gospel of John:

The mother of Jesus (2.1–12; 19.25–27) at the wedding at Cana and the crucifixion = Mary of Clopas	Mary Magdalene (19.25; 20.1–18) at the crucifixion and by the garden tomb, the first witness to the resurrection
Martha (chapter 11, especially 11.20–28), a resident of Bethany; Martha declares Jesus 'the Messiah, the Son of God' and he tells her that he is the 'resurrection and the life'	Mary (11.1–12.6, especially 11.28–33), a resident of Bethany; Mary anoints Jesus after the raising from the dead of her and Martha's brother, Lazarus
The 'elect lady' of 2 John verse 1	The 'elect sister' of 2 John verse 13

Therefore, the theme of sisters plays an important part at key moments in John's Gospel, and it may not be a coincidence that the same writer refers to two churches as sisters. This may have helped to shape the sister theme in the gospel. While Mary the mother of Jesus and Mary Magdalene were historical persons with individual contributions to the mission of Jesus, over time they may have come to be associated with a pair of prominent churches, one of which was obviously at Jerusalem.

---

[24] It has usually been assumed that the 'elect lady' is the church community to whom John is writing and the 'elect sister' the church community *from* which he is writing. On the other hand, it has also been suggested that the lady is a distinguished individual in the early Church, and that attempts to make her a metaphor detract from the role of women in the apostolic period. Despite this, the signature verse of 2 John suggests the first answer to be most likely, i.e., that the ladies are metaphors for individual churches.

Having mentioned the sisters Mary and Martha in John's Gospel (they also appear in Luke 10.38–42), we now move to the anointing narratives, which appear in all four gospels. The anointing woman is unnamed in three gospels, but in the Gospel of John she is Mary of Bethany.

12

The Anointing:
The Woman in Mary's Image

THE ANOINTING AND THE TOMB

The anointing at Bethany in the Gospels of Mark, Matthew, and John is important, because it clearly acts as a precursor to the story of the empty tomb. The mother of Jesus is not mentioned in association with this story, but we will see that it is nevertheless relevant to a discussion of her role in the gospels.

An anointing of Jesus by a woman appears in all four gospels, although in Luke, the setting is completely different to the other three. We will give the Markan version in full, as it is likely to be the oldest. It comes after the plotting of the chief priests and scribes to kill Jesus, and before the decision by Judas Iscariot to betray him; therefore, its context is the growing tension leading up to the final week of Jesus' ministry. After this comes the Last Supper, the Passover Feast in Jerusalem just a few miles from Bethany. Mark therefore intends the reader to see the anointing in the context of the inevitability of the crucifixion of Jesus; it is a scene that prepares for the Passion narrative.

> While he was at Bethany in the house of Simon the leper, as he sat at the table, a woman came with an alabaster jar of very costly ointment of nard, and she broke open the jar and poured the ointment on his head. But some were there who said to one another in anger, 'Why was the ointment wasted in this way? For this ointment could have been sold for more than three hundred denarii, and the money given to the poor.' And they scolded her. But Jesus said, 'Let her alone; why do you trouble her? She has performed a good service for me. For you always have the poor with you, and you can show kindness to them whenever you wish; but you will not always have me. She has done what she could; she has anointed my body beforehand for its burial. Truly I tell you, wherever the good news [gospel] is proclaimed in the whole world, what she has done will be told in remembrance of her.'
>
> (Mark 14.3–9)

The story tells us the following explicitly:

- That Jesus' community were not afraid of mixing with those with diseases which are generalized in the word 'leper', as we read elsewhere in the gospels;
- That Jesus' community were concerned about the poor, which once again is verified in other passages;
- That the death and burial of Jesus is being anticipated.

We might also infer that the anointing on the head is symbolic of the messianic status of Jesus, although anointing of the head could also be an action of hospitality. Given that Jesus is the

'Christ' (Greek) or 'Messiah' (Hebrew), the 'anointed one', the lack of any anointing elsewhere cannot but lead us to think that Mark's Gospel is suggesting a symbolic reference to it here.[25] In Mark's Gospel, Jesus tries to keep secret his status as the Messiah in the early part of the ministry in Galilee (especially when Peter declares it in Mark 8.27–30); then, after travelling to Jerusalem including the stay at Bethany where the anointing takes place, he boldly declares it to the Sanhedrin (14.62) and is condemned as a result.

The position of the anointing during the last week in Jerusalem confirms what the reader already knows but about which many characters in the gospel are still unsure: the Messianic identity of Jesus. It is known only to outcasts and to disciples, although the latter do not understand its implications. Jesus being the 'Son of David', hence Messiah, is declared by a blind man (Mark 10.47). Later, Jesus is anointed in the house of a leper by a woman whose actions have overtones of impropriety in the culture of the time, a woman anointing a male guest at a meal unannounced. These passages are powerful reminders of the context for Jesus' mission, the marginalized people of Israel as in other gospels: the Messiah is the one who heals the poor, blind, lame, lepers, etc. (Matt. 11.5, 15.31, 21.14; Luke 7.22, 14.13, 14.21; John 5.3, and the healings in Acts).

The anointing woman understands what Jesus' Messianic mission is about: he will have to suffer death. As has been noted in feminist biblical analysis, there is a strange discrepancy between the high praise and promised legacy of this woman and the fact that she remains anonymous. We do not know whether she was one of those who travelled from Galilee, or

---

[25] This is supported by Santiago Guijarro and Ana Rodriguez in *Biblical Theology Bulletin* 41.3. One of the first scholars in recent decades to suggest the Messianic anointing of Jesus in the Markan and Matthean accounts was one of my tutors at the University of Leeds, J.K. Elliott, *Expository Times* 85.4.

whether she was a member of the host's household, but Jesus' response to her suggests that she is to be considered a true disciple. It is not surprising, therefore, that John identifies her as Mary of Bethany, whom we know from Luke 10.38–42 is associated with discipleship and 'sat at the Lord's feet'. In John and Luke, unlike Mark and Matthew, the anointing is of the feet.

The anointing in Mark begins the story of the Passion which ends with the empty tomb story. The fact that the woman has anointed Jesus anticipates concerns about the manner of his burial. In the synoptic gospels, Joseph of Arimathea wraps the body in a 'clean linen sheet', but it would seem that, because Jesus had been executed at the command of the Sanhedrin as well as the Roman governor, the appropriate rites are omitted, according to the custom of the time for condemned criminals. The women observe but do not seem to mourn properly. They collect spices and return to the tomb on the third day to try to carry out the anointing having rested on the Sabbath. But, of course, he will not be there. Therefore, the anointing narrative has two symbolic layers added to a story about hospitality to an honoured guest. It is both Messianic and anticipates the need for burial rites as they will not be possible after death. It functions as an excellent vehicle for proclaiming the executed, buried, and raised Jesus as the Messiah.

In terms of the anointing, Matthew's Gospel follows Mark reasonably closely as it often does, and John's Gospel is different in its approach to this story as it often is. The anointing of Jesus' body before burial is completed in John 19.38–42 and carried out, surprisingly, by males who do not appear to be family members of Jesus, and quite excessively so, a Johannine device to remind us of Jesus' kingly status. This is odd in light of the fact that, in the anointing story of John 12.1–8, Mary of Bethany has purchased the oil for Jesus' burial and has already anointed him with it, but it is a much smaller amount, a hundredth of that used by Joseph and Nicodemus. We also have a different sequence in John's Gospel, which places the anointing before Jesus' entry into Jerusalem rather than after it.

Luke takes the anointing somewhere else entirely. Now the anointing is in Galilee, and it comes immediately before the introduction of the women who have been healed and follow Jesus. The anointer is a 'sinner' from the 'city' (it is not clear which city this is). The fact that she might be of questionable status could be inferred from the account in Mark and Matthew, but it is not made explicit there as it is in Luke. Luke neither tells us which sins she has committed nor her name, but Western tradition identified her as a prostitute, put her together with the Mary who anointed Jesus in John, and then conflated her with Mary Magdalene, who was healed of seven demons and introduced in the very next passage. Thus, the repentant prostitute Mary Magdalene was born, although not until the sixth century! This has been reversed in Roman Catholicism recently, which now accepts the Eastern view that these are three distinct women.

There is a certain confusion about all the gospel Marys which spills over into the Christian apocrypha of following centuries. It is not surprising that the early Church began to confuse Mary Magdalene and Mary of Bethany, as their roles with respect to the burial and the recognition of Jesus as the crucified Messiah are close, and they both have allusions to the Bride of the Song of Songs: Mary of Bethany with her costly ointment (Song of Songs 1.12) and Mary Magdalene as the seeker and finder of Jesus (3.1–4, 5.6, 6.1), who attempts to hold onto him (3.4) in the garden (4.12–5.1, 6.2). In the apocrypha, the name 'Mary' when it has no further identifying information, might be Mary the mother of Jesus, Mary Magdalene, or Mary of Bethany.

What is interesting is that one of the women who follow Jesus is 'Joanna, the wife of Herod's steward Chuza' (Luke

8.3). A woman who had lived in the entourage of Herod's court and enjoyed its fruits might well be a better candidate for a reformed sinner from the city than Mary Magdalene; just before this passage, we have heard Jesus talk about John the Baptist, referring to his greatness, and he is the one who will be beheaded by Herod.

Of course, we will never know whether a particular woman was behind this story; most likely, the anointing woman in Luke is a representative of women converts generally for the purposes of the narrative. Many converts – both men and women – will have regarded their past lives as sinful, some probably with better reason than others. The power of Jesus to forgive is at the heart of this story, and so the woman is an ideal disciple; the anointing serves as a precursor to the healing of the women followers which follows directly after this scene in Luke 8.1–3.

The table overleaf demonstrates the main differences in the three anointing stories.

The anointing in its position in Mark begins the story of the Last Supper and Passion, and may have been taken from earlier sources, probably oral, in which the Passion was recited. It is intimately linked to the empty tomb story because of the reference to oil and burial, and the anointing along with the empty tomb form the bookends within which the Passion narrative is placed. There are two meals at which Jesus prepares his disciples and companions for the imminence of his death, this one in Bethany and the Last Supper in Jerusalem. In John, the action of Mary of Bethany, anointing Jesus' feet, comes before him washing his disciples' feet. This seems to be one of those instances where Luke and John have some interdependence, as Luke 10.38–42 tells us that Mary sat at Jesus' feet while Martha prepared the meal, a situation repeated in different circumstances in John 12.1–8. The possibility that Mary and Martha are fictitious ideal types is suggested by

	MARK 14.3–9 AND MATT. 26.6–13	LUKE 7.36–50	JOHN 12.1–8
WHO?	'a woman'	'a woman in the city, who was a sinner'	Mary, sister of Martha and Lazarus
WHERE?	Bethany	Galilee	Bethany
WHOSE HOUSE?	Simon the leper	Simon, a Pharisee	Lazarus, Martha, and Mary
HOW?	On the head	On the feet	On the feet
WHO OBJECTS?	'Some there' (Mark); the disciples (Matt.)	Simon the householder	Judas Iscariot
WHY DO THEY OBJECT?	The cost of the oil which could be used for the poor	The woman's reputation	The cost of the oil which could be used for the poor
WHAT DOES THE ANOINTING REPRESENT?	Jesus' burial	The woman's repentance and faith; she is forgiven	Jesus' burial
HOW WILL THE WOMEN BE REMEMBERED?	Wherever the gospel is preached	Not specified	Not specified
WHAT HAPPENED BEFORE?	Jesus is in Jerusalem and the scribes and chief priests are plotting	Jesus speaks about John the Baptist	Jesus is in Bethany and the scribes and chief priests are plotting after the raising of Lazarus
WHAT HAPPENED AFTERWARDS?	Judas goes to the priests to betray Jesus, and then there is the Last Supper	Jesus goes through Galilee with the twelve disciples and women, both those healed and those who provide for him	The plot to kill Lazarus and the entry into Jerusalem on a donkey

the fact that their names only differ by one letter in Greek, and this might also be the same for Lazarus, whose name is associated with resurrection in Luke 16.19–31.

WHAT HAS THE ANOINTING GOT TO DO WITH MARY THE MOTHER OF JESUS?

At first sight, there is no obvious link between the anointing and Mary the mother of Jesus. In John's Gospel, the woman is called Mary, but she is the sister of Martha and Lazarus; they all live in Bethany. Because we know from the crucifixion stories that women followed Jesus from Galilee, it would be reasonable to suppose that the evangelists imagined them to be close at hand when this incident occurred, but the text does not say this. Mary the mother of Jesus and Mary Magdalene are only tangentially connected to the anointing through their observing the burial of Jesus in the synoptic gospels which is prefigured in this episode. The woman does not keep the oil for the burial because she has used it for the anointing, so we cannot presume that the writer of Mark intends us to think that she may have been at the burial.

However, the purpose of the story is to link the death of Jesus and his Messiahship, which we know was very difficult for the Jewish tradition, as evidenced by Paul's statement:

For Jews demand signs and Greeks desire wisdom, but we proclaim Christ crucified, a stumbling block to Jews and foolishness to Gentiles, but to those who are the called, both Jews and Greeks, Christ the power of God and the wisdom of God.

(1 Cor. 1.22–24)

Burial and anointing are connected in all four gospels:

MARK AND MATTHEW	LUKE	JOHN
There is an explicit reference to the anointing being an anticipation of the burial of Jesus	The anointing comes immediately before the introduction of the women who are to follow Jesus from Galilee to the empty tomb	The anointing has a reference to Jesus' burial, but also comes immediately after the story of Lazarus being raised from the tomb

The anointing stories therefore create an interplay between Jesus as Messiah and Jesus, the one who is raised from the dead, and who is resurrection and life in person in John's Gospel (11.25). In all four gospels, the link that is made between the Messianic vocation of Jesus and the fact that he will die, be buried, and raised again on the third day is made prophetically by women. We hear that this is 'in accordance with the scriptures' (1 Cor. 15.4, quoted in the Nicene Creed), which admittedly is something of a mystery if we apply this just to the third day, as it is only alluded to in Hosea 6.2: 'After two days he will revive us; on the third day he will raise us up, that we may live before him', but this reference is to the Lord raising up stricken Israel rather than being raised himself. We could possibly add Exodus 19.11–16 when the Lord comes down on Sinai on the third day. But generally, 'in accordance with the scriptures' repeated twice in this Pauline passage relates to the whole process of death, burial, and raising up, to which the Psalms and the Suffering Servant passage in Isaiah 52.13–53.12 have ample reference in one form or another. It is with the fulfilment of this prophetic tradition that the women are associated.

Luke's is the one gospel that does not refer to the anointing as a Messianic prophetic action, but the revelation of the Messianic mission of Jesus to a woman is elsewhere in Luke. In the events of the conception and birth of Jesus, Mary his mother, like the anointing woman, understands by divine revelation Jesus' Messianic vocation in advance and that she will suffer through it. She is praised in the same way as the anointing woman. In the conception stories, the person who does the praising is Elizabeth: 'Blessed are you among women, and blessed is the fruit of your womb' (Luke 1.42), whereupon Mary utters the *Magnificat*, in which she declares that 'all generations will call me blessed' (1.48). In the anointing, it is Jesus who offers the praise: like Mary, the anonymous woman will be remembered wherever the gospel is preached. Both women are prophets.

Luke, the great evangelist of the poor, has reconfigured the anointing story possibly because he dislikes the idea that 'you always have the poor with you', in the sense that poverty will endure, and the implication that it was better to spend the money on the oil. Yet, whether it was Luke's intention or not, the fact that he has removed the prophetic anointing but has added the story of Mary as the prophetic mother of the Saviour helps us to see an equivalence between these two. The women who followed Jesus and supported him, including Mary, are the ones who are most astute in understanding what the mission will mean. The conception and birth narrative presents a parable of the faithfulness of the women disciples as they journey towards the cross, where they will be present even in the absence of the twelve disciples. Among them, we can imagine that the mother of Jesus will have had an important role, one that continued after the events of Easter as is suggested by mention of the 'certain women, including Mary the mother of Jesus, as well as his brothers' (Acts 1.14).

This means that all four gospels have a story in which a woman takes the initiative at a crucial moment in the ministry of Jesus. This creates an important thematic pattern which links the anointing with narratives in which Mary the mother of Jesus is the main subject:

MARK AND MATTHEW	LUKE	JOHN
The anointing woman, in a prophetic action, introduces the Passion story by showing that the Messiah will die; she is one of the very few people praised by Jesus in this gospel	The woman with initiative is Mary the mother of Jesus in the conception and visitation stories; she is made aware of the sorrow that awaits and reflects on the events The anointing in this gospel precedes the first mention of the women who were healed and who follow Jesus to the crucifixion and tomb	The mother of Jesus asks Jesus to perform the first miracle of his ministry at Cana The anointing by Mary follows the story of the raising of Lazarus and the statement that Jesus is the resurrection and the life, the Messiah and Son of God, in conversation with Martha

The consistent testimony to the anointing stories in all four gospels suggests that women were associated with anointing in pre-gospel traditions. The early Church could easily have created a story of the Messianic anointing of Christ by a man, following the tradition of Old Testament anointers Moses, Samuel, Zadok, Nathan, Elijah, the young prophet instructed by Elisha in 2 Kings 9.1–13, and Jehoiada and his sons, but they did not; the nearest equivalent is the baptism of Jesus by John the Baptist. Here, as in the virgin conception story, women stand in where men have become secondary: Jesus is anointed by God and by women but not by men. This creates another connection between the anointing and the virgin conception. Thus, the anointing woman is in the image of Mary the virgin mother of the Lukan account; both stories are parables that tell us about real women in Jesus' community and historical actions in a compelling and memorable way.

What do we know about the participation of these women in the mission of Jesus? Having considered all the New Testament passages which include Mary as well as other important women, we need to consider what we know of Jesus' ministry before we can go on to evaluate how Mary and her female companions may have contributed to it.

13

Jesus' Ministry and Mary's Vocation

SEEKING THE HISTORICAL JESUS

Reconstructing the history of the life of Jesus is an extremely difficult task which has occupied scholars for the last two hundred years. We can attempt to sketch some outlines but with awareness that we are dealing with gospel texts that developed over some decades. We are looking at history but through the thick lens of the faith of the early Church.

The first step in a historical construction is to note how little the life of Jesus impacted on the historical records of the ancient world in contrast to the growing Christianity of some decades later, which is referred to by Tacitus, Suetonius, and Pliny the Younger, all of whom were born after the year 55 CE; therefore, their testimony comes much later than Jesus' life, although they refer back to events as early as the reign of Claudius (41–54 CE). The only record of Jesus' life outside the New Testament is one short piece in the books by Flavius Josephus.

Josephus' section on Jesus is brief; it is referred to as the *Testimonium Flavianum*. It reads:

> Now there was about this time Jesus, a wise man, if it be lawful to call him a man, for he was a doer of wonderful works, a teacher of such men as receive the truth with pleasure. He drew over to him both many of the Jews, and many of the Gentiles. He was the Christ, and when Pilate, at the suggestion of the principal men among us, had condemned him to the cross, those that loved him at the first did not forsake him; for he appeared to them alive again the third day, as the divine prophets had foretold these and ten thousand other wonderful things concerning him; and the tribe of Christians, so named from him, are not extinct at this day.
>
> (Josephus, *Antiquities of the Jews* Book XVIII: 3.3)

This text is the subject of much discussion. Josephus was not in favour with the Jews, whom he had betrayed during the Jewish War, and so his work was handed down by Christians interested in the history of the Jews during the period that Christ lived. Origen is known to have held a copy in the third century. It presents a positive view of Jesus by one whose testimony was considered authoritative and contemporaneous. For this reason, there is much suspicion that the text was either (a) edited or expanded by Christian redactors to include those aspects which are clearly based on Christian belief, or (b) inserted wholesale by them into an existing narrative (certainly the next verse follows on quite logically from the preceding verse). Scholarly opinion is that one of these two is the case, with the majority view favouring (a). Yet, even if all or part of the text was original to Josephus, it does not take up much space in his historical works.[26] The section on Jesus is shorter than the one on John the Baptist (*Antiquities* Book XVIII: 5.2).

There are many clues in the Acts of the Apostles that the Church was fast growing. The story of Pentecost (Acts 2.1–13) suggests a period of successful conversion summarized in this account; Acts 2.47 talks about the expansion of the Church and 4.4 suggests that there were five thousand converts at the time of the arrest of Peter and John. This growth continues in 5.14, and so on (6.1, 6.7, 9.31). The idea that Christianity made great strides in mass events is corroborated by Paul's testimony that more than five hundred saw the risen Jesus (1 Cor. 15.6), and its growth is illustrated in parable form by the mustard tree, the seed of which is small but the fully grown plant extensive (Matt. 13.31–32; Mark 4.30–32; Luke 13.18–19).

The record of the progress of the Church in relation to the lack of non-Christian records of Jesus strongly suggests that Jesus' movement was originally quite small. Although the impact of his life was nuclear, there will not have been a large following in his lifetime. This is another indication that, as we have suggested, the truly miraculous events claimed of Jesus are mythical descriptions of what he means to Christians, metaphorical ways of describing salvation. If we take out those, what do we have left?

JESUS IN HISTORY: THE NON-VIOLENT PREACHER

Jesus grew up and practised his ministry as a Jewish man of his time, observing the Jewish *Torah* and its customs. While the cities were multicultural, rural Galilee was predominantly

---

[26] Greater detail on Josephus has been given in Chapter 8.

Jewish. We do not know whether Jesus or Mary were literate in the sense that they could read and write fluently, although we may suspect that they might, given Jesus' teaching, but they were certainly very familiar with the Jewish Scriptures which most rural Galileans knew orally if not in writing.

During Jesus' lifetime, there was a period of relative peace under Herod Antipas, son of Herod the Great, who reigned over the one third of Israel that included Galilee from about 4 BCE to 39 CE. He was, relative to other rulers of that time, a successful king who maintained order, and there were few Roman soldiers visible in that region during his reign. He tried not to offend Jewish religious sensitivities. However, Herod Antipas' rulership was not all harmonious. The people of Galilee will have remembered the many crucifixions by the Romans following the occupation of Sepphoris in Galilee by a certain Judas in about 6 CE. Around twenty years later, Herod Antipas had John the Baptist executed and the gospels tell us that he also plotted against Jesus, who is said to have referred to him as 'that fox' (Luke 13.32). Therefore, he was a ruler who aroused indignation, and there was constant fear of revolt by Jews against an authority that they did not recognize: Herod was Idumean, like his father, imposed by Rome, and not regarded as a suitable ruler for the Jewish people. People outside the ruling classes – and that is the great majority – were poor and lived a day-to-day existence. Many continued to follow apocalyptic preachers like John the Baptist.

It is very likely that Jesus practised *non-violent* resistance to both the Roman occupation and to the Jewish authorities when they appeared to collude with Rome and/or regard their own survival as more important than the spiritual health of the Jewish people. During Antipas' reign, non-violent resistance was a natural response in a time when the overwhelming oppression and poverty that leads to full blooded revolution was not in evidence.

The practice of what we would now call non-violent resistance is evidenced in the gospels in sayings such as 'turn the other cheek' and 'if someone asks you to walk with him one mile, walk with him two' (Matt. 5.38–41). Mark Wilde in *Crossing the River of Fire* shows that these were ways in which subjugated Jews showed their refusal to be bowed down by the Roman military; the story of the Gerasene swine rushing into the sea suggests that Jesus, like other Jews, longed for liberation from the Romans (Mark 5.1–13). The swine were metaphors for the Roman legions as the spirits that possessed them were called 'Legion'; the boar was a common symbol among the Roman military.

Nevertheless, it is not necessary to move to the conclusion that Jesus was violently opposed to Roman occupation and promoted armed revolution. We know from the history of the Jewish War (66–73 CE) and the Bar Kochba revolt in the following century (132–5 CE) that such a policy was unsuccessful, leading to the destruction of the Temple and the loss of the Jewish homelands. It is an unnecessary step to take to move from the belief that Jesus understood the Roman occupation as damaging and oppressive, to the conclusion that he was part of an armed insurrection. In situations of subjugation by one's own rulers or foreign powers, there are different ways of responding, which include passivity, collusion, non-violent resistance, and revolution. It might be anachronistic, perhaps, to talk of non-violent resistance based on twentieth-century examples like Mahatma Gandhi, Martin Luther King, and Eastern Europe. Yet, in all times and places, non-violent revolution is the most likely to be successful under oppression as opposed to direct violence which, unless it is pragmatic and ultimately successful, plays into the hands of those holding power, giving them a rationale for greater repression.

Non-violent resistance has various implications which makes it a likely fit for how the historical Jesus perceived his ministry:

(a) It attracts condemnation from two groups of fellow countrymen at once: those advocating violent revolution, and those discouraging any kind of resistance, such as the chief priests. This makes sense of the way that Jesus was apparently abandoned and condemned by some fellow Jews as the crucifixion came nearer.

(b) It is the approach that is most likely to gain supporters among members of the dominant culture, that is, it would have been attractive to countercultural elements among the Gentiles. Witness the popularity of Gandhi and Luther King among Europeans and Americans in recent decades. We know that Christianity was adopted at an early stage by Gentile converts.

(c) It is the best option for the more vulnerable sectors of the oppressed culture, the poor and the meek who are praised by Jesus as the inheritors of the Kingdom in the Beatitudes and elsewhere.

One point that could be raised in favour of Jesus as an armed revolutionary is that Jesus had a disciple named Simon 'the Zealot', according to Luke 6.15 and Acts 1.13, and also that the name Judas 'Iscariot' may imply a member of the Sicarii, the dagger-wielding assassins among the Jewish insurgents. However, this argument quickly falls apart. It would be strange if particular followers of Jesus were given these titles if Jesus and *all* his disciples were either Zealots or Sicarii (or an equivalent kind of violent revolutionary, as these terms belong to the 60s CE and may be anachronistic for c. 30 CE). It is more likely that Jesus' movement attracted people from other Jewish groups and that they bore names indicating their origin; the conversion of a person to a different cause can be celebrated in this way. Perhaps they put forward the argument for a violent revolution among non-violent people who disagreed with them. We do not know for sure who these men were, but the names do not in themselves imply anything for the whole movement. It also shows that the gospel writers did not systematically eradicate any mention of insurrectionists among Jesus' followers, and so their presence was not necessarily an embarrassment, which contradicts any theory that the gospels hid the violent past of Jesus in order to appease the Romans.

There is no convincing argument that can be made that Jesus was originally some kind of violent revolutionary, which would lead to its corollary that the picture of Jesus in the gospels is therefore wholly inaccurate. This is the kind of conspiracy theory that we rejected in Chapter 1.

To say that Jesus was non-violent does not lead to the conclusion that he was continually gentle and mild. If the gospels contain accurate echoes of Jesus' teaching, we find some very fierce sayings which prophesy a *spiritually violent* overthrowing of the powers and demons of this world, and the raising up of the poor through divine intervention. This spiritual revolution demanded a response and the choosing of sides.

JESUS IN HISTORY: THE PREACHER RESTORING HOPE AND IDENTITY

Jesus was therefore a non-violent preacher and teacher with disciples, one who taught the reality of God's presence as the answer to the many ills that were befalling the Jewish society under the Romans, Herodians, and Jewish priestly castes. Jesus communicated a powerful message that the God of Israel was a living God intimately involved in the fate of the nation and its people, and could be accessed simply through prayer rather than elaborate ritual. This brought about a radical change of attitude among people who were desperate and downtrodden, giving them meaning and hope. We get a sense of Jesus' feeling about the hopelessness in Jewish society in Matthew 9.36: 'When he saw the crowds, he had compassion for them, because they were harassed and helpless, like sheep without a shepherd.' Oppressive power divides and conquers, but the gospel narratives reveal Jesus' work of reintegrating people into the community of Israel: the lepers, the tax collectors, the prostitutes, the impoverished. Jesus did not limit his message to the religiously faithful, the ritually clean, or the upstanding and moral; he understood that many of the outcasts of Jewish society were in that position due to the social situation which led to abuses of all kinds.

Biblical references that illustrate the ministry to the outcast include the great banquet of Luke 14.15–24, in which 'the poor, the crippled, the blind, and the lame' are invited. This passage recalls Micah 4.6–7 which refers to the return from the Exile, but which will have served as a proof text for Jesus' ministry:

> In that day, says the LORD, I will assemble the lame
> and gather those who have been driven away,
> and those whom I have afflicted.
> The lame I will make the remnant,
> and those who were cast off, a strong nation;
> and the LORD will reign over them in Mount Zion
> now and for evermore.

If you believe in God, really believe in God, then the things that crush you in life can be overcome, at least internally. Jesus' positive message of affirmation for the poor may well have resulted in healings and what were then regarded as exorcisms, in cases where a change of heart or outlook led to physical or mental healing (while the more dramatic healings of incurable diseases or raisings from the dead are part of the mythology of the post-Easter Jesus). The gospels are full of symbolic ways of describing in picture form this sense of belief and realignment: the dead are raised, the sick healed, demons exorcized, the poor lifted up in spirit, water becomes wine, and so on.

The transformed society that Jesus encouraged and represented was described as 'the Kingdom of God' (or, in Matthew, 'the Kingdom of Heaven'). Jesus followed John the Baptist in calling for repentance because of the imminence of the Kingdom of God, and this of course is what baptism is: it takes a rite used for the entry of Gentile sympathizers into the Jewish faith and asks Jews to re-enter their own faith in this way. This was probably interpreted by many Jews as an insult. It is unlikely that Jesus regarded baptism as the substitution for circumcision that Paul claimed it to be later; nevertheless, the practice of asking people to radically renew faith does sow the seeds for Paul's later arguments. Jesus' and Paul's ways of understanding baptism were different but not contradictory.

Jesus taught that the Kingdom of God was both 'among you' (Luke 17.21) and coming soon as a great judgement of the world. This would fulfil the prophecies of Daniel with the coming of the Son of Man (Mark 14.62, quoting Dan. 7.13) who represented, expressed in modern terminology, humane society. The Kingdom was both in the present, here and there, as it could be found in various instances of positive and healing human interaction, and in an imminent future. Jesus' own death and resurrection heightened this apocalyptic expectation and it continued into the ministry of Paul, where we see that the first Christians expected the second coming of Jesus. This urgency is also reflected in the gospel parables which discuss the Kingdom and the coming of Jesus as the Bridegroom. We can see an alternative version of this in the book of Revelation. Sanders' reconstruction of Jesus' ministry, *The Historical Figure of Jesus*, suggests that we can be confident of Jesus' own teaching if those before him, such as John the Baptist, are in agreement with those after him, such as Paul.

This is true for the belief that God's intervention was to occur within a generation. Jesus' ministry and the teaching of the very earliest Church form the continuous link between John the Baptist and Paul.

Jesus, like Jews both before and contemporaneous with him, saw God's Kingdom as a restoration of Israel. The twelve disciples were symbols of the twelve tribes of Israel, and they would be the leaders and judges of the tribes (Matt. 19.28), although as servants to them (Matt. 10.26; Mark 10.43). The Son of Man of Daniel's prophecy would bring a humane kingdom replacing the dominance of the Greeks and Romans, and it would be a Jewish kingdom. However, the means for achieving this for Jesus was a call to conversion among the whole Jewish population anticipating divine action and not via a radical sub-group of revolutionaries.

Jesus' teaching drew on the prophets, the *nevi'im*. There is a prophetic challenge to Israel in these books, in which justice and righteousness are indispensable for monotheistic faith and its rituals and festivals (see, for example, Jesus referring to himself as the servant of Isaiah 42.1–4 who establishes justice, quoted in Matt. 12.18–21). This prophetic challenge was, like its forerunners, filled with a strong critical judgement on those who did not understand the imminence of the coming of the Kingdom of God, particularly those who paid lip-service to true faith or gained power and status through religion.

The people around Jesus had a growing understanding that his message was Messianic in nature, and Jesus' claim to a Davidic lineage would have encouraged that. Jesus was not only the preacher of the Kingdom of God but at the same time the one who was called to be its King. The Kingdom may not have been destined to overthrow the Romans; instead, it was inscribed into people's hearts, lives, and practices. The situation did not practically allow for the possibility of armed revolution, as the Jews eventually discovered in the Jewish

War. Only God could bring about the change that Jewish people desired.

Jesus was, like other groups such as the Essenes, very critical of Jewish leadership, particularly the Temple priests, whom he regarded as abandoning the heritage of Israel in order to survive under the Roman regime. It is interesting that Caiaphas survived as high priest for eighteen years, according to Josephus, when the average tenure under the Romans was much shorter, suggesting that Caiaphas may have been a particularly Machiavellian figure. The high priest held power over everyday life in Jerusalem and its surrounding districts in Judea, the Roman army only being called in when circumstances threatened disorder, particularly during major feasts such as Passover. Therefore, it is quite plausible that the high priest had a hand in the death of Jesus, even if the sentence was carried out by the Romans.

Jesus' ministry was essentially a rural enterprise except when he visited Jerusalem.[27] The New Testament includes no record of him preaching and healing in the cities of the Galilean region, like Sepphoris and Tiberias. It was also an itinerant ministry, and Jesus' followers travelled light, as we read in Mark 6.8–9: 'He ordered them to take nothing for their journey except a staff; no bread, no bag, no money in their belts; but to wear sandals and not to put on two tunics.' The itinerant mission relied on the hospitality of people in the towns visited, and this continued into the early Church, as we can see in 1 Corinthians 9, when Paul argues that he should receive this hospitality as well as the apostles and brothers of Jesus. It could not have involved a large group, as to be a member required a radical renunciation of wealth, trade, and extended families. This will have been too great a challenge

---

[27] There are also the 'cities' through which Jesus passed, as mentioned in Luke 8.1, but there is nothing specific included that identifies them.

for most people (for example, the rich man of Matt. 19.16–22; Mark 10.17–22; and Luke 18.18–25).

In the rural culture of Galilee, a Messianic theology inspiring a movement that reached out to the poor was born. It is not surprising that many in Israel, even the authorities, saw this as a good thing; they may have welcomed, much as we do today, a movement that was prepared to tackle some of the more difficult problems suffered in the community. Perhaps Jesus' fieriness and public statements of condemnation took it in too political a direction for some of them; perhaps his brother James, according to the reconstructions of later history an upstanding member of the Jerusalem community known as the 'Just', was more moderate, and so he survived for much longer until eventually suffering assassination by an opportunist high priest. We can only speculate on this. Yet, however we conceive of its development, the movement centred on Jesus gave meaning and purpose to the marginalized, as well as much needed funds to the poor and, as we have seen, it was supported and funded, perhaps even initiated, by women of means.

John Dominic Crossan, in *Jesus: A Revolutionary Biography*, argues that Jesus' ministry was subversive of many of society's boundaries: table fellowship; association (for example, healing and touching lepers); family; class; hierarchy; patronage. According to Crossan, Jesus was a Jewish version of the Cynics in Greek society who likewise abandoned social systems. Itinerancy and minimal baggage were clear ways of marking this refusal to accept the restrictions of social interaction prescribed by the establishment.

Jesus' ministry was therefore *liminal*: it remained on the margins of society, as John Meier indicates in the title of his book, *Jesus: A Marginal Jew*. Liminality is difficult to maintain; in the early Church, Crossan suggests, boundaries and hierarchies began to make their way back into the once radical community. In the same way, Elisabeth Schüssler Fiorenza's feminist analysis of the New Testament, *In Memory of Her*, argues that Jesus' mission was marked by a radical egalitarianism in terms of gender which had begun to break down by the time that the New Testament was written. Just how far Jesus' ministry differs in its social outlook from the early Church at the time of writing of the New Testament epistles and gospels is one of the great debates of New Testament study. As we have seen, Paul seems to reflect this original equality in Galatians 3.28 ('There is no longer Jew or Greek, there is no longer slave or free, there is no longer male and female; for all of you are one in Christ Jesus') in a way that other epistles attributed to him do not.

Jesus was a miracle-worker, like many others in the ancient world; miracles were generally accepted, although there were some sceptics at that time just as there are today. Probably, gossip and high expectation made more of them than an impartial observer would have recorded, and we have seen how much they are part of the mythology of the New Testament. Nevertheless, Jesus must have had a reputation in this respect. Sanders says that Jesus' miracles were unremarkable in themselves; what was more important is that they were signs of the impending divine intervention. For the New Testament, the resurrection is the proof of Jesus' divine status, not the miracles. To achieve the glory of the resurrection, Jesus first had to die.

Jesus was one would-be Messiah among many in an era of fervent apocalyptic expectation, prophetic calculations, and popular belief that God was about to act to institute a new kingdom for the Jewish people. Why then was Jesus the one whose legacy survived the catastrophic Jewish wars in which these hopes were dashed? This is a question which requires hindsight or faith, or both. The belief in his resurrection was unique and it resolved the difficult question of death and failure. The way in which Jesus' message transcended the Jewish nationalist cause, and touched on the human condition for people of all races, attracted great numbers of Gentiles to the movement. Then, of course, believing that Jesus really was the Incarnate Son of God, and the one who sends the Holy Spirit, leads to the conclusion that generations of people keeping his memory and believing in him would be inevitable.

MARY'S VOCATION

In terms of the contribution of women to Jesus' ministry, here is a summary of the arguments that have been developed in this book:

- The downplaying of women in patriarchal texts in that time and culture tells us that the participation of women would have been much greater than the gospels suggest.
- What the gospels do state is that Mary and other women supported the ministry and accompanied Jesus to the cross. Mary and other women acted as inspirers and initiators at important moments in the ministry of Jesus and belief in the resurrection. While we cannot be sure of the historicity of each one of these narratives, there is nothing in the New Testament that contradicts this overall impression, and many passages that support it.
- Mary is often mentioned along with the brothers of Jesus who, it is clear, were leaders in the early Church, working with the apostles; among them, James was foremost and Mary was associated with him in the cross and tomb narratives.

Therefore, Mary was a participant in the life and death of Jesus, and in the resurrection faith. She was not just a passive bystander. However, we should not detach Mary from the other women in the movement as so many devotional and theological writings do. While she, as mother figure in the Jerusalem community, will have had a more prominent role, with that exception what can be said of her is also applicable to them. We have seen how the anointing narratives indicate the importance of women in understanding and declaring the Messianic mission of Jesus.

If we imagine what life was like for Mary as far as a twenty-first-century person can do, then clearly there must have been a period of contemplation and decision for Mary as Jesus entered adult life. He may not have taught the rabbis in the Temple at the age of twelve, but certainly he was a remarkable person to have been able to carry out the ministry that led him to Jerusalem and the cross in the company of his followers, who risked a great deal to travel with him. At some point, whether Jesus was aged twelve or later, Mary must have realized that he had a unique vocation. She may have encouraged this and helped to shape it as he grew. There is nothing in the New Testament to suggest that she did not; the stories of her reflecting in Luke and asking Jesus to undertake the miracle at Cana in John do support a general assumption that Mary was influential in the formation of Jesus' mission. In other words, there was a memory of Mary in the early Church that allowed the evangelists to create stories around her that were appropriate to her legacy.

The narratives about Mary presented in the gospels of Luke and John show her understanding something of Jesus' vocation before his mission began and reflecting on the realities of life around her and the possibility that Jesus could make an impact on that reality. Along with the brothers, she participated in Jesus' ministry, realizing that the mission was dangerous. While this is composed of material that is not necessarily historically accurate, it supports rather than contradicts the view that Mary was influential, and so it may have been true to folk traditions about her.

In Chapter 7, we discovered material in Mark's Gospel that brings us closer to the life of Mary in history. Mark's reluctance to allow the mother and brothers any special importance in the passing on of the gospel of Jesus tells us that many Christians in the early Church probably did the opposite, and they may have been those who preferred to adhere to the Jewish *Torah*. Luke-Acts and John both confirm the memory of the mother (and not the father) and brothers of Jesus as a family unit at the very beginning of the Church. Mary, as Jesus' mother, was known to the early Church to have been an active participant in the ministry of Jesus, accompanying him on his journey to the cross. As one of the older members of the movement supporting Jesus, and especially being his mother, she must have made a conscious decision to become involved in what was a dangerous undertaking in the society of the time.

The social project of Jesus' community, in its reaching out to the poor and insistence on non-violent resistance is, to generalize, one that will have resonated with women. This is not to say that men will not also have had the insight that this is the best strategy in an oppressive society. However, in a patriarchal, binary world, the male response is often more head-on: violent resistance, as with those later called Zealots, voluntary exclusion, as with the Essenes, or maintenance of the cultural traditions through compromise and negotiation, as with the priests. These are outward-facing strategies. An approach that is more inward, that is, looking back into the community in order to strengthen and bring unity to it, while following a peaceful avoidance of direct confrontation is, in a patriarchal society, more likely to be the province of females. The success of this strategy will then attract males who, once again bearing in mind the patriarchal world in which all of this was taking place, begin to take control and leadership of the movement as it grew.

In Luke 1.39, we hear that Mary travelled in haste to visit her kinswoman Elizabeth, who lived in the Judean hill country. This would have been a dangerous journey to a country occupied by soldiers, revolutionaries, and bandits. Even if we accept that it might never have happened in history, it would nevertheless be an appropriate metaphorical way to describe the journey made by Mary and the women of Jesus' community from Galilee to Jerusalem in support of a claimed Messiah. Such an undertaking is most likely to be a historical reality, even if the visitation to Elizabeth is not, and it may have occurred several times because of the various feasts in Jerusalem and the demands of the itinerant ministry of Jesus and his disciples. Membership of the Church community will have been even more dangerous after the crucifixion.

Mary, along with other women and men in the community, must have decided at some point that Jesus' ministry was worth these risks. Without them, Jesus would probably have been forgotten. He is unlikely to have been able to pursue an itinerant ministry in isolation. Hypothetically, it is possible for a single figure to make an impact, travelling and preaching, relying on local hospitality, but the New Testament makes it clear that this was not the case for Jesus. He was surrounded by a supportive community. We can agree, therefore, that the image of Mary in Luke's narrative as an exemplar for hearing the word of God and acting on it is an appropriate one for the historical Mary, the original followers of Jesus, and those who came after them in circumstances which included rejection from their own communities and sometimes civic persecution. The sacrifices involved are summed up in the dialogue between Jesus and Peter in Mark 10.28–30:

> Peter began to say to him, 'Look, we have left everything and followed you.' Jesus said, 'Truly I tell you, there is no one who has left house or brothers or sisters or mother or father or children or fields, for my sake and for the sake of the good news, who will not receive a hundredfold now in this age...'

For all these reasons, 'Virgin' might well be an appropriate metaphorical description for Mary. Prominent among a community of women and men, Mary conceived a Messianic mission unlike anything before it and there is no record of her requiring any male mentor: Joseph is a shadowy figure in the birth narratives but then disappears, and Jesus, according to the earliest testimony, was 'the son of Mary'. But to use a term like 'Virgin' as a metaphor for Mary should not result in the suppression of sexuality and the relegation of consummated marriage to a spiritual second best. Neither should marriage be promoted above celibacy; both are different ways of living out one's life journey. What seems to be the case is that Mary was a married woman with a family, a Davidic family with a unique claim to lead the Messianic movement, and in which the mantle of everyday leadership passed from Jesus to James after the crucifixion. However, belief in the resurrection meant that Jesus was proclaimed the Lord, remaining the spiritual leader of the community through the gift of the Holy Spirit.

14

The Death and Resurrection of Jesus

THE EXECUTION OF JESUS

As a source of consolation to the poor, Jesus' non-violent movement would have been welcomed by all sections of Jewish society, the Romans probably unaware of its more subtle belittling of them. A non-confrontational group might have been able to coexist, uncomfortably, with the 'world' of Roman and Herodian rule by serving its underclasses. Later Christian communities did flourish in this way as social helpers in times of communal distress such as plague.

However, Jesus and his followers could not avoid the political element which caused them to clash with the authorities. It was inevitable because of the theological vision of a restored Israel – restored Messiah, restored Temple, restored people. A Messianic movement had to be centred on a male leader who constituted a threat. It was inevitable that a desire for the betterment of the poor as opposed to simply consoling them, in tandem with a visionary, parallel system of authority in which God ruled through a Messiah in anticipation of an imminent divine overthrowing of the present powers, would eventually come into conflict with governor and priests.

The execution of a non-violent person is all the more shocking because of its sheer injustice. A violent insurgent would not be surprised to die at the hands of the authorities; indeed, he may welcome this as a martyr. Perhaps the story of Barabbas arose to indicate that even violent bandits were not hounded as much as Jesus, the non-violent man. However, non-violent resistance along with the refusal to accept social boundaries can become more effective than insurrection and therefore more threatening to those in power. If Jesus did adopt rituals and practices that suggested to the authorities, both Jewish and Roman, that he saw himself as the Messiah, that will have concerned them. So, we read that Pilate wanted him to be designated 'King of the Jews' on the cross. This could be an aspect of the narrative that emerged in the oral tradition, a folk cultural way of showing that Pilate thought himself to be ironic but actually stated the truth without realizing it. Or it could be historical, the act of a governor wanting people to know the inevitable result of Messianic claims. Pilate's message proclaimed loud and clear that there was only one place for the King of the Jews: on the cross. They had a ruler, Tiberius Caesar, represented locally by the Herodians in the north and his governor/prefect, Pilate, in the south. Anyone else with claims to thrones in the region was destined to death.

Scholars of the New Testament have discussed the accuracy of the texts concerning Jesus' self-perception of his mission and there are many different views. Did he see himself as the Messiah, the Son of God, or even God? Was he aware of his impending death as the gospels suggest? Did he think that God would intervene first? How can we know anything about Jesus' own thoughts and plans?

Let us start from first principles. What Jesus and his disciples certainly knew was that Israel as a nation had understood itself to be blessed by God despite its lowliness, especially in the two major events of its history: Exodus and Exile. In both cases, Israel had been subjugated to foreign domination; in the first, its people had been slaves, in the second, their home city and sacred temple destroyed with the leading citizens killed or led away as prisoners. Yet this was the nation that God had chosen to be a light to the world, and so they were liberated, sent across the desert to the promised land in both cases.

Therefore, the Exile is associated with the Exodus in the Hebrew Scriptures, both narrating the great story of Israel's most desperate times followed by its revival. The greatest prophecy of redemption is to be found in the long prophetic book of Isaiah, in that part known as 'Deutero-Isaiah' (chapters 40–55), the 'Second' Isaiah, because it appears to have been written during a later time than when Isaiah himself lived. Its author prophesied after the defeat of Babylon by Cyrus when the Jews were being allowed home (some of them chose not to go):

> Comfort, O comfort my people, says your God. Speak tenderly to Jerusalem, and cry to her that she has served her term, that her penalty is paid, that she has received from the Lord's hand double for all her sins. A voice cries out: 'In the wilderness prepare the way of the Lord, make straight in the desert a highway for our God. Every valley shall be lifted up, and every mountain and hill be made low; the uneven ground shall become level, and the rough places a plain. Then the glory of the Lord shall be revealed, and all people shall see it together, for the mouth of the Lord has spoken'.
>
> (Isa. 40.1–5)

This became a proof text for the redemption brought about by Jesus. While many Hebrew prophets are quoted and remembered in the New Testament, there is no section more relevant to the way in which Jesus' mission was understood than Deutero-Isaiah.

Later in Deutero-Isaiah comes the 'Suffering Servant' passage of Isaiah 52.13–53.12 (see also Isa. 50.4–11). It is worth quoting this in full:

See, my servant shall prosper; he shall be exalted and lifted up, and shall be very high. Just as there were many who were astonished at him – so marred was his appearance, beyond human semblance, and his form beyond that of mortals – so he shall startle many nations; kings shall shut their mouths because of him; for that which had not been told them they shall see, and that which they had not heard they shall contemplate.

Who has believed what we have heard? And to whom has the arm of the LORD been revealed? For he grew up before him like a young plant, and like a root out of dry ground; he had no form or majesty that we should look at him, nothing in his appearance that we should desire him. He was despised and rejected by others; a man of suffering and acquainted with infirmity; and as one from whom others hide their faces he was despised, and we held him of no account.

Surely he has borne our infirmities and carried our diseases; yet we accounted him stricken, struck down by God, and afflicted. But he was wounded for our transgressions, crushed for our iniquities; upon him was the punishment that made us whole, and by his bruises we are healed. All we like sheep have gone astray; we have all turned to our own way, and the LORD, has laid on him the iniquity of us all.

He was oppressed, and he was afflicted, yet he did not open his mouth; like a lamb that is led to the slaughter, and like a sheep that before its shearers is silent, so he did not open his mouth. By a perversion of justice he was taken away. Who could have imagined his future? For he was cut off from the land of the living, stricken for the transgression of my people. They made his grave with the wicked and his tomb with the rich, although he had done no violence, and there was no deceit in his mouth.

Yet it was the will of the LORD to crush him with pain. When you make his life an offering for sin, he shall see his offspring, and shall prolong his days; Through him the will of the LORD shall prosper. Out of his anguish he shall see light; he shall find satisfaction through his knowledge.

The righteous one, my servant, shall make many righteous, and he shall bear their iniquities. Therefore I will allot him a portion with the great, and he shall divide the spoil with the strong; Because he poured out himself to death, and was numbered with the transgressors; yet he bore the sin of many, and made intercession for the transgressors.

We cannot be sure as to whom Deutero-Isaiah was referring when these words were written: Israel as a nation, its king, or perhaps one of the Exilic prophets, like Jeremiah? This remains a mystery, but what we can be certain of is that early Christians applied this prophecy to Jesus, as Acts 8.32–33 attests. The gospels tell us that he understood he was destined to die, and that he accepted the fatal mission to which he had been called. There is no clearer passage than the Suffering Servant to explain why the early Church claimed that Jesus had been crucified 'for our sins' (1 Cor. 15.3). Whatever the intentions of its original author, the importance of this passage in the prophetic collections of Jewish tradition meant that it allowed for the unthinkable to be regarded as a blessing: the death of the Messiah as a cursed criminal. In addition, there are also passages in the Psalms where the psalmist suffers first and is then raised up, such as Psalm 22, which Jesus quoted on the cross according to the Gospels of Mark and Matthew.

There is no reason to doubt that Jesus may have understood these passages as referring to himself and the unavoidable death that was the consequence of his ministry. This strengthens the argument that his mission was non-violent. Jesus emphasizes his servant role in Mark 10.35–45, and here we read that his greatest act of service was to die 'as a ransom for many'. At the very least, it was one of the first insights of the infant Church contemplating the horrors of the destruction of someone who stood for life and justice, doing no harm to anyone. But the prophecy has a happy ending: the servant would be raised up and, drawing on the equally influential prophecies of Daniel, taken into heaven as the Son of Man who would return to judge the world.

It is interesting that John's Gospel includes the high priest Caiaphas sharing the view that Jesus' death could have some benefit for the Jewish people (11.47–53): 'to gather into one the dispersed children of God' (11.52). Clearly, John does not think that Caiaphas had a proper understanding of the significance of Jesus, but it is nevertheless the case that the idea of a sacrificial victim was prevalent and may have been drawn from Isaiah's Suffering Servant. According to John's Gospel, the disciple with Peter in the courtyard of the high priest during Jesus' trial, presumably the beloved disciple, 'was known to the high priest' (John 18.15–16); if so, it may have been believed that he had an insight into Caiaphas' thinking about Jesus' fate.

Alternatively, another idea in circulation at that time was that the death of a just man could bring condemnation onto the nation, which is rather the opposite of Caiaphas' view in John. The idea of the death of Jesus being a curse on generations to come is there in Matthew 27.25. Eusebius (*Church History* II.23.19) records that the 'more sensible' of the Jews attributed the siege of Jerusalem to the unjust death of James the Just, brother of Jesus; Josephus, nearer in time to the events, does not go this far but still records the concern that some Jews had at the murder of James and others by the high priest Ananus (*Antiquities* XX.9.23). The idea that an unjust execution could taint a city was certainly extant.

Why did the authorities regard Jesus as so dangerous that he had to die? There are many who think that the events of the Passover visit to Jerusalem are based on real history. We concluded in Chapter 8 that the objections of Pharisees to Jesus' interpretations of the *Torah* were not enough to lead to execution, despite what the gospels imply. Much more serious were the threats to social and political order. If Jesus really did make a statement by riding into the city on a donkey at this major feast, and then tried to eject the money changers from the Temple (although John has this event on a visit earlier than the synoptic gospels), then this would have been sufficient for a nervous and suppressive regime to have him executed. Jesus claimed to have divine authority, and so he undermined political authorities. His attack on the Temple was symbolic; as an observant Jew, he would not have wanted to threaten the sacrificial business of the Temple which its money changers represented. Therefore, it was all the more threatening. Sanders, in *The Historical Figure of Jesus*, points out that it is likely that Jesus really did prophesy the Temple's destruction (Mark 14.58; Matt. 26.61; John 2.19), and thereby angered the priests. The Temple was not *wholly* destroyed by the Romans in 70 CE, and therefore a prophecy which is not fulfilled in all its detail is unlikely to be invented.

Caiaphas would have wanted to prevent the situation from getting out of hand. He did have responsibility for public order, and so the gospel narratives may represent the historical core, if not the precise detail, of his involvement. However, as far as Pilate is concerned, the Passion stories are less likely, as he would barely have taken the trouble with this Jewish offender. His sentence was most likely a summary one, fitting the rather brutal and impatient image that we have of him from Philo and Josephus. Jesus can only have been regarded as a criminal by many Jews, not because he was executed by the Romans, but because of the condemnation of the high priest and the Sanhedrin. As we have seen, Jesus would have been denied the honour of a proper Jewish burial.

The probability that the Passion narratives were constructed from folk memory because of ignorance of the details does not change the likely historical core of the Passion story: that Jesus was crucified by the Romans for threatening the peace, while some Jews concurred because he claimed superiority over the scribes and priests. He may have made Messianic claims like that in Mark 14.61–62 which would have led to a charge of blasphemy. It is not antisemitic to think that the involvement of the Jewish authorities may have been historical, although the implications for persecuted Jews down the centuries were wholly unwarranted. The history of religion in all corners of the world shows us that religious power in any culture can be every bit as brutal as its secular counterpart. We have already suggested that Caiaphas may have been more likely than other high priests to work with the Romans rather than against them. But ultimately, it was a Roman rather than Jewish execution, unlike the Jewish killings of Stephen (Acts 7.54–60) and James the Just (recorded by Eusebius).

We will never know how prepared the companions of Jesus were for this violent end to an enlightened and liberating ministry. The gospels tell us that he gave his disciples many warnings, but we do not know whether these were presumed only after the event. Was the whole affair a terrible shock from which only the resurrection appearances and careful contemplation of scriptures such as the Suffering Servant helped the disciples to recover? Did Jesus anticipate it? Did the anointing woman in the Gospels of Matthew, Mark, and John foretell it in her symbolic relating of Messiahship, hospitality, and death? It is not possible to know the answers to these questions. Many scholars have tended to emphasize the post- rather than pre-Easter origin of the interpretations of the scriptures that inspired the early Church, which would mean that Jesus and the disciples may have anticipated the coming of the Kingdom of God as an irruption into history before anything happened to Jesus, but then the crucifixion occurred and caused them to think again. On the other hand, the fact that they will have known Isaiah 52–53 and its Suffering Servant passage might cause us to be cautious about ruling out the possibility that Jesus and others may have seen his death beforehand as a realization of this prophecy, something that needed to be gone through *before* the Kingdom of God would be triumphant. As Crossan in *Jesus: A Revolutionary Biography* points out, faith did not begin with the resurrection; it was more that the resurrection confirmed the faith in Jesus that already existed.

Mary is appropriately called the 'Mother of Sorrows', the *Dolorosa*, subject of the *Stabat Mater*, the mother standing at the cross in torment. For me, to find her there in the synoptic gospels has been very important. The idea that this was found in one gospel alone, that of John, and that there it may have been a symbolically contrived scene, was never satisfactory. The fact that she is present at the crucifixion in all four gospels, even if forced to observe from 'far off' in three of them, confirms the importance of her presence in the early Christian tradition before the gospels were written. Of everything that we read in the gospels, the fact that Jesus was crucified is one of the hard facts, the undeniable history, as reliable as anything historical can be. And, therefore, it is undeniable that Mary suffered acutely before she and her community came to the realization that God's promises really were being fulfilled in the resurrection of her son Jesus.

WOMEN AND THE RESURRECTION

The *Magnificat*, the hymn of praise which Mary recited in Elizabeth's house, may have arisen at an early point in the life of the Church, or it may have been authored by the writer of Luke's Gospel. Yet even if the latter is true, it would still have been very appropriate to the joyous and courageous faith of the resurrection shared by women and men in the nascent Church community which will have faced constant dangers in the wake of Jesus' crucifixion. The man put to death at the hands of the Romans with the collaboration of the Jewish authorities had risen and was reigning in heaven, and thereby God had raised up those who had waited for deliverance. Were hymns like this the way in which women celebrated the resurrection?

Kathleen Corley is a researcher into the role of women in the early Church. Her book *Maranatha: Women's Funerary Rituals and Christian Origins* shows how several of the New Testament stories, such as the anointing, some healings, and the miraculous feedings may have had their origins as women's narratives at communal meals in the very earliest Christian community. Women in the ancient Mediterranean created songs and stories that remembered the dead; these might lie behind the empty tomb traditions in the gospels. They held ritual commemorative meals in which the presence of the dead was welcomed and food offered to them, and would have visited the tomb for this purpose on the third, ninth, and thirteenth day after death and then annually. Corley provides us with an impressive piece of analysis which confirms the existence of women's traditions that fed into the New Testament. However, she sees these as having an existence prior to belief in the resurrection and concludes that the Christian proclamation of the risen Jesus is secondary to women's lamentations and rituals. The resurrection faith is regarded as being appended to an original tradition about Jesus and his community.

The problem with this is that the powerful message of the resurrection and its joyful tidings for humanity, announcing a reality in which the poor find meaning and vindication and oppressive power structures melt away, then becomes a male enterprise. The resurrection need not be detached from the tomb traditions in this way. It is the genius behind the relating of the concepts of Messiah, death, empty tomb, and God's presence in these events that in many cultures has transformed conceptions of leadership, power, and social responsibility (which is not to deny that Christianity has had a shadow side which has undermined that teaching in some terrible and long-lasting ways). That genius can and should be attributed to women as well as men in the early Church.

Given women's prominence in stories that directly relate to the resurrection, it is reasonable to conclude that women were instrumental in the early growth of the resurrection faith. The cross and resurrection is at the heart of several stories discussed in this book that centre on female characters:

1. The birth of Jesus. We have seen when considering the text of Revelation 12 and the Gospel of John that Jesus' crucifixion and resurrection were symbolized by a painful but ultimately joyous birth, symbolism which has precedents in the Hebrew Scriptures. The Lukan

narratives of the birth of Jesus contain anticipations of the cross and resurrection: the sorrowful prophecy of Simeon concerning the sword that will pierce Mary's heart; the baby wrapped in 'bands of cloth' as he would be later in the tomb; the hymns of thanksgiving and praise which have no meaning apart from the resurrection, the *Magnificat*, *Benedictus*, and *Nunc Dimittis*. Matthew's birth story anticipates the burial of Jesus with the inclusion of myrrh among the gifts of the magi.

2. The marriage at Cana, with its allusions to the 'third day' and the wine. Jesus' 'hour' has not yet come, but the wedding anticipates the marriage of the Lamb and the coming of the Bridegroom (a theme across the gospels, and especially in John and Revelation).

3. The anointing, and its symbolic connection with Messiahship and the tomb.

4. The cross at which only women are present save for the beloved disciple in John.

5. The empty tomb, after which the announcement of the resurrection is made by the women in all four gospels and they also see Jesus first in the Gospels of Matthew, John, and the later, longer version of Mark.

The experience of the resurrection is one that would have been difficult to capture in doctrinal terms in earliest Christianity. Its best articulation comes in poetic forms, in stories and symbols, in explanations of the fulfilment of prophecy. It will have been an ecstatic experience. Paul talks about being 'caught up to the third heaven—whether in the body or out of the body I do not know; God knows ... caught up into Paradise and heard things that are not to be told, that no mortal is permitted to repeat' (2 Cor. 12.2–4). Paul also talks about the gift of prophecy (1 Cor. 12.10) and the involvement of women in prophesying (1 Cor. 11.5).

What if ecstatic experiences stand behind the two pivotal moments for the two Marys in John's Gospel: Cana and the garden tomb? Both are related to the resurrection. One can only speculate on whether we can reconstruct anything of the women's experience of the resurrection using the New Testament texts. It is more an act of the imagination than one of systematic research (see Appendix 6 for a creative reconstruction of passages from John's Gospel).

The story of Cana is an account of a wedding, prefiguring the marriage of the coming Bridegroom, the risen Christ returning as the Son of Man. Mary tells Jesus about the wine, but he says that it is 'not yet' the right time (2.4). Despite this, he turns the water into wine. The drinking of fine wine is an apt description of the ecstatic encounter with the risen Jesus. Perhaps, rather than narrating an everyday wedding and a miracle during Jesus' ministry, this story has its origin in the resurrection encounter of Mary and others like her 'on the third day', which is the greatest miracle of all.

In the garden, after seeing the empty tomb, Mary Magdalene meets the risen Jesus. Mary Magdalene wants to touch Jesus, but he is 'not yet' ascended (20.17). The 'not yet' in both these passages might be a clue as to the evolution of women's traditions into male text. The women experienced the resurrection as something immediate, an ecstasy in which the things imagined in an eschatological future were already in the present: the marriage of the Lamb, the direct encounter with the risen and ascended Jesus, the coming of the new Jerusalem. The texts, however, add in the 'not yet' which distances the Marys from the culmination of their experience and from the realization of God's promises. If, in the early Church, women were directly associated with these things, then the gradual formalization under male leadership will have diminished the direct relationship between the risen Jesus and female ecstatic experience.

The story of the cross, burial, and resurrection is so familiar in the Christian tradition that it is easy to lose sight of the sheer desperation experienced by Jesus' family and followers at his execution, and then the supreme joy caused by encounters with the risen Jesus that convinced these people that he had been raised from the dead by divine action. They came to the understanding that his death was not meaningless and tragic, but in fact the most meaningful event in history. The gospel was the best news that there could possibly be: human lives are not swept away by the tide of history, and social and political suppression do not have the last word, but each and every one of us has their purpose and final destination in God's Kingdom.

One can imagine trying to articulate such an ecstatic realization in some form that is communicable to others. One can see why it would have been likened to the wonder and pleasure of holding a newborn child after a particularly painful and life-threatening delivery. There is every reason to think that this metaphor was more likely to have arisen among women in Jesus' community, and from there the idea of the virgin birth took root. The resurrection is like a birth where the only father is God, who has brought it about not by sexual relations, as in some of the Greek myths where deities mate with humans, but through the power of the Holy Spirit.

And then the anointing, which may have been based on an actual event, but is certainly a powerful metaphorical story regardless. This is an image of a meal at which women, in the normal run of things, will have had duties in the provision of hospitality, which may have included anointing with perfumed oil after a long journey. The mundane act of anointing takes on momentous significance: it is the anointing of the very person who is the Messiah, the 'anointed one', and it is also a prophetic recognition of the fact that this Messiah is going to die and be buried before he comes into his kingdom; his death will be so shameful that the normal burial rites will not be possible to carry out.

Finally, the empty tomb, which is the story of a group of women, quietly and avoiding attention, walking to the tomb in the darkness in the early morning of the third day. They are afraid, as anyone would be, and they are not ready for what is to unfold. Matthew's and John's accounts in which women encounter the risen Jesus are more likely to have formed the original traditions than those of Mark (the original, shorter version) and Luke, where the women simply pass on the message of angels. Why would folk memory omit to place the risen Jesus outside the tomb, manifesting himself to his loyal followers now that the resurrection is a reality? Are Mark and Luke presenting us with another example of the 'not yet' to the women, their experience delayed, waiting on male ratification?

In each of these cases: birth, anointing, and responsibilities associated with death rites, activities associated with the female in that culture became the cornerstone of the popular understanding of the resurrection faith. No doctrine or scholarly exegesis of the Scriptures could do the job of conveying that experience in a more powerful way than narratives such as these.

15

Mary, Founder of Christianity

JESUS' MOVEMENT AND HIS FAMILY

We can summarize the characteristics of Jesus' movement that we have explored in the previous two chapters as follows:

1. Non-violent resistance to tyranny of all kinds, both against Roman military rule but also in opposition to Jewish collusion under the dominance of the high priest and his retinue;
2. The belief that God would intervene to bring justice to the nation in the very near future;
3. The belief that, in anticipation of this, one could build God's kingdom, not politically but in the midst of communities, and by doing so, one could overcome the oppressive effects of tyranny;
4. A conviction that spiritual malaise could be countered by giving people a sense of purpose and meaning through their relationship to a real and loving God;

5. A strong commitment to the poor, especially those forced to become outcasts by the social and religious system, and a rejection of worldly status;

6. All of this underpinned by faith in the Messiah who had to die for his people for new life to grow, that is, a servant Messiah, which is the key to Jesus' movement; it did not seek to dominate people but to lead them by serving them. In this respect it presents a devastating critique of authorities who do the opposite.

What were Jesus' main influences in shaping this movement? What inspired him as he grew up? It is customary to think of him being in direct communication with God and needing no human instruction. This is contradictory to the doctrine of the Incarnation. Jesus was human, and therefore needing to learn and grow like anyone else. If you doubt that this is a true reflection of what is said in the Bible, read Luke 2.52: 'And Jesus increased in wisdom and in years, and in divine and human favour.' There are obvious influences on Jesus' understanding of his mission:

- The Hebrew Scriptures. They were not in the final Jewish canon that we know now, which was not agreed until the late first century, but Jesus as a teacher, a rabbi, will have known all the texts in detail.

- The ministry of John the Baptist. Jesus was baptized by John and was clearly a member of his community as he formulated his own mission. The first gospel, Mark, makes this clear, even if the later gospels try to water down the basic fact that Jesus was a follower of John and not the other way round. Jesus' teaching, like John's, continued the centuries-old Jewish tradition of preaching repentance in anticipation of God's forgiveness. Jesus was not as strict with fasting as John (according to Mark 2.18 and parallel passages) and it is clear that Jesus, after John's death, developed his own unique approach to mission, but his debt to his predecessor is clear from the way in which the New Testament tries to explain away or justify it.

However, we should not overlook the fact that parents were important teachers in the Jewish tradition. Luke 2.51 says that, after upsetting his parents by staying in Jerusalem aged twelve, Jesus 'went down with them and came to Nazareth and was obedient to them'. The intimacy of Luke's description of the annunciation and birth of Jesus encouraged Christians to think that Luke may have known Mary, and that she passed on her recollections to him. There are works of art that are ascribed to Luke; it is imagined that he painted the Madonna and Child as they sat for him. We may regard such stories as charming but highly unlikely cultural legacies. However, one aspect of Luke's story that inspired the idea that the evangelist knew Mary is that he records her reflecting on events on two occasions. The first is at Luke 2.19: after the shepherds visited the baby Jesus and reported the praising of the angels that they had experienced, 'Mary treasured all these words and pondered them in her heart.' Then, after Jesus aged twelve was found engaging with the teachers in the Temple at Jerusalem, at Luke 2.51, we read: 'His mother treasured all these things in her heart.' While we may doubt that the writer of Luke ever met Mary, he would have been party to traditions and memories that led him to think that this was an appropriate detail to add in, despite it being unnecessary; the story works perfectly well without it. Therefore, the fact that he did include it is significant. At the very least, he regarded this as a means of describing what the very first hearers of Jesus must have been involved in: that is, reflecting and considering what the appearance of Jesus in the world might mean, and how they should respond to it.

As Joseph's influence on Jesus is not mentioned in the Bible, we only have the testimony about Mary reflecting on her son's vocation and then initiating the first miracle at Cana (John 2.3). Although these verses occur in passages that are unlikely to represent actual history, all we can say is that the gospels corroborate and do not contradict the suggestion that Mary instructed Jesus and gave some shape to his understanding of his mission; mothers were and are important teachers of the *Torah* in the Jewish tradition.

Mary is often referred to as 'the first disciple' in the modern Catholic Church, drawing on the idea that Mary is an exemplar and type of the Church. However, while the logic of this description is clear, it can be misleading. A disciple is a *follower* and a *learner*. Mary, on the other hand, was Jesus' *predecessor* and, as his Jewish mother, his *teacher*. In Jewish tradition, the mother played an important role in teaching the faith to the young child (for example, Prov. 1.8). Indeed, Wisdom who teaches is imagined in a female form (Prov. 1.20), and Mary is seen in Catholic and Orthodox tradition as the embodiment of Wisdom.

The principle that people in Jesus' movement may have preceded him is worth emphasizing. Mary Rose D'Angelo, in her book edited with Ross Shepard Kraemer, *Women and Christian Origins*, suggests that Mary Magdalene may have been Jesus' predecessor.[28] We do not know one way or another, but this would dovetail nicely with the view in this book that Mary Magdalene was some kind of sister to Mary the mother of Jesus, who certainly preceded Jesus. In a Messianic age, Jesus was anointed as the Messiah by the popular movement around him; he was not chosen by God alone as one reading of the gospels might suggest. The gospels also tell us that

---

[28] In Chapter 5, 'Reconstructing "Real Women" from Gospel Literature: The Case of Mary Magdalene', pp. 105–28.

women, in partnership with God whose voice they heard, were the human initiators of this divine calling.

In Church tradition, there are many images of Mary's mother (named Hannah or Anne in the *Protevangelium*) teaching her to read; in particular, she will have been taught the scriptures by her mother. The line of women and mothers is important. There is a gender issue here. How would we understand the relationship between Joseph and Jesus were Joseph to have been active in Jesus' ministry and the early Church? Perhaps we would have imagined Joseph as Jesus' father to have been someone who had inspired Jesus, and not merely a follower or disciple? Why then do we not say the same for Mary?

Indeed, if we count passages where Jesus' action or understanding is directly affected by another person, we are left with very few. It has been suggested that Mary of Bethany's action in anointing Jesus' feet in John 12.1–8 is the inspiration for him washing the disciples' feet in John 13.3–11, which is an interesting and satisfying conjecture, although the two actions are understood quite differently. Jesus does do healing miracles when asked to on several occasions; the most notable where Jesus learns from someone is the story of the Syrophoenician or Canaanite woman (Mark 7.24–30; Matt. 15.21–28). Here Jesus learns that the Gentiles as much as Jews yearn for his healing, and it is notable that a woman acts as his teacher. However, Cana remains the one instance in the gospels where Jesus responds with a miracle not instigated by the person who is the beneficiary (for example, the parent of an ill child), but asked of him by his mother. The writer of John's Gospel therefore accepts that Mary had an influence on Jesus that goes beyond the immediate; it would not be unusual for any ordinary adult were their parent to give them direction, but for the divinely inspired Jesus of the gospels, it is notable.

And does John also record his brothers encouraging Jesus to act in John 7.1–16?

After this Jesus went about in Galilee. He did not wish to go about in Judea because the Jews were looking for an opportunity to kill him. Now the Jewish festival of Booths (Tabernacles) was near. So his brothers said to him, 'Leave here and go to Judea so that your disciples also may see the works you are doing; for no one who wants to be widely known acts in secret. If you do these things, show yourself to the world.' (For not even his brothers believed in him.) Jesus said to them, 'My time has not yet come, but your time is always here. The world cannot hate you, but it hates me because I testify against it that its works are evil. Go to the festival yourselves. I am not going to this festival, for my time has not yet fully come.' After saying this, he remained in Galilee.

But after his brothers had gone to the festival, then he also went, not publicly but as it were in secret. The Jews were looking for him at the festival and saying, 'Where is he?' And there was considerable complaining about him among the crowds. While some were saying, 'He is a good man,' others were saying, 'No, he is deceiving the crowd.' Yet no one would speak openly about him for fear of the Jews.

About the middle of the festival Jesus went up into the temple and began to teach. The Jews were astonished at it, saying, 'How does this man have such learning, when he has never been taught?' Then Jesus answered them, 'My teaching is not mine but his who sent me...'

(John 7.1–16)

The line 'For not even his brothers believed in him' and the sentences that immediately follow have the look of an editorial insertion into what may have been an older source.

Overall, the story has parallels to Cana; once again, Jesus does what his family asks of him after appearing to resist. This occasion is later than Cana in the ministry; this is not Jesus' first visit to Jerusalem, and he has already made a name for himself there. In John 2.13–25, he cleansed the temple (much earlier than in the synoptics) and in 5.1–43, his second visit includes the healing of a paralytic on the Sabbath and the controversies that ensued. The story in John 7 is difficult to explain on this basis: why do the brothers think that Jesus is keeping his acts a secret when he has already been very open in his confrontation with the authorities in Jerusalem on two previous occasions? Why are the 'Jews' so astonished when he has been there before and taught?

We cannot answer these questions, but these are clues as to the influence of the family on the ministry of Jesus. It was a family led by the mother as far as we can see in the gospel texts: the 'mother and brothers'. Everything therefore points to Mary having a considerable influence on the ministry and mission of Jesus. Mary's vision, whether she willed it or not, led to the cross, the brutal facts of history powerfully summed up in the legends of the early chapters of Luke, in which Simeon says to her, 'This child is destined for the falling and the rising of many in Israel, and to be a sign that will be opposed so that the inner thoughts of many will be revealed – and a sword will pierce your own soul too' (Luke 2.34–35).

HISTORY AND MYTHOLOGY IN THE STORY OF MARY

The foundation for Christianity is both historical and mythological. We can relate the mythical Mary to the real woman who lived in Galilee all those centuries ago. Historical speculation is more likely to have some meaning for the Christian story if it relates in some demonstrable way to the metaphorical passages which present Mary as exemplar and archetype.

The idea that legendary material is appropriate to the history, even if it does not describe how events actually occurred (which we can never reconstruct), is an important one in accepting the New Testament narratives as theological truth. *Myth* is truth.

The New Testament is truth about the Word of God, but it is also a truth shrouded in the cultural assumptions of the day in which the voices of women were largely absent from social, political, and religious discourse. Even with that consideration, the figures of the various Marys still come out larger than life, and we may suppose that the actual reality behind the texts will turn out to be an even greater female contribution than the gospels suggest.

Many of the passages that include Mary, most of which are in the Gospels of Luke and John, belong to myth rather than history. However, this is also true of many of Jesus' miracles. Yet, while the sensational feats of walking on water, stilling the storm, or raising the dead did not happen in history, they were appropriate metaphors for what Jesus did achieve. He preached the reality of God's Kingdom to people who felt oppressed by the religious, social, and political context of the time, and presented a theology in which God reached out to the humanity of the vulnerable. This led to a renewed sense of purpose and meaning which may well have led to healing, some of which may have been experienced as miraculous. The important point is that Christians through time can achieve these ends in their own ages and cultures using the equivalent means; they will not be able to walk on water, still storms, or raise the dead, but they can preach the Kingdom and the reality of God's presence.

The same can be said of Mary. One cannot follow her by becoming a virgin mother! She was not a virgin in any physical sense except, like other Jewish women, during the brief liminal period which separated girlhood and the consummation of marriage. The narratives of the annunciation and virgin birth of Jesus locate Mary in a mythological space, describing conversations and actions that probably did not take place historically, but which are full of cosmic significance in the Christian tradition. Luke's conception narrative overlaid with John's prologue places Mary in a new garden of Eden, as the bearer and mother of the one through whom all things were created and by whom creation is to be restored ('recapitulated', according to Irenaeus). Mary heard God's word and set the events of redemption in progress; in the Christian Eden, the new Eve preceded the new Adam. Mary the young woman was taken up into the liminal space that is the door through which the Incarnation takes place, the meeting place of heaven's eternity and earth's history. In Christian tradition, she has been described as the New Eve, Ark of the Covenant, Temple, Wisdom, Bride of the Holy Spirit, and Daughter of Zion. The New Testament does not actually say any of these things explicitly, although some are clearly implied by the setting of Luke's conception and birth narratives.

Luke's story of the annunciation, birth, and infancy of Jesus with Mary as its heroine is a symbolic theological story that speaks about the Jewish people waiting on God for deliverance. Mary's counterparts in the story are Elizabeth, Zechariah, Simeon, and Anna; old in years, they recognized the arrival of their salvation in Jesus Christ. Mary is the one through whom this deliverance came; she represents the newness of God's initiative in acting in a way that was unanticipated, his Son the Messiah being born among the poor ('no place for them in the inn') and destined for a painful death.

We will never know one way or the other whether the Mary of history met with an angel. It is possible that she did experience visions; on the other hand, the angelic encounter is a standard form of announcing a future miracle in the Hebrew Scriptures, and so it is a natural way for an evangelist to express the events in a theologically symbolic form. Luke is clear that, to face the challenges ahead of her, Mary needed God's grace and favour. Yet Mary was not a passive recipient of this grace; theologians quite rightly have made much of the fact that she responded to the angel: 'Here am I, the servant of the Lord; let it be with me according to your word' (Luke 1.38). Mary is therefore the archetypal believer who accepts the will of God and acts upon it, an exemplar for each and every Christian, female and male. While this statement reflects Church tradition as it has evolved through the centuries, it is not at all unreasonable to find its basis here in Luke, and to argue that something along these lines was the intended reading of the author of this gospel.

The table opposite relates theological symbolism to history. On the left, there is the portrayal of Mary as an exemplar in metaphorical narratives in the gospels. On the right, we have the facts that we can be reasonably confident about with respect to the history of the woman who was the mother of Jesus. These relate to one another.

WOMEN'S LEADERSHIP IN EARLY CHRISTIANITY

Mary was therefore very influential in Jesus' mission and ministry, but was she some kind of leader? After all, we have seen that she was an important person in the Jerusalem community that came into being after the events of the death and resurrection of Jesus, so much so that leading apostles were associated with her as mother, beginning with her son James but also those, like Clopas and possibly also John Mark, who were not her children. The New Testament only hints at this possibility and requires us to use speculative analysis to reconstruct the possible role of Mary.

MARY AS EXEMPLAR (LUKE AND JOHN)	MARY IN HISTORY (MARK FOLLOWED BY OTHER GOSPELS)
The one who accepts the will of God and acts upon it (Luke)	Mother of a large family, including James the successor to Jesus as leader, which believed itself to have a Davidic heritage and Messianic mission
Representative of faithful Israel awaiting God's intervention and deliverance (Luke)	The only active member of the generation before Jesus (as far as we know; Clopas and Mary Magdalene are possible exceptions), and probably a widow
Archetype of the Church community bringing Christ into the world (Luke)	Companion and prominent member of the women from Galilee who supported the ministry of Jesus
The one who instigates the miracle at Cana, the anticipation of the cross and resurrection (John)	The mother of Jesus and his predecessor and teacher in the Jewish faith
Mother of 'new birth' in Christ (John)	Associated at an early stage of the Church, along with Mary Magdalene and other women, with the stories of the death, burial, and empty tomb of Christ and the original proclamation of the resurrection
Defining member of the new family of Jesus born at the cross (John)	Remembered as being present in the very earliest Church community at Jerusalem and associated with leading apostles

However, there are also post-biblical sources. The absence of females explicitly referred to at important moments in the gospels provided a gap which later literature tried to fill. Christian apocryphal gospels and writings include accounts of the events of the lives of Jesus, Mary, and the apostles that were not received into the New Testament canon, either because they were not regarded as apostolic or because they appeared after the canon was established in the fourth century. They include descriptions of Jesus' ministry which refer to a woman called Mary in a position of some authority or leadership and having recourse to a certain amount of knowledge. Because the exact identity of 'Mary' is not established, this is assumed to be Mary Magdalene, but Stephen Shoemaker's research (in, for example, *Mary in Early Christian Faith and Devotion*) has led him to argue that to identify her as Mary the mother of Jesus is equally possible. He suggests that quite probably Christians in the early centuries did not always distinguish Mary and Mary Magdalene, so that there was an indefinite sense that a woman called Mary had been an important member of Jesus' itinerant community. Another candidate is Mary of Bethany, who was also important in post-biblical Christian writings along with her sister Martha.[29]

Tony Burke says of Mary as she is depicted in the apocrypha, including the so-called 'lives' of Mary:

> Together, all of these texts show that Mary of Nazareth is a much more nuanced figure in Christian literature than one might expect from reading the canonical gospels alone. She is wife and mother, yes, but also disciple, visionary, matriarch, heavenly sojourner [i.e., taken into heaven by assumption], and mediator.
>
> (*Oxford Handbook of Mary*, p. 40)

---

[29] For Mary of Bethany, see the work of Mary Ann Beavis, especially the volume edited with Ally Kateusz: *Rediscovering the Marys: Maria, Mariamne, Miriam*.

Of course, the fact that a female figure was exalted in texts does not mean that women in general were always respected in the communities that produced and maintained them. Nevertheless, the apocryphal testimony to the importance of Mary in the first centuries of Christianity is compelling.

Ally Kateusz, in her book *Mary and Early Christian Women: Hidden Leadership*, explores Christian apocryphal writings and early Christian art to analyse how women may have had a role in Church leadership during the initial centuries of Christianity.[30] In these sources, women including Mary are involved in evangelizing, preaching, teaching, baptizing, working miracles and cures, performing exorcisms, prophesying, leading prayer, wearing priestly garments, breaking the communion bread, making offering to God with incense and prayer, and using censers during liturgy. In summary, these are all activities traditionally ascribed to male apostles, bishops, and priests. These manuscripts go against the general trend of marginalization of women in texts, and consequently they are very interesting.

What adds to the mystery is that some of these texts have variants which show that the activities of the women were edited out by scribes in some cases; sometimes Mary was replaced by Peter. This process of what is known as 'redaction' (the editing of texts) shows that women's leadership in the early Church was suppressed at an increasing rate as time went by. Yet, as Kateusz demonstrates, there is plenty of evidence for women leaders before this process intensified. This is substantiated by the condemnation of women's leadership in the works of various theologians, including Irenaeus,

---

[30] The apocrypha which Kateusz considers in particular are the *Gospel of Mary*, the *Gospel* (or *Questions*) *of Bartholomew*, the *Six Books Dormition Apocryphon* which describes the death of Mary the mother of Jesus (known as the 'dormition', i.e., the 'falling asleep'), the *Acts of Philip*, and the *Acts of Thecla*.

Tertullian, and Epiphanius; of course, this denunciation of an active role for females has its origin in some of the epistles of Paul, as we noted earlier. One does not oppose something that is not occurring. It can be supposed that the leadership role of females in the pastoral practice and liturgy of Christian churches extends right back to the New Testament period. It is unlikely to have begun spontaneously.

Yet, it might be asked whether we should take any notice of the apocrypha. They are nowhere near as well attested in early Christian writers as the canonical texts. Surely, they were written so long after the New Testament witness that they comprise only speculation and fanciful, imaginative fiction?

There is some truth in this but it is not the whole story. The growing belief in Mary as a lifelong virgin will have encouraged some of the ideas that she had special spiritual powers. Mary's supposed status as a lifelong virgin is not present in the New Testament; it is a metaphorical description without any basis in history and derived from Greco-Roman tradition, as we have seen. However, the possibility of Mary as a matriarch and leader is much more easily derivable from the gospel accounts: Mary was included both with women, the female followers of Jesus from Galilee, and men, the brothers of Jesus. We should remember that most writers of what we call apocryphal texts were reading the same gospels as we are. While they had devotional reasons for promoting Mary's powers and attributes, they would have also been subject to the same requirement that these ideas did not flatly contradict the gospels and also reflected life in the churches that they knew. While specific details may not have satisfied these criteria in every case, the overall picture of Mary and other women, like Mary Magdalene, holding a leadership role in the community around Jesus nowhere runs contrary to the gospel witness.

Other evidence for women's leadership in the early centuries of the Church can be found in inscriptions and documents.

Ute E. Eisen, in *Women Officeholders in Early Christianity*, shows that women were referred to as prophets, teachers of theology, stewards, and even as being in ordained ministry: bishops, priests, and deacons. While these are scattered instances, they show that women's leadership in the churches could exist. An order of widows was also very important in the pastoral ministry of the churches.

During the same period in Judaism (about the first six centuries CE), Bernadette J. Brooten's research in *Women Leaders in the Ancient Synagogue* locates inscriptions to women as heads of the synagogue, 'mothers of the synagogue', elders, and priests. She concludes that the functions practised by such women included keeping the synagogue congregation faithful to the *Torah*, planning and organizing services, being representatives of the congregation, scholarship, teaching, and looking after the buildings. Those women with resources will have donated them to the work of the synagogue and its assets.

These testimonies to women's participation in both Christian and Jewish communities in the centuries after Christ establish the principle that women's leadership, while not equal to men's in scale and frequency, was nevertheless neither unknown nor impossible in that age. We are not going beyond the evidence to imagine Mary, Mary Magdalene, and the other women in their circle baptizing new converts, organizing and leading worship, laying on healing hands, or exorcizing. Jesus' community formed a means for the poor and marginalized to experience and access the blessings of the divine in a way that the Temple and priesthood in Jerusalem did not. Marginalized and unofficial communities are freer to move beyond the margins of what is 'normal'.

While we might have expected Mary as a leader in the early Church to receive more of a mention in the New Testament than she does, we have already investigated the contextual factors leading to the gospel writers being cautious about conceding too much authority to, first, a prominent member of the family of Jesus, and second, a woman. Therefore, there is a strong case for women's leadership in the churches before and during the period in which the New Testament was written. Male objections to women's initiative in founding the Christian faith begin with the reactions in the story of the anointing and continue in the apocryphal gospels, where Peter, regarded as the male leader, is usually the one who raises the issue. These objections are to something real and tangible, the co-leadership and important contribution of women in the early Church.

MARY'S INITIATIVE

Mary the mother of Jesus was one of those women who came with him from Galilee to Jerusalem, and we know that Jesus' Galilean ministry was mainly based in rural contexts. It is not unreasonable to suggest that the movement of the non-violent servant Messiah originated with influential women from a rural environment. Might it not have been more likely to have been women who (a) believed in the absolute certainty of God's presence and coming Kingdom; (b) sought to provide meaning and hope to those most affected by oppression and injustice; (c) found neither hope nor compassion in the violence of revolutionary movements; (d) did not wish to separate from the common people, unlike the Essenes; and (e) expressed their theology in terms of the pastoral folk culture in which the parables came to be formed? Among these women, Mary had a leading role as the mother of a family which had some claim to Davidic Messianic inheritance.

Mary had considerable influence in Jesus' ministry and in the very earliest Church. The relating of the name Mary to mother figures occurs in all four gospels and in Acts 12.12.

It is quite probable that all these references derive from the importance of Mary in early traditions. We know that she was associated with the Jerusalem Church; authority in that Church had a relationship to her, perhaps it even derived from her. However, the memory of the leadership of real women transmuted into symbols, familiar in the ancient world, of mythical females representing community cohesion. In time, Mary became the symbol of the Church itself. The female representation of communities has its origins in the New Testament period, as attested to by the descriptions of churches as female figures in the second epistle of John and the first epistle of Peter. Yet the attestation to female leadership in the Church did continue in some of the apocrypha.

The frequent but mysterious references to 'Mary the mother of...' in the New Testament represent a shadowy memory of a mother figure and matriarch from whom authority derived in early Christian Jerusalem. Like the queen mother of the ancient Israelite monarchy, she – the 'mother of the Lord' – had a special privilege. But her relationship to other women, and the testimony to their part in the Messianic mission, confirms that she did not reserve to herself the authority that came with being mother of the leader. As the gospels state, her motherhood of Jesus was not the only source of her important position. It was that, like other women in Jesus' community, she 'heard the word of God and obeyed it' (Luke 11.28). It is not that 'obedience' is confined to women, either; Jesus in Gethsemane prayed, 'not what I want, but what you want' (Mark 14.36). Obedience to God, and not to corrupt human authority, means independence, creative thinking, and rebellion.

The theory that the mantle of leadership passed from Jesus to James his brother is now commonly held among scholars of the early Church, and we have followed that line here so far, but in actual fact it represents a patriarchal take on history based in traditional assumptions that men will be pastors, leaders, bishops. Perhaps we need to revise this. If Mary already held a position of authority before the crucifixion, then there would have been no need for anything to be passed on at the death of Jesus; Mary was still alive and retained her leadership role until her death. Perhaps she could be referred to as the 'first bishop' of Jerusalem, an anachronistic title but one that is given to her son James, who succeeded her. That is not to deny that she would have recognized Jesus her son as the risen Lord who had been taken up to God's throne, and the coming Son of Man. She had already understood that he was to be the Messiah who would be the saviour of Israel. Yet, she is the one person who could claim to have conceived of his mission before he did, and to have shaped it.

When we read the New Testament with a critical eye in respect of its downplaying of women and the family of Jesus, it becomes clear that understanding Mary as the initiator of the Christian faith is fully justified. She was the first to realize the power of the Messianic vision that is the root from which Christian mission grew. She is the mustard seed of the parable. Yet she did not act alone; she is the prominent member of the women in the community that proclaimed Jesus as Messiah, but others were remembered too.

In Mary's image, several other females are remembered in the New Testament: most prominently, Mary Magdalene. Mary may have regarded Mary Magdalene as a sister in some sense; they accompanied each other to the cross and tomb. Perhaps Mary Magdalene did find meaning and healing in the message that Mary the mother of Jesus and her family were proclaiming. Her possession by 'seven demons', as recorded by Luke, may have been due to her deep awareness of social disaster and the catastrophes awaiting in the future; this indicated that she had the spiritual sensitivity to become a major visionary of the Christian movement, and perhaps she – as three of the gospels suggest[31] – emerged as the first witness of the resurrection. She was the first woman mentioned at the cross and tomb in each of the lists in Mark, Matthew, and Luke which suggests a leadership role.

Mary Magdalene is thought to be from Magdala by the Sea of Galilee but there is doubt as to whether this location would have been easily recognized in the mid-first century. She may just as easily have been Mary 'of the Tower', as *magdala* meant Tower in Aramaic.[32] After all, Peter was nicknamed by Jesus 'the Rock' and the sons of Zebedee 'Sons of Thunder'. If so, Mary Magdalene may have been associated with the Jerusalem Church just like Mary the mother of Jesus, as the most obvious reference to 'tower' in the Hebrew Scriptures derives from Micah 4.8:

And you, O tower of the flock, hill of daughter Zion,
to you it shall come, the former dominion shall come,
the sovereignty of daughter Jerusalem.

A second Mary emerged, Mary of Bethany, who may or may not have been a fictional ideal type created in the Gospels of Luke and John along with her sister Martha, another pair of sisters who embodied certain tendencies: the bold, active Martha who declared Jesus to be the Messiah, and the quieter, contemplative Mary, who understood that he had to die. In their own ways, they were images of the original Mary, the mother of Jesus, and they represented various other women in the movement.

Therefore, the ancient instinct in Christian traditions both East and West that Mary had an important participatory role

---

[31] Probably only two of the original gospels, as the longer ending of Mark (in which Mary Magdalene was the first witness to the resurrection) is thought to be a later addition and based on the other gospels.

[32] See Joan E. Taylor's article in the *Palestine Exploration Quarterly* 146.3.

in the events of salvation as a co-redeemer has a biblical basis and, we have argued, a historical one. She is revered as the New Eve, Jesus' 'helper' as Eve was intended to be for Adam, but much more than a helper: an inspiration, a teacher, a mother. In short, she has an even greater claim than Jesus to be the founder of what we understand as Christianity, while accepting that the New Testament contains more than either Mary or Jesus could ever have envisaged on their own as individuals. She was the one who understood what Messianic leadership could represent: it served the poorer members of the Jewish community under oppression and occupation, and it gave people meaning and purpose because they were encouraged to believe that God was truly working among them, and that God's perspective was the only one that mattered; obedience and conformity to human rulers were pragmatic and not absolute. It was a non-violent Messiahship, the way of life of the Suffering Servant, the key text in making sense of such a role. It was the only positive way forward in the circumstances in which the Jewish people found themselves. Mary, probably because the family claimed Davidic inheritance, understood that her son Jesus could fulfil this role of Messiah, and at some point came to realize that it would lead to a violent death because it was too radical for the authorities to tolerate when it came to their notice.

16

Mary and the Incarnation

It might be asked where the analysis in this book leads
with respect to the status of Mary in Christian theology.
If she has the pre-eminent role that we have ascribed
to her, might this not have an implication for a Christian
understanding of Jesus as the unique individual who is at
the same time the eternal Word of God, two natures, divine
and human, in one person? In what I am about to write, I am
not seriously suggesting that the Churches for whom Mary
is important, the Catholic and Orthodox, will somehow be
inspired to change centuries-old traditions of Jesus-centred
Christology which are at the same time the main point of
contact with the Protestant traditions and probably the only
hope for ecumenism. Rather, I am addressing free thinkers in
the Christian tradition, asking whether we have arrived at an
important crossroads after several decades of social change
and radical theological thinking.

One of the great problems of the human political world is
the tendency to believe that a single great man can resolve

all manner of social problems. The twentieth century experienced some acutely tragic consequences of this thinking, Hitler, Mussolini, and Stalin paramount among them. The rising to power of a charismatic man who promises to solve the complex issues of the day continues to bedevil the twenty-first century. Indeed, the word 'messianic' is often used to describe the illusory and persistent trust that people place in a person who is, more often than not, either the subject of self-delusion or a power-grabbing charlatan.

In the first century, Roman emperors were ancient examples of this tendency to exalt a male leader. Yet we have learned that the political importance of Jesus was that he opposed the deification of the emperors and established the Christian belief that a truly divine human being would be one who was a servant, an outcast, and ultimately a victim of the social world, not one who gained supreme power by it (summed up in the story of Jesus being tempted by the devil). The raising of Jesus to 'the right hand of the Father' as the King of Heaven is based, as Luther argued, firmly in the servant Jesus; the two images are interdependent on each other. Jesus is expressly *not* a role model for the dominant male leader.

Unfortunately, however, the glorified Jesus can easily transmute back into the idea that we need to look for an inspired and isolated male leader to solve our problems and to bring us salvation: this is realized not only in politics, but also in religious movements, especially sectarian ones where individuals gain great power over their followers. It has also been a tendency in the Catholic Church, where the pope as the 'vicar of Christ' and 'infallible' can be exalted as the one person, the only priest in the Church, who is above corruption. The cult of the pope is often a barrier to the Church carrying out its gospel mission.

To some extent, the gospels do encourage this tendency: Jesus is the miracle worker, he needs no helper, no one understands him, only God. This is because the gospels were written in a time when the Jews, along with other cultures, looked for an inspired sacred king to lead them. This is a hierarchical and patriarchal view of leadership which modern society is slowly, painfully, and quite rightly, discarding. Belief in Jesus implies a critique of this ancient model. The Christian vision initiated a long development in Europe and the Mediterranean in which kingship or imperial power moved from semi-divine in the Roman Empire, to having divine prerogative in the Byzantine and medieval periods, to being understood as a human constitutional construct in early modernity, and finally to democracy and the limitation or eradication of royal power. Although it took many centuries, the coming of Jesus sounded the death knell to belief in divine status for royal leaders, usually male.

It is clear how much Jesus depended on those who supported and followed him. This, of course, is true of any leader, either good or evil. The Incarnation could not have been a reality without Mary, Mary Magdalene, Peter, James, and the other disciples, both female and male. Human beings are social to their very core. Therefore, one cannot limit the Incarnation to an individualized reality in which Jesus alone as a male individual is the Word of God. Incarnation is better interpreted as a communal experience in which the Word takes flesh in a movement, in a community that formed itself around Jesus, died, buried, and risen. An understanding of the communal aspect of the Incarnation is not new; it was handed down in traditional theological concepts such as the Church and the community of saints, yet, of course, in this theology, no one is divine and human except Jesus alone, Jesus of Nazareth, the individual male person. But more recently, late-twentieth-century theologies such as the feminist and liberationist have recognized and expanded upon the importance of Jesus' community in the work of salvation.

In a modern world in which we desperately need to escape the delusion of male and hierarchical supremacy, it is right that the idea of God being incarnate in an individual, enclosed male person is challenged. While many people would refute the idea that God could become incarnate at all, Christianity's great value has been that it affirms that such an incarnation occurs among the poor and powerless, in the one who is the servant of all. God is the servant and sustainer of everyone and everything, a powerful theology which has helped Christian society in stages and over a great arc of time challenge notions of absolute human power, presenting a transcendence in which moral truth is governed by service and the universal inclusion of people irrespective of their situation in life. For this reason, the gospel has inspired resistance to corrupt systems of power throughout Christian history and, one could argue, is at the very heart of democracy, anti-slavery, and human rights.

However, the idea of Jesus as a lonely and inspired individual has become problematic in the modern world in which we are right to critique the assumptions of previous generations in order to progress, two steps forward and one back, through the centuries. As feminist theologians have pointed out, 'where God is male, the male becomes God'. God in Christianity, of course, is not male but beyond gender, yet the language of God as Father and the Incarnation of God in male form makes it difficult for Christians to escape from the 'He' who is God.

Jesus was part of a community of suffering servants, which included women and men. While respecting the modern recognition that the binary of genders is inadequate to describe the diversity of human beings, nevertheless the bringing together of the male and female creates a powerful and ancient symbol of wholeness, partnership, equality, and diversity, from Adam and Eve onwards. The people we can identify in the gospels as presenting no hindrance to the work of Jesus are the women in the community, unlike Peter's denial, the pretensions of the sons of Zebedee, Thomas' doubt. In some ways, the lack of negative female role models in the gospels (apart from Queen Herodias) is another indicator of their male-centred nature.

Jesus extended his idea of family to include all the disciples, but there are several indications that Mary remained the mother figure. At Cana, the text that we have handed down to us suggests that Jesus seems to be uncertain of Mary's intervention, but it goes on to say that the changing of water into wine was 'the first of his signs, in Cana of Galilee, and revealed his glory; and his disciples believed in him' (John 2.11). It anticipated the resurrection and the marriage of the Lamb.

The Incarnation of God in human flesh has a wider scope than the individual Jesus; it is focused upon him in Christian tradition with his life, death, and resurrection its unchanging central point but, represented by the person of Mary, the Incarnation overflows into human society so that we cannot tell what its extent might be, and neither should we ever try to judge. It includes all those who proclaim the gospel of the reality of the loving God and live the servant vocation in which leadership consists of laying down one's life.

The first people to be included in this communal vision of the Incarnation proceeding out from Jesus and Mary would certainly be the women in Jesus' community, primarily Mary Magdalene, whose close relationship to Mary the mother of Jesus is confirmed in the narratives of the crucifixion and tomb. To object by saying that she was possessed by seven demons, according to Luke 8.2, is to suppose that such a state implies sinfulness or excessive frailty. However, the point of the Incarnation is the 'emptying' of divine power (*kenosis* in Greek), as Philippians 2.7 confirms. Jesus' divinity did not render God's raising him unnecessary. Just as Jesus was subject in his servant state to the horrors and agony of crucifixion and death, so Mary Magdalene suffered from what the ancient world called 'demons'. In the modern world, we now know that mental anguish does not mean the sufferer is culpable or weak; sensitivity to the terrible conditions that people face in the world suggest rather a heightened empathy and spiritual awareness. Perhaps, like Jesus, in the depths of her struggle Mary Magdalene cried out, *'Eloi, eloi, lema sabachthani?'* (Mark 15.34 and Matt. 27.46: 'My God, my God, why have you forsaken me?'). Then she too was raised from death to life.

Jane Schaberg's book, *The Illegitimacy of Jesus*, caused something of a scandal by suggesting that the idea of Mary's virginal conception could have evolved from an original memory of an illegitimate birth, possibly due to rape by a Roman soldier, as suggested in early anti-Christian polemic. Schaberg's biblical historical research does not really convince, in my opinion, as the birth narratives are clearly mythological and we do not have to find any historical kernel behind them (except to say, as we have in this book, that they are appropriate and describe Mary's life through metaphor). However, the challenge that Schaberg's research raised was profound. While Mary the rape victim offended sensibilities around sexuality and virginity, it also placed her with Jesus as the one whose life was marked by violence and tragedy, but through that trauma she brought the Word of God and hence the resurrection into being. Mary understood in this way becomes, like Jesus, one who takes the place of those who suffer most in the world and stands in solidarity with them. So, while I think that Schaberg's thesis is on shaky ground historically – as I believe that the virgin conception narrative was always intended to be metaphorical – I do nevertheless appreciate the symbolic resonance of the image of Mary as victim of violence, and how this might form a parallel to Jesus' crucifixion and also Mary Magdalene's seven demons.

At the core of my understanding of the Incarnation stands the union between Jesus and his mother Mary which makes any distinction of status between them unnecessary. The Catholic official view that her contribution was vital and yet 'inferior' or 'subordinate' is a simple projection of the desired gender relations of the Catholic hierarchy. The Incarnation of God in human history comes into being in the union of Mary and Jesus through the Holy Spirit. The unity in relationship between Jesus and Mary opens out to include others in their community, like Mary Magdalene; it is not exclusive. To use Catholic terminology, Mariology is both *Christocentric*, in that Mary is understood in relation to Jesus Christ and in union with him, and also *ecclesiocentric*, in that the union of Jesus and Mary is the dynamic heart of the Church (in Greek and Latin, *ecclesia*), which includes all those who have faith in them. By this I mean an active faith which follows what they stood for in the Incarnation, and *not* a simple identification of Mary with the Catholic Church and its hierarchy, which is rightly a major problem for Protestants. The Church that transcends denominations is not exclusive, either: Mary and Jesus are the Incarnate centre of the whole human race, not the reason for Christian superiority, but rather for Christian solidarity with others outside the faith.

The problem with the traditional association between Mary and the Church is that *Christ* is the paramount symbol of the Church in the New Testament. He is the 'True Vine' (John 15.1) and the Church is his body (1 Cor. 12 and elsewhere in the Pauline literature). The Church is not the Church unless it is conformed to Christ. Why is the image of Mary as the Church necessary? This symbolic association can be regarded as detracting from the Christocentric understanding of Church. The dilemma is resolved by seeing Jesus Christ and Mary in union. As we have seen, Luke's conception and birth narratives present Mary as the Church in embryo, and the mother of the Messiah is a symbol of the persecuted Church in Revelation 12, whereas the Church is the body of

Christ in Pauline theology. Mary and Jesus belong together as a figure of the Church just as they were united in history with a shared mission which grew into an influential movement and eventually into Christianity as a world faith. This is relevant to all Christian denominations.

Radical unity between Jesus and Mary is not simply the modern and rational innovation based on equal opportunities that it might appear to be. It is also the latent yearning in the heart of Christian history. The Orthodox and Catholic Churches have said everything but not quite this, sentiments close to endowing Mary with divinity but held back by the New Testament focus on Jesus alone as the Saviour. It has been on the tip of the ecclesiastical tongue. The honours bestowed on Mary hardly knew any bounds in the Byzantine and medieval Catholic periods which provided the heritage for Marian devotion today. From the fourth century, Mary was proclaimed as having been assumed into heaven at her death, body and soul, a doctrine still firmly held in Orthodoxy and Catholicism. Over the same period, she has been regarded as sinless and flawless in both East and West, although this is expressed in different ways (in Catholicism, using the doctrine of the Immaculate Conception). And for all Christians, she is the *Theotokos*, Mother of God.

In Orthodoxy, Mary is known as the *Panagia*, the 'All Holy One' and, in the high Marian veneration of eighth-century Byzantium, she was called 'Lady of All Created Things' (John Damascene, *On the Orthodox Faith* 4.14), 'Queen of Humanity' (Andrew of Crete, *Oration 13: On the Dormition of Holy Mary 2*), and 'Queen above Everything' (Germanus of Constantinople, *Oration 3: On the Presentation of the Theotokos 1*). In Catholicism, she is known as the 'Queen of the Universe' and 'Queen of Heaven'. A major strand of modern Catholic spirituality declares that the hearts of Jesus and Mary are in union; Catholics in past centuries have speculated on the unity of Jesus and Mary in the sacrament of the Eucharist. Pope Benedict XVI expresses official Catholic Mariology by stating that Mary demonstrates God's motherliness.[33] A sizeable Catholic movement today campaigns for the definition of Mary as 'Co-Redemptrix, Mediatrix, and Advocate' (none of these titles are innovations nor are they heterodox, but they have not yet been declared as dogma).

It is difficult to know how to avoid saying that a life thus described was one in which God was wholly and fully present, in such a way that Incarnation is the best theological articulation of it. Otherwise, what does 'full of grace' mean?[34] We do not need to abandon the Christian focus on Jesus as Son of God and Messiah as, in this thinking, Jesus is united with Mary in life and in eternity, no part of either separate from the other. Jesus of Nazareth, like all other human beings, was not an island.[35]

We can either avoid the whole conundrum and agree with Protestantism that Mary should cease to be the object of high veneration, and Jesus Christ alone will remain the focus of Christian devotion because that is what it appears to say in the New Testament, or we need to accept what many Christians have been straining to say: that the Incarnation has its basis in the lives of Jesus *and* Mary, male and female together, the image of God just as it is in Genesis 1.27. Although humanity

---

[33] This is explored in several places in Mary Frances McKenna's *Innovation within Tradition: Joseph Ratzinger and Reading the Women of Scripture*. The idea can be found elsewhere in approved Catholic Mariological writing.

[34] The translation of *kecharitōmenē* (Luke 1.28) in Catholicism, e.g., the 'Hail Mary'. This is why other translations (such as 'favoured one' in the NRSV) have been preferred in Protestantism!

[35] This unity of Jesus and Mary is not the same as the deification of Mary (*theosis* in Greek) which is the destiny of all Christians, to be partakers in the divine nature (2 Peter 1.4; expressed in eucharistic prayers). Although Mary has been regarded as the supreme example of deification in Christian tradition, East and West, the union of Jesus Christ and Mary in the Incarnation is a different concept, saying something more substantial about Mary as the locus of divine presence.

is made in the image and likeness of God, it is only in Jesus Christ that humanity achieves the perfect image of God (2 Cor. 4.4, 6). By locating that perfect image in the union of Jesus and Mary – *both* of whom are flawless in the Orthodox and Catholic tradition – we avoid the patriarchal sexism inherent in proclaiming a new Adam who is divine and human, and a new Eve who is purely human. Pope John Paul II spoke about the Church needing to breathe with its two lungs, meaning the Catholic and Orthodox Churches (*Ut Unum Sint* 54). One could argue that the two lungs are also good analogies for female and male.

In this final chapter, we have moved from biblical history to its implications for theology. If we accept the argument that Mary founded, or at least co-founded, the Christian movement in its earliest beginnings, it is not a large step to suggest that the Catholic description of her as Co-Redemptrix is on the right lines, but it does not go far enough. Jesus as the Word made flesh lived in a network of human beings among whom certain women, most prominently his mother Mary, were instrumental in the bringing into being of his ministry and mission, and with him they proclaimed the good news of the Kingdom of God. The Word dwelled in them as it did in him.

17

Concluding Summary

If you are interested in Christianity, then you will be interested in Jesus of Nazareth, his life and mission. You might prefer to regard the gospels as narrating pure history told from four different perspectives, but if you heed the advice of the majority of biblical scholars today, some of them representing the Churches, then you will accept that there is a large element of myth and legend, material that is not historical but which expresses theological truths in symbolic forms. If so, then the passages that narrate the virgin conception and birth of Jesus are among the strongest candidates to be regarded as metaphorical and not historical.

However, that would include the majority of verses in the New Testament which speak about Mary. Where does that leave us in terms of understanding the Mary of history? In this book, we have shown that there is enough evidence in the gospels and Acts to construct a portrait of her. These are drawn from traditions that reflect her importance in the earliest Church that emerged after the resurrection appearances of Jesus.

Despite the image of the isolated figure that meets the angel in the annunciation narrative, Mary was remembered as being in the company of others. In the gender demarcated society of the first century (one that continues into Eastern Mediterranean culture today), Mary was intimately associated with:

- The brothers of Jesus, who worked with the apostles in preaching the gospel of Jesus, and of whom at least James was given authoritative status in the Jerusalem Church;
- The women in the community who followed Jesus from Galilee to the cross, some of whom were able to provide resources which funded and supported the ministry of Jesus; of these, Mary Magdalene was the most prominent.

The Gospel of John confirms that Mary the mother of Jesus could be understood in the first century as the adopted mother of an important apostle, the 'disciple whom Jesus loved'. We have shown that this idea extended further back in history beyond simply being a symbolic device for John to express the idea of Jesus' family of faith. Mary was the mother not only of James and Joses (plus Judas and Simon), who were most probably her actual children, but she is also described as being of the household of Clopas, and perhaps also the mother of John Mark. All of these people were associated with the Jerusalem Church. For a man to hold authority in the Jerusalem Church in the first decades of Christianity, he needed to call Mary his mother.

The writer or compilers of the Gospel of Mark, for reasons that made sense to them in terms of the requirements of the Gentile mission, preferred to stress that Mary and the brothers of Jesus were unnecessary mediators for faith in Jesus. The other gospels followed suit, but they reinstated Mary when utilizing and developing traditions about the birth of Jesus and the wedding at Cana. In addition, all the gospels contain traces of her involvement in the crucifixion and the events that followed.

Mary preceded Jesus; the Gospels of Luke and John had no difficulty with the inclusion of passages portraying her reflecting on Jesus' mission while he was still a child and, at Cana, providing the initiative for it. Therefore, we can acclaim her as the original founder of the Christian vision. Doubtless, she had her own sources of inspiration but, beyond the Hebrew Scriptures and possibly the movement behind John the Baptist, we do not know what these were. The New Testament generally attributes to women the initiative for understanding the mission of Jesus as the non-violent Messiah who was destined to be executed, and believing that he was risen from the dead. Mary's involvement in the origin of Jesus' mission is remembered, but not Joseph's.

The metaphor of the Virgin is appropriate but far too easily misleading in describing the woman who stood at the crossroads of history; it says nothing about sexuality and everything about the profound inspiration of her vision and that of her son. It is extremely likely that she was the mother of several children; the New Testament says so and it takes a convoluted argument to deny it. She is the 'Ever Virgin' because her decision to undertake the mission to the poor and disadvantaged of ancient Israel belongs to eternity as well as history, but it is not a statement about her attitude to sex. As there is no mention of Jesus being married in the gospels, he is a better role model for the celibate than Mary.

What this means for the theology of Mary will be a matter for debate; the Churches in East and West have tended to see Mary in union with Jesus as a mother figure for Christianity, never quite fully divine but a figure of supernatural power and quality, nonetheless. The Protestant Reformation took the cue from Mark's Gospel in seeing Mary's mediation as unnecessary. This had the unfortunate consequence of Mary being associated too closely with hierarchical models of the Church in Roman Catholicism.

Christian theology and doctrine evolve. Recent social development in terms of gender equality renders the concept of a New Adam who is divine and human, as opposed to a New Eve who is human and subordinate, extremely problematic. This theology of creation is no longer plausible. While Mary's divine-human nature has been latent in devotion over the centuries, Christianity is leaving it to New Age Goddess worshippers to take the final step that the Churches could never quite countenance because of the testimony of the New Testament that Jesus Christ alone was the incarnate God.

Our modern understanding of humans as social beings might lead us to wonder what it might mean for God to be incarnate in a male individual. This belongs to an ancient world of belief in sacred kings. Some radical modern theologies, the liberationist and the feminist, have emphasized and expanded upon the ancient doctrine that incarnation and salvation are communal and relational. The Incarnation, overflowing beyond the individual person Jesus, begins its journey with Mary the mother of Jesus, in company with the women and men of her community.

Appendix 1

The Development of the New Testament

PAUL'S LETTERS	The earliest documents in the New Testament are some of the epistles attributed to Paul; they can be used as a check on what might be concluded from the gospels. In particular, the epistles to the Corinthians (two), Galatians, Philippians, Romans, and Thessalonians (two) are regarded as the genuine letters of Paul to the churches in the titles; they were most likely to have been written during the 50s CE. Mary is not mentioned in these epistles, although Paul confirms that Jesus was a Jew and 'born of a woman' (Gal. 4.4).
MARK'S GOSPEL	Among the gospels, Mark's is the earliest, the only one that might have been completed before 73 CE, the end of the seven-year Jewish War of revolution against Roman rule. It is not clear that Mark's Gospel is a 'book' in the sense of a finalized, complete edition, as Matthew and Luke were quite content to expand on Mark's Gospel and amend it. In Mark, Mary is mentioned along with brothers and sisters of Jesus (although the sisters are not named). Other Marys appear in the texts involving the crucifixion, burial, and empty tomb of Jesus.

MATTHEW AND LUKE	Matthew and Luke used Mark as a source and may have been written very roughly around 80 CE, Matthew appearing first. They also used a collection of Jesus' teachings that they seem to have shared (including sections like the Beatitudes, for example) but, if such a source existed, it is no longer in existence. Matthew and Luke include the only narratives in the New Testament about the conception, birth, and childhood of Jesus and Mary's part in them. They also develop Mark's information about the women at the cross and tomb. The three gospels Matthew, Mark, and Luke have a good deal of material in common that leads to them being known as the 'synoptic gospels'.
JOHN'S GOSPEL	John's Gospel was completed last, perhaps towards the very end of the first century CE, but some of the material that fed into it may be much earlier. There are clearly some traditions that John shares with Matthew, Mark, and Luke. However, it is radically different from the synoptic tradition in some areas, such as the timing of the crucifixion with respect to Passover. In John's Gospel, Mary is referred to as 'the mother of Jesus' without a name; she appears in texts describing the wedding at Cana and the crucifixion. The cross and tomb stories also include other Marys.
THE GOSPEL AUTHORS	The naming of the authors of the gospels was not established until the second century among the churches; no one knows whom first-century Christians reading the original texts regarded as the authors, as they are not named in the gospels themselves. It is clear that the most important criterion in the second century was that the writer was a key witness to the ministry of Jesus in some way: thus Matthew and John were assumed to have been the disciples with these names, Mark the scribe of Peter, and Luke a physician and follower of Paul (a Mark and a Luke are mentioned in the Pauline epistles at Col. 4.10–14; 2 Tim. 4.11; Philemon v. 24; and a Mark at 1 Peter 5.13).
ACTS OF THE APOSTLES	The Acts of the Apostles was clearly written by the same author as the Gospel of Luke. The presence of passages in the first person ('we') in Acts chapters 16, 20, 21, 27, and 28 suggests that the writer either accompanied Paul on some of his travels or that his testimony fed into the final text. Mary the mother of Jesus is mentioned just once, after the Ascension and before Pentecost at 1.14, although there is another Mary at 12.12.

NEW TESTAMENT LETTERS OVERALL	All epistles in the New Testament bar Hebrews and the three letters attributed to John are explicitly ascribed to an apostolic author: Paul, James, Jude, or Peter. It cannot be proven that these were written by the claimed authors, but the ascription of a work to an author who did not actually write it was not the fraud that it would be considered in the modern world. It was a means of honouring the person named and an attempt to discern the spirit of his teaching as applied to a later generation. We can be confident that the three letters of John were written by the same author as the Gospel.
REVELATION	Revelation was the final book of the New Testament to be accepted into the canon; it was ascribed to John, but it is unlikely to have been written by the same person as the author of the epistles and gospel. It was probably written during a time of Roman persecution, and the 90s CE is the dating most favoured by scholars, but the book also refers back to suppression during the reign of Nero in the 60s CE. There is a vision of the mother of the Messiah in chapter 12, which is a mythical description of the events at the origin of the Church.

NOTE: We should also consider the development of the manuscripts on which the New Testament was written. The complete manuscripts are dated no earlier than the fourth century, when the New Testament canon was finalized. However, there are many sizeable sections of text produced in an earlier time than this, and there are also quotes from the New Testament in the work of second and third-century Christian theologians. Generally, the evidence suggests that the original books of the New Testament, written mostly in the first century, do not deviate substantially from the earliest manuscripts that we have, although some of the fine detail may have been affected by scribal alteration. There are two exceptions: Mark 16.9–20 and John 7.53–8.11, whole sections which do not appear to have been in some of the earlier manuscripts, so we can assume them to have been inserted at a later point. In the case of Mark's Gospel, this was for the purpose of including resurrection appearances which were missing in Mark; the original form of this gospel would have been the only one where the risen Jesus is not clearly manifest in the narrative.

Appendix 2

References to Mary in the New Testament

H ere is a list of all the references to Mary in the New Testament. Also included are mentions of other women called Mary in the gospels and Acts [in square brackets].

EVENT	BIBLICAL REFERENCE
The Annunciation by Gabriel to Mary in Nazareth; Mary gives assent to her commission and reflects on the events	Luke 1.26–38
The Visitation of Mary to her relative Elizabeth in the hill country of Judea; this includes Mary's famous hymn, the *Magnificat*	Luke 1.39–56
Mary is included in Matthew's genealogy as Joseph's wife	Matt. 1.16
Joseph is disturbed by Mary's pregnancy but is reassured by a dream in which he sees an angel; he takes her for his wife	Matt. 1.18–25

EVENT	BIBLICAL REFERENCE
Mary and Joseph, betrothed, travel to Bethlehem from Nazareth because of the census	Luke 2.1–5
The birth of Jesus in Bethlehem (visited by shepherds in Luke)	Matt. 1.25; Luke 2.6–20
Jesus is circumcised and named after eight days	Luke 2.21
The visit of the magi to Bethlehem	Matt. 2.1–12
The flight to Egypt; the massacre of the infants; the return of Jesus' family who now settle in Nazareth	Matt. 2.13–23
The ritual in the Jerusalem Temple which comprises both the Purification of Mary and the Presentation of Jesus forty days after birth	Luke 2.22–38
Jesus grows to twelve years old and deserts his parents in Jerusalem at the Passover in order to teach; Mary is anxious but reflects on the events	Luke 2.40–52
Jesus' ministry begins with the miracle of water and wine at the marriage of Cana, which is initiated by 'the mother of Jesus'; after this, he stays with her, his brothers, and disciples in Capernaum for a few days	John 2.1–12
The adult Jesus is approached by his mother and brothers, but he refers to his disciples and 'those who do the will of God / hear the Word' as his mother and brothers	Mark 3.31–35; Matt. 12.46–50; Luke 8.19–21
While Jesus is in Nazareth (near the Sea of Galilee in John), the local people identify him as the son of Mary (Mark) or of Joseph and Mary (Matthew) (or of Joseph – Luke and John)	Mark 6.1–6; Matt. 13.54–58; (Luke 4.16–30; John 6.41–51)
Jesus says that it is not the body of his mother which is blessed, rather those who 'hear the word of God and obey it'	Luke 11.27–28
[Jesus' female followers include Mary Magdalene, Joanna the wife of Herod's steward Chuza, and Susanna]	[Luke 8.1–3]

EVENT	BIBLICAL REFERENCE
[A woman anoints Jesus at Bethany; she is unnamed in Mark and Matthew, but in John, she is Mary, the sister of Martha in the story of the raising of their brother Lazarus; these sisters and an anointing also appear in Luke but in very different contexts]	[Mark 14.3–9; Matt. 26.6–13; John 11.1–12.6; Luke 7.36–50 and 10.38–42]
In John, 'the mother of Jesus' is at the cross with Mary (wife?) of Clopas, Mary Magdalene, and the disciple whom Jesus loved [In the synoptic gospels, women observe the crucifixion from far off and these include Mary Magdalene, 'Mary mother of James and Joses', and Salome (Mark) or the mother of the sons of Zebedee (Matthew)]	John 19.25–27; [Mark 15.40–41; Matt. 27.55–56; Luke 23.49]
[Mary Magdalene and 'Mary of James' or 'of Joses' – 'the other Mary' in Matthew – are at the burial of Jesus, and then visit the empty tomb in the synoptic gospels with Salome (Mark) and Joanna (Luke)] [In John, no women are mentioned at the burial and only Mary Magdalene of the women features in the tomb story]	[Mark 15.46–47, 16.1–8; Matt. 27.59–61, 28.1–10; Luke 23.53–56, 24.1–10; John 20.1–18]
Mary and Jesus' brothers, his disciples, and 'certain women' pray between Ascension and Pentecost	Acts 1.14
['Mary mother of John whose other name was Mark' has a house in Jerusalem where Peter goes after escaping prison]	[Acts 12.12–17]
[Paul asks the Romans in his letter to 'Greet Mary, who has worked very hard among you']	[Rom. 16.6]

Appendix 3

Instances of the Word 'virgin' in the Hebrew Scriptures and the Greek Old Testament

The following table gives the total number of places where the word for 'virgin' in Hebrew (*betulah*) or in Greek (*parthenos*) appears, comparing these with the English New Revised Standard version. Sometimes other words in Greek translate the Hebrew *betulah*, and occasionally the Hebrew uses other words which the Greek nevertheless translates to *parthenos*. The New Revised Standard version in English uses a range of expressions including 'virgin' to translate *betulah* and *parthenos*.

In all cases, however, these words refer to a female who is in the transition from girlhood to womanhood (completed at the consummation of marriage). This is a liminal state and is therefore rich in symbolic significance. We can conclude that this liminal state in the life cycle is what the evangelists intended to convey to their readers: that Mary had not yet completed this transition when she became pregnant. There is no hint of a commitment to a permanent state of virginity.

HEBREW SCRIPTURES IN THE JEWISH CANON	GREEK VERSION OF THE HEBREW SCRIPTURES (SEPTUAGINT)	ENGLISH NEW REVISED STANDARD VERSION: OLD TESTAMENT
Hebrew *betulah* = virgin	Greek *parthenos* (or *parthenikos*) = virgin	English 'virgin'
49 times (not including duplicates, i.e., Lev. 21.3 and Ezek. 44.22; 2 Kings 19.21 and Isa. 37.22)	51	32

Instances where these three words coincide in the translations (i.e., *parthenos* translates *betulah* and the NRSV gives 'virgin'): 30

Other combinations:

betulah, *parthenos*, 'young woman' 11
betulah, *parthenos*, 'young girl' 3
betulah, *parthenos*, 'girl' 2
betulah, *parthenos*, 'maiden' 1
betulah, *thugatēr* (Greek for daughter), 'virgin' 2
'almah (Hebrew for young woman), *parthenos*, 'young woman' 2
(famously, one of these is Isaiah 7.14; the other describes Rebekah when she meets Isaac)
na'ara (Hebrew for girl), *parthenos*, 'girl' 2

There are also these combinations:
'almah, *neanis* (Greek for young woman), 'young woman' 4
'almah, *neotētos* (Greek for young person), 'young woman' 1

Appendix 4

Describing Relations in Greek: Mother, Wife, and Daughter

There are words in Greek to describe clearly that someone is a mother (*mētēr*), wife (*gunē*) or daughter (*thugatēr*). However, if the meaning is clear, it is acceptable in Greek to describe someone simply as 'X of Y' where X is the mother, wife, or daughter of a male Y. It is more problematic when the meaning is not clear, as with Mary of Clopas.

In the New Testament, excepting Mary of Clopas for a moment, there is only one place where 'X of Y' refers to a wife. This is in Matthew 1.6 when the English 'And David was the father of Solomon by the wife of Uriah' reads literally in Greek, 'And David begat Solomon from her of Uriah'. Here there can be no doubt that this is the wife of Uriah; we know this from the Hebrew Scriptures and her name was Bathsheba.

There are seven other places where someone is described as the wife of X, and in all these cases the word 'wife' is added. Every single reference to someone being the daughter of X in the New Testament (there are eight of them) uses the word 'daughter'.

There are just three places in the New Testament where 'X of Y' denotes a mother without explicitly stating so. These are Mark 15.47 and 16.1 where Mary of Joses and Mary of James respectively are assumed to refer to mothers, because Mark 15.40 has already told us that Mary was the mother of James the Younger and Joses, and the proximity of the later verses suggest that the same person is being referred to. There is also Luke 24.10, which follows Mark 16.1.

All other references to someone being the mother of X (either Mary the mother of Jesus, Mary the mother of James and Joses, Mary the mother of John Mark, Elizabeth the mother of John the Baptist, and Herodias the mother of Salome) include the word 'mother' explicitly.

Therefore, there are only five instances in total of the expression 'X of Y' where X is a female in an unspecified relationship to a male Y. In four of these, the meaning is clear (admittedly, in the case of Luke 24.10, only because of the parallel with Mark 16.1), and therefore 'Mary of Clopas' is something of an anomaly.

Appendix 5

Words Used for Mary in the Greek New Testament: 'Maria' or 'Mariam'

There are many manuscripts of the New Testament which vary in their detail; the study of textual criticism is the discipline that attempts to discover the most likely original form based on the age of the manuscript and its comparisons to other manuscripts. In this appendix, we show the places in the New Testament where *Maria* (Greek) and *Mariam* (Aramaic) are used for the name translated 'Mary' in English, drawing on ancient manuscripts.

Mark, who prefers *Maria*, only includes the lists at the cross, burial, and tomb (plus the one other place at 6.3 where Mary is named in passing). Matthew, Luke, and John follow Mark's usage *Maria* for the lists at the cross, burial, and tomb but prefer *Mariam* for the story narratives. [There is an exception: the three evangelists use the Greek *Marias* for the genitive case while *Mariam* is used in the nominative, vocative, and accusative cases; the genitive case is also used in Mark 6.3: 'son of Mary'.] This leads us to the overall argument that *Maria* is predominantly used in the gospels for the lists of women at the cross, burial, and tomb, and *Mariam* for the longer stories in Matthew, Luke, and John which feature a person called Mary.

Here is the detail, using the standard text book for comparing manuscript variants of the New Testament, the Nestle-Aland *Novum Testament Graece* (28th revised edition, edited by B. and K. Aland, J. Karavidopoulos, C.M. Martini and B.M. Metzger, Stuttgart: Deutsche Bibelgesellschaft, 2012).

MATTHEW

The conception and birth of Jesus: Mary is mentioned at 1.16, 1.18, 1.20, 2.11. These are all in the genitive (*Marias*) except 1.20, which is accusative. Nestle-Aland prefers the Greek *Marian* at this point, but there are many ancient manuscripts which give the Aramaic *Mariam*.

Jesus in Nazareth: 13.55 (parallel to Mark 6.3). Here Matthew uses *Mariam* and there are no given textual alternatives.

The cross and tomb: 27.56 (twice), 27.61 (twice), 28.1 (twice). Nestle-Aland gives *Maria* for four of the six instances and *Mariam* for two mentions of Mary Magdalene at 27.61 and 28.1. However, there are several manuscripts which prefer *Maria* in these latter two places. Given the proximity of these references, it is difficult to imagine that the original will have alternated between two ways of writing the name. Therefore, *Maria* is likely for all six.

MARK

Jesus in Nazareth: 6.3. It is genitive, *Marias*.

The cross and tomb: 15.40 (twice), 15.47 (twice), 16.1 (twice). Nestle-Aland gives *Maria* for all these instances. Manuscripts giving the alternative *Mariam* are few.

The longer ending: 16.9. Also, *Maria*.

LUKE

The conception, birth, and childhood of Jesus: 1.27, 1.30, 1.34, 1.38, 1.39, 1.41, 1.46, 1.56, 2.5, 2.16, 2.19, 2.34. These are all *Mariam* without any variants, except for 1.41, which is genitive, and there are a few manuscripts which give *Maria* at 2.19 but Nestle-Aland stays with *Mariam*.

Introducing Mary Magdalene: 8.2. This is *Maria* without any manuscripts giving the alternative, but this does not contradict the argument, as this is a list and clearly prepares the reader for the tomb story at 24.10.

Mary and Martha: 10.39, 10.42. Nestle-Aland gives *Mariam*, despite some manuscripts which have *Maria*.

The tomb: 24.10. *Maria* without the alternative reading.

ACTS

Mary after the Ascension: 1.14. Again, *Mariam* but with the alternative reading in some cases.

Mary mother of John Mark: 12.12. *Marias*, genitive.

JOHN

The raising of Lazarus with Martha and Mary at Bethany: 11.1, 11.2, 11.19, 11.20, 11.28, 11.31, 11.32, 11.45, 12.3. Nestle-Aland gives *Mariam* in all these verses, except for 11.2, which is genitive. There are instances of manuscripts reading *Maria* in all cases, however.

The cross: 19.25 (twice). Nestle-Aland prefers *Maria*, although there are a few manuscripts which give *Mariam*.

Mary Magdalene in the garden: 20.1, 20.11, 20.16, 20.18. This is confusing, as Nestle-Aland gives *Maria* for the first two verses and *Mariam* for the second two. However, there are many manuscripts, including quite ancient ones, which prefer *Mariam* throughout. One could see the version *Maria* as a scribal attempt to be consistent with 19.25, perhaps.

ROMANS

The only other instance of the name Mary is at Romans 16.6. Nestle-Aland suggests *Maria* but there are many manuscripts which have *Mariam*. This is immaterial to the argument, but it provides another example of the way in which manuscripts vary between the two versions of the name.

Appendix 6

A Creative Rewriting of the Resurrection Experiences in John 2 and 20

I have combined and edited the texts of John 2.1–11 (the wedding at Cana) and John 20.11–18 (the garden tomb) and created an imagined, pre-gospel tradition of Mary the mother of Jesus and Mary Magdalene encountering Jesus on Easter Day. This is not meant to represent a historical reconstruction, but a narrative by which women expressed their powerful ecstatic experiences of the resurrection. In doing this, I am attempting to counter the minimalizing or reframing of women's experiences in the gospels, which were written from a male perspective, and so I have removed all the references to Jesus distancing himself from the women and saying, 'not yet'. The idea that the two Marys together saw the risen Jesus corresponds to Matthew 28.9–10.

On the third day when Jesus rose from the dead, the mother of Jesus saw him as the bridegroom at a great wedding in heaven. The mother of Jesus said to him, 'We have no wine.' Now standing there was a jar of water. Jesus said to her, 'Fill the jar with water.' And she filled it up to the brim. She tasted the water that had become wine, and said to him, 'You have kept the good wine until now.' Jesus did this and revealed his glory. When the mother of Jesus told the disciples about this, they believed in him.

Mary Magdalene had been standing weeping outside the tomb. As she wept, she bent over to look into the tomb; and she saw two angels in white, sitting where the body of Jesus had been lying, one at the head and the other at the feet. She turned around and saw Jesus standing there. Jesus said to her, 'Mary!' She turned and said to him, 'Rabbouni!' Joyfully, she embraced Jesus. He said to her, 'Go to my brothers and say to them, "I am ascending to my Father and your Father, to my God and your God."' Mary Magdalene went and announced to the disciples, 'I have seen the Lord'; and she told them that he had said these things to her.

Compare these with an actual text, a resurrection appearance to James the brother of Jesus which is not found in the New Testament. It comes from the *Gospel of the Hebrews*, probably second century, quoted by Jerome in *Illustrious Men* 2; an English translation is given in Bart D. Ehrman, *Lost Scriptures: Books that did not make it into the New Testament* (Oxford University Press, 2003, p.16).

...[the Lord] went and appeared to James. For James had taken a vow not to eat bread from the time he drank the cup of the Lord until he should see him raised from among those who sleep ... The Lord said, 'Bring a table and bread'... He took the bread and blessed it, broke it, gave it to James the Just, and said to him, 'My brother, eat your bread. For the Son of Man is risen from among those who sleep.'

Bibliography

This bibliographical list includes sources mentioned in the book and those that have been consulted for general research.

Biblical quotes are from the *New Revised Standard Version* (Oxford University Press, 1995).

Allen, Nicholas P.L. 2017. 'Josephus on James the Just? A re-evaluation of *Antiquitates Judaicae* 20.9.1'. *Journal of Early Christian History* 7.1: 1–27.

Anderson, Paul N. 2019. 'Why the Gospel of John is fundamental to Jesus research' in *Jesus Research: The Gospel of John in Historical Inquiry*, edited by James H. Charlesworth and Jolyon G.R. Pruszinski. London & New York: T & T Clark.

Athans, Mary Christine. 2013. *In Quest of the Jewish Mary: The Mother of Jesus in History, Theology, and Spirituality*. Maryknoll NY: Orbis.

Barker, Margaret. 2008. *Christmas: The Original Story*. London: SPCK.

Bauckham, Richard. 1999. *James: Wisdom of James, Disciple of Jesus the Sage*. London & New York: Routledge.

——2002. *Gospel Women: Studies of the Named Women in the Gospels*. Grand Rapids MI & Cambridge: Wm. B. Eerdmans.

——2004. *Jude and the Relatives of Jesus in the Early Church*. London & New York: T & T Clark.

——2007. *The Testimony of the Beloved Disciple: Narrative, History, and Theology in the Gospel of John*. Grand Rapids MI: Baker Academic.

Beavis, Mary Ann. 2012. 'Reconsidering Mary of Bethany'. *The Catholic Quarterly* 74: 281–97.

——2013. 'Mary of Bethany and the hermeneutics of remembrance'. *The Catholic Quarterly* 75: 739–55.

Beavis, Mary Ann and Kateusz, Ally, editors. 2020. *Rediscovering the Marys: Maria, Mariamne, Miriam*. London: Bloomsbury/T & T Clark.

Berg, InHee C. 2017. 'The Gospel traditions inferring to Jesus' proper burial through the depictions of female funerary kinship roles'. *Biblical Theology Bulletin* 47.4: 216–29.

Bernheim, Pierre-Antoine. 1997. *James the Brother of Jesus*. London: SCM.

Bockmuehl, Markus. 2011. 'The Son of David and his Mother'. *The Journal of Theological Studies* 62.2: 476–93.

Borg, Marcus J. and Crossan, John Dominic. 2008. *The First Christmas: What the Gospels Really Teach about Jesus' Birth*. London: SPCK.

Boring, M. Eugene. 2012. *An Introduction to the New Testament: History, Literature, Theology*. Louisville KY: Westminster John Knox Press.

Boss, Sarah Jane. 2000. *Empress and Handmaid: On Nature and Gender in the Cult of the Virgin Mary*. London & New York: Cassell.

Brooten, Bernadette J. 1982. *Women Leaders in the Ancient Synagogue: Inscriptional Evidence and Background Issues*. Atlanta: Scholars Press (Brown Judaic Studies 36).

Brown, Raymond E. 1993. *The Birth of the Messiah: A Commentary on the Infancy Narratives in the Gospels of Matthew and Luke*. London: Geoffrey Chapman.

——1994. *The Death of the Messiah: From Gethsemane to the Grave: A Commentary on the Passion Narratives in the Four Gospels*, Vol. 2. New York: Doubleday.

Brown, Raymond E., Donfried, Karl P., Fitzmyer, Joseph A. and Reumann, John. 1978. *Mary in the New Testament*. London: Geoffrey Chapman.

Brown, Raymond E. and Meier, John. 1983. *Antioch and Rome: New Testament Cradles of Catholic Christianity*. New York & Mahwah NJ: Paulist Press.

Burke, Tony. 2019. 'Mary and the Apocrypha' in *The Oxford Handbook of Mary*, edited by Chris Maunder. Oxford: Oxford University Press.

Carey, Greg. 2013. 'Moving things ahead: a Lukan redactional technique and its implications for Gospel origins'. *Biblical Interpretation* 21.3: 302–19.

Chilton, Bruce and Neusner, Jacob. 1995. *Judaism in the New Testament: Practices and Beliefs*. London: Routledge.

——editors. 2001. *The Brother of Jesus: James the Just and His Mission*. Louisville KY, London & Leiden: Westminster John Knox Press.

Collins, Adela Yarbro. 2007. *Mark: A Commentary*, edited by Harold W. Attridge. Minneapolis: Augsburg Fortress.

Corley, Jeremy, editor. 2009. *New Perspectives on the Nativity*. London & New York: T & T Clark.

Corley, Kathleen E. 2002. *Women and the Historical Jesus: Feminist Myths of Christian Origins*. Santa Rosa CA: Polebridge.

——2010. *Maranatha: Women's Funerary Rituals and Christian Origins*. Minneapolis: Fortress Press.

Crossan, John Dominic. 1994. *Jesus: A Revolutionary Biography*. San Francisco: Harper Collins.

Croy, N. Clayton and Connor, Alice E. 2011. 'Mantic Mary? The Virgin Mother as prophet in Luke 1.26–56 and the early Church'. *Journal for the Study of the New Testament* 34.3: 254–76.

Davidson, John. 2005. *The Odes of Solomon: Mystical Songs from the Time of Jesus*. Bath: Clear Press.

Dei Verbum. 1965. *Dogmatic Constitution on Divine Revelation*, Second Vatican Council, at www.vatican.va/archive/hist_councils/ii_vatican_council/documents/vat-ii_const_19651118_dei-verbum_en.html

Dijkhuizen, Petra. 2011. '*Buried shamefully*: Historical reconstruction of Jesus' burial and tomb'. *Neotestamentica* 45.1: 115–29.

Eisen, Ute E. 2000. *Women Officeholders in Early Christianity: Epigraphical and Literary Studies*, translated by Linda M. Moloney. Collegeville MN: Michael Glazier/The Liturgical Press.

Elliott, J.K. 1974. 'The Anointing of Jesus'. *Expository Times* 85.4: 105–7.

——2015. 'Christian apocrypha and the developing role of Mary' in *The Oxford Handbook of Early Christian Apocrypha*, edited by Andrew Gregory and Christopher Tuckett. Oxford: Oxford University Press.

Eusebius of Caesaria. *Church History*, New Advent version at www.newadvent.org/fathers/2501.htm, translated by Arthur Cushman McGiffert, from *Nicene and Post-Nicene Fathers, Second Series*, Vol. 1, edited by Philip Schaff and Henry Wace. Buffalo NY: Christian Literature Publishing Co., 1890. Revised and edited for New Advent by Kevin Knight.

Evans, Craig A. 2005. 'Jewish burial traditions and the resurrection of Jesus'. *Journal for the Study of the Historical Jesus* 3.2: 187–202.

Fehribach, Adeline. 1998. *The Women in the Life of the Bridegroom: A Feminist Historical-Literary Analysis of the Female Characters in the Fourth Gospel*. Collegeville MN: The Liturgical Press.

Foskett, Mary F. 2002. *A Virgin Conceived: Mary and Classical Representations of Virginity*. Bloomington IN: Indiana University Press.

Gaventa, Beverly Roberts. 1999. *Mary: Glimpses of the Mother of Jesus*. Edinburgh: T & T Clark.

Gorman, Michael J., editor. 2005. *Scripture: An Ecumenical Introduction to the Bible and its Interpretation*. Peabody MA: Hendrickson.

Graef, Hilda and Thompson, Thomas A. 2009. *Mary: A History of Doctrine and Devotion*. Notre Dame, IN: Christian Classics.

Grafton, Thomas E. 2011. 'Just as it was spoken: Annunciation type-scenes and faithful response in Luke's birth narrative'. *Conversations with the Biblical World* 31: 143–61.

Guijarro, Santiago and Rodríguez, Ana. 2011. 'The "Messianic" anointing of Jesus (Mark 14:3–9)'. *Biblical Theology Bulletin* 41.3: 132–43.

Gundry, Robert H. 1993. *Mark: A Commentary on His Apology for the Cross*. Grand Rapids MI & Cambridge: Wm. B. Eerdmans.

Hartin, Patrick J. 2004. *James of Jerusalem: Heir to Jesus of Nazareth*. Collegeville MN: Liturgical Press.

Hurtado, Larry W. 2009. 'The Women, the tomb, and the climax of Mark' in *A Wandering Galilean: Essays in Honour of Seán Frayne*, edited by Zuleika Rodgers, Margaret Daly-Denton and Anne Fitzpatrick McKinley. Leiden: Brill.

Hylen, Susan E. 2019. *Women in the New Testament World*. New York: Oxford University Press.

Ilan, Tal. 1999, *Integrating Women into Second Temple History*. Peabody MA: Hendrickson.

Johnson, Elizabeth. 2003. *Truly Our Sister: A Theology of Mary in the Communion of Saints*. New York & London: Continuum.

——2009. 'Galilee: a critical matrix for Marian studies'. *Theological Studies* 70: 327–46.

Josephus, Flavius. *The Complete Works of Flavius Josephus*, translated by William Whiston, 1860. London: T. Nelson & Sons.

Kateusz, Ally. 2019. *Mary and Early Christian Women: Hidden Leadership*. London: Palgrave Macmillan.

Kraemer, Ross Shepard and D'Angelo, Mary Rose. 1999. *Women and Christian Origins*. New York: Oxford University Press.

Kraemer, Ross Shepard. 2010. *Unreliable Witnesses: Religion, Gender, and History in the Greco-Roman Mediterranean*. New York: Oxford University Press.

Kuhn, Karl Allen. 2015. *The Kingdom according to Luke and Acts: A Social, Literary and Theological Introduction*. Grand Rapids MI: Baker Academic.

Larsen, Matthew D.C. 2018. *Gospels before the Book*. New York: Oxford University Press.

Levine, Amy-Jill and Robbins, Maria Mayo, editors. 2005. *A Feminist Companion to Mariology*. Cleveland OH: Pilgrim.

Lieu, Judith M. and De Boer, Martinus C., editors. 2018. *The Oxford Handbook of Johannine Studies*. Oxford: Oxford University Press.

Lincoln, Andrew T. 2005. *The Gospel according to St John*. London & New York: Hendrickson/Continuum.

——2013. *Born of a Virgin?: Reconceiving Jesus in Bible, Tradition and Theology*. London: SPCK.

Maunder, Chris. 1996. 'Mother or disciple: the quest for the historical Mary'. *The Month* 29: 494–9.

——2007. 'Mary in the New Testament and Apocrypha' in *Mary: the Complete Resource*, edited by Sarah Jane Boss. London & New York: Continuum.

——2008. 'Origins of the cult of the Virgin Mary in the New Testament' in *Origins of the Cult of the Virgin Mary*, edited by Chris Maunder. London & New York: Burns & Oates.

——2019. 'Mary and the Gospel narratives' in *The Oxford Handbook of Mary*, edited by Chris Maunder. Oxford University Press.

McCane, Byron R. 2002. '"Where no one had yet been laid": The shame of Jesus' burial' in *Authenticating the Activities of Jesus*, edited by Bruce Chilton and Craig A. Evans. Leiden: Brill.

McKenna, Mary Frances, 2015. *Innovation within Tradition: Joseph Ratzinger and Reading the Women of Scripture*. Minneapolis: Fortress Press.

Meier, John P. 1991. *A Marginal Jew: Rethinking the Historical Jesus* Vol. I. New York: Doubleday.

Michaels, J. Ramsey. 2010. *The Gospel of John*. Grand Rapids MI & Cambridge: Wm. B. Eerdmans.

Moloney, Francis J. SDB. 2013. *The Resurrection of the Messiah: A Narrative Commentary on the Resurrection Accounts in the Four Gospels*. New York: Paulist Press.

Nortjé-Meyer, Lilly. 2009. 'The "Mother of Jesus" as analytical category in John's Gospel'. *Neotestamentica* 43.1: 123–43.

Rahner, Karl SJ. 1983. *Theological Investigations*, Vol. 19, translated by Edward Quinn. London: Darton, Longman & Todd.

Ricci, Carla. 1994. *Mary Magdalene and Many Others; Women who Followed Jesus*, translated by Paul Burns. Tunbridge Wells: Burns & Oates.

Sanders, E.P. 1993. *The Historical Figure of Jesus*. London: Penguin.

Schaberg, Jane. 1987. *The Illegitimacy of Jesus: A Feminist Theological Interpretation of the Infancy Narratives*. San Francisco: Harper & Row.

Schüssler Fiorenza, Elisabeth. 1983. *In Memory of Her: A Feminist Theological Reconstruction of Christian Origins*. London: SCM.

——editor. 1994. *Searching the Scriptures: Volume 1, A Feminist Introduction*. London: SCM.

——editor. 1995. *Searching the Scriptures: Volume 2, A Feminist Commentary*. London: SCM.

——2011. *Transforming Vision: Explorations in Feminist The*logy*. Minneapolis MN: Augsburg Fortress.

Shoemaker, Stephen J., editor and translator. 2012. *The Life of the Virgin: Maximum the Confessor*. New Haven & London: Yale University Press.

——2016. *Mary in Early Christian Faith and Devotion*. New Haven & London: Yale University Press.

Sissa, Giulia. 1990. *Greek Virginity*, translated by Arthur Goldhammer. Cambridge MA: Harvard University Press.

Soulen, Richard N. 2009. *Sacred Scripture: A Short History of Interpretation*. Louisville KY: Westminster John Knox Press.

Tabor, James D. 2006. *The Jesus Dynasty*. London: Harper Element.

——2020. *Marie: De son enfance juive à la foundation du christianisme*, translated by Cécile Dutheil de la Rochère and Nathalie Gouyé-Guilbert. Paris: Flammarion.

Taylor, Joan E. 2014. 'Missing Magdala and the name of Mary "Magdalene"'. *Palestine Exploration Quarterly* 146.3: 205–23.

The Interpretation of the Bible in the Church. 1993. Pontifical Biblical Commission, at https://catholic-resources.org/ChurchDocs/PBC_Interp.htm

Vuola, Elina. 2019. *The Virgin Mary across Cultures: Devotion among Costa Rican Catholic and Finnish Orthodox Women*. London & New York: Routledge.

Westerholm, Stephen and Westerholm, Martin. 2016. *Reading Sacred Scripture: Voices from the History of Biblical Interpretation*. Grand Rapids MI & Cambridge: Wm. B. Eerdmans.

Wilde, Wilf. 2006. *Crossing the River of Fire: Mark's Gospel and Global Capitalism*. London: Epworth.

Index

Index of Textual References

NEW TESTAMENT

Mark 8.27–30 159
Mark 8.28 51
Mark 9.2–13 19
Mark 10. 5–6 100
Mark 10.17–22 180
Mark 10.28–30 185–6
Mark 10.35–45 126, 192
Mark 10.43 178
Mark 10.46–48 27
Mark 10.47 159
Mark 10.52 85
Mark 12.34 85,99
Mark 12.43 85
Mark 14.3–9 133,
    157–68, 243

Mark 14.6 85
Mark 14.17 19
Mark 14.25 111
Mark 14.36 219
Mark 14.58 193
Mark 14.61–62 194
Mark 14.62 159, 177
Mark 14.64 134
Mark 15.34 123
Mark 15.39 102, 127
Mark 15.40 87, 92,
    129, 248, 251
Mark 15.40–1 124,
    138, 243
Mark 15.41 126, 136

Mark 15.43 133–4
Mark 15.46–47 124–5,
    243
Mark 15.47 128, 138,
    248, 251
Mark 16.1 87, 128,
    138, 143, 248, 251
Mark 16.1–2 125
Mark 16.1–8 134,
    243
Mark 16.6–7 134, 137
Mark 16.7 119
Mark 16.8 134n.20
Mark 16.9 251
Mark 16.9–20 239

Luke

Luke 1–2 26–34, 53–69,
    71–5, 79–82, 115
Luke 1.5 28, 29
Luke 1.27 251
Luke 1.28 231n.34
Luke 1.30 251
Luke 1.34 251
Luke 1.36 92
Luke 1.38 75, 91, 212,
    251
Luke 1.39 185, 251
Luke 1.41 251
Luke 1.42 34, 166
Luke 1.43 82
Luke 1.45 74
Luke 1.46 251
Luke 1.46–55 63
Luke 1.48 166
Luke 1.56 251
Luke 1.67–79 198
Luke 2 21
Luke 2.1–5 242
Luke 2.5 80, 251
Luke 2.6–20 242
Luke 2.16 251
Luke 2.19 205, 251
Luke 2.21 242
Luke 2.22–38 242
Luke 2.28–32 198
Luke 2.34 251

Luke 2.34–35 209
Luke 2.36–38 17
Luke 2.40–52 242
Luke 2.41–51 93
Luke 2.51 205
Luke 2.52 204
Luke 3.23 87
Luke 4.16–30 242
Luke 4.22 59, 87
Luke 6.15 174
Luke 7 147
Luke 7.11–17 39
Luke 7.22 159
Luke 7.34 30
Luke 7.36–50 157–68,
    243
Luke 8.1 179n.27
Luke 8.1–3 162, 242
Luke 8.2 227, 251
Luke 8.2–3 21, 126,
    131, 136
Luke 8.3 162
Luke 8.19–21 90, 242
Luke 9.19 52
Luke 9.28–36 19
Luke 10.38–42 21,
    155, 160, 162,
    243
Luke 10.39 251
Luke 10.42 251

Luke 11.27–28 90–1,
    242
Luke 11.28 219
Luke 11.42–44 99
Luke 13.1 97
Luke 13.18–19 171
Luke 13.32 172
Luke 14.13 159
Luke 14.15–24 176
Luke 14.21 159
Luke 16.19–31 164
Luke 17.21 177
Luke 18.18–25 180
Luke 19.1–10 49
Luke 20.45–47 99
Luke 22.14 19
Luke 22.18 111
Luke 23.35 136
Luke 23.49 125–6,
    143, 243
Luke 23.53–56 243
Luke 24.1–10 243
Luke 24.5 135
Luke 24.6–7 137
Luke 24.10 126, 128,
    131, 248, 251
Luke 24.11 138
Luke 24.18 119
Luke 24.22–25 138
Luke 24.34 119

Romans

Rom. 1.3 27
Rom. 16.1 19
Rom. 16.6 243, 252

1 Corinthians

1 Cor. 1.11 19
1 Cor. 1.12 108
1 Cor. 1.22–24 164
1 Cor. 1.23 43
1 Cor. 7 58
1 Cor. 9 179
1 Cor. 9.5 91, 92
1 Cor. 11.5 198
1 Cor. 12 229
1 Cor. 12.10 198
1 Cor. 14.34–35 15
1 Cor. 15 107, 120, 132
1 Cor. 15.3 191
1 Cor. 15.3–7 137
1 Cor. 15.4 165
1 Cor. 15.5 42
1 Cor. 15.6 171
1 Cor. 15.17 39

2 Corinthians

2 Cor. 4.4 232
2 Cor. 4.6 232
2 Cor. 11.2–3 65
2 Cor. 11.24 99
2 Cor. 12.2–4 198

Galatians

Gal. 1–2 42, 94, 104
Gal. 1.19 92, 104
Gal. 2.6 105
Gal. 2.7–8 41
Gal. 2.7–9 101
Gal. 2.7–10 105
Gal. 2.9 104
Gal. 2.11–12 104
Gal. 2.12 92
Gal. 2.13 151
Gal. 3.28 15, 181
Gal. 4.4 86, 237
Gal. 4.25–26 151

Ephesians

Eph. 5.27 65

Philippians

Phil. 2.6–8 38
Phil. 2.7 227

Colossians

Col. 4.10–14 238
Col. 4.15 19

1 Thessalonians

1 Thess. 2.14 99

1 Timothy

1 Tim. 2.12–14 15

2 Timothy

2 Tim. 4.11 150n.23, 238

Philemon

Philemon v.24 150n.23, 238

1 Peter

1 Pet. 5.13 150n.23, 154, 238

2 Peter

2 Pet. 1.4 231n.35

2 John

2 John v.1 154
2 John v.13 154

Revelation

Rev. 12 77–82, 197, 229, 239
Rev. 12.1–6 77
Rev. 19 65, 78
Rev. 19–21 79
Rev. 19.9 111
Rev. 21 65